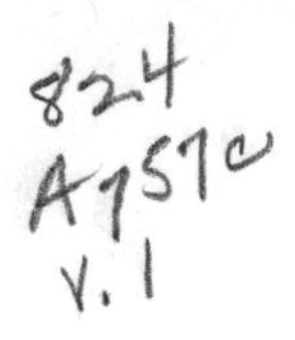

[THE COMPLETE PROSE WORKS OF MATTHEW ARNOLD]

I

On the Classical Tradition

MATTHEW ARNOLD

ON THE CLASSICAL TRADITION

Edited by R. H. Super

ANN ARBOR THE UNIVERSITY OF MICHIGAN PRESS

Third printing 1971
ISBN 0-472-11651-7
Library of Congress Catalog Card No. 60-5018
Published in the United States of America by
The University of Michigan Press and simultaneously
in Don Mills, Canada, by Longman Canada Limited
Manufactured in the United States of America

Printed in the United States of America by
Vail-Ballou Press, Inc., Binghamton, New York

Editor's Preface

The present edition proposes to print in about ten volumes every one of the writings in English prose that Arnold published or prepared for publication, whether in books or periodicals. Books on education which he himself published will be included; his official reports to his superiors in the Education Office will not, even though parts of them were published unofficially after his death. His letters, likewise, except of course those to the public press, will not be a part of this edition.

The canon of Arnold's writings is perhaps not yet complete, but it has been established with reasonable accuracy. The bibliography by T. B. Smart as revised for the final volume of the deluxe edition of 1903–4 has not been seriously challenged in its listing of Arnold's books, except for its failure to include certain American editions. There have been additions to Smart's list of Arnold's periodical writings, most notably by Marion Mainwaring, Fraser Neiman, and myself in *Modern Philology* (XLIX, 189–94, February, 1952; LV, 84–92, November, 1957; LVI, 268–69, May, 1959). Though further search of the files of nineteenth-century periodicals may bring to light more items from his pen, the most likely sources of further discoveries are his letters and his diary-notebooks. The latter have been transcribed and edited by William B. Guthrie at the University of Virginia; their publication will be most valuable for Arnold scholars. Meanwhile, Mr. Guthrie has very kindly placed in my hands a typed copy of his transcript, and the Yale University Library has supplied photographs of the originals. Arnold's letters to his publishers, insofar as they concern his writings, are the basis of William E. Buckler's monograph, *Matthew Arnold's*

Books: Toward a Publishing Diary (Geneva, 1958). Professor Arthur Kyle Davis, Jr., of the University of Virginia, whose assiduous assembling of original letters and copies will eventually, it is to be hoped, lead to an edition of Arnold's entire correspondence, has generously made his collection available to me for whatever light it might throw on Arnold's publications. With the addition of writings discovered in recent years and those known earlier but omitted from the deluxe edition, the present will be the most complete collection of Arnold's prose works.

His writings will be printed in the order of their first appearance (except in a few instances in which they are known to have been written some years earlier than their publication; such works will take their place according to the date of composition). This arrangement will do some violence, though less than might be expected, to Arnold's final order when he collected his essays into books, but the place of each essay in his collected volumes will be indicated in the Textual Notes.

Critical and Explanatory Notes are provided to explain Arnold's topical references and to indicate his sources and throw some light on the way he worked; these will be as complete and helpful as I can make them, with the assistance of the available scholarship upon Arnold. Such notes will, I hope, be useful to the general reader and will save future scholars some steps, but they are only a beginning of the study of Arnold's methods and his meaning. His style is richly allusive: classical, Biblical, and Shakespearean phrases especially are always at the tip of his pen, and these I have identified when I recognized them for what they were, but many such allusions no doubt remain hidden in the text. The notes that describe Arnold's sources should, from one point of view, make use of the editions Arnold himself used; from another point of view, they become more convenient if they refer to editions that are likely to be most generally available today. There is of course one controlling force—the accessibility of the book to the editor. This it is that accounts for the occasional use of an American edition of an English book or periodical, an annoyance (for I hope it will in fact be very little inconvenience) for which I must apologize to

Arnold's Countrymen. It may be worth remarking generally that Arnold had a sharp eye for what he could use, wherever he saw it: it is very likely that some allusions here traced to books reached Arnold through the medium of a review or magazine article. I have failed more often than I like to think in my search for the sources of statements and allusions, and shall be most grateful for my readers' help in filling the gaps. Meanwhile, it is a pleasure to acknowledge the assistance in these matters of Mr. Kenneth Allott, Professor Arthur M. Eastman, Professor Robert L. Lowe, Professor George E. McCracken, Professor William A. Madden, Professor Thomas M. Raysor, and Miss Marjorie G. Wynne.

The Critical and Explanatory Notes for each work are headed by a brief comment on the circumstances under which the work was composed and some indication of the most valuable scholarship upon it. The notes printed at the bottom of the page in the text are Arnold's own.

The basic text in each case is the last one over which Arnold is known to have (or may be presumed to have) exercised any supervision; ordinarily this is the last version printed in his lifetime. All respects in which the language of other texts differs from the one adopted are indicated in the Textual Notes; variations in punctuation and spelling, which are as likely to be the work of printer or publisher as of the author, are usually not recorded. The Textual Notes are introduced by adequate bibliographical information so that the history of the text can easily be traced. So far as the works in this volume are concerned, there has been little textual problem; three of the essays were not reprinted by Arnold and the others underwent very little revision. Arnold was not a remarkably accurate proofreader, and the history of these texts has been largely the accumulation of misprints. Twice Arnold attempted to illustrate by quotation the involvement of Elizabethan prose style, for instance, and both times the printer, by omitting a few words, made a difficult passage quite opaque. On the assumption that Arnold never intended to print nonsense, I have corrected these and other errors (leaving a record of them in the Textual Notes). More than once in the past the pedants have seized upon such blunders as evidence of Arnold's ignorance; at worst they are the fruit of his negligence.

Each volume will be indexed, in the hope of providing useful cross references from one to another of Arnold's works.

This edition owes much to the constant interest shown by the Horace H. Rackham School of Graduate Studies at The University of Michigan, which through generous grants has underwritten the editorial expenses and helped to provide free time for the work. The continuance of the project has been assured by a fellowship from the American Council of Learned Societies.

Ann Arbor, Michigan

Contents

Preface
to First Edition of *Poems*

(1853)

In two small volumes of Poems, published anonymously, one in 1849, the other in 1852, many of the poems which compose the present volume have already appeared. The rest are now published for the first time.

I have, in the present collection, omitted the poem from which the volume published in 1852 took its title. I have done so, not because the subject of it was a Sicilian Greek born between two and three thousand years ago, although many persons would think this a sufficient reason. Neither have I done so because I had, in my own opinion, failed in the delineation which I intended to effect. I intended to delineate the feelings of one of the last of the Greek religious philosophers, one of the family of Orpheus and Musæus, having survived his fellows, living on into a time when the habits of Greek thought and feeling had begun fast to change, character to dwindle, the influence of the Sophists to prevail. Into the feelings of a man so situated there entered much that we are accustomed to consider as exclusively modern; how much, the fragments of Empedocles himself which remain to us are sufficient at least to indicate. What those who are familiar only with the great monuments of early Greek genius suppose to be its exclusive characteristics, have disappeared: the calm, the cheerfulness, the disinterested objectivity have disappeared; the dialogue of the mind with itself has commenced; modern problems have presented themselves; we hear already the doubts, we witness the discouragement, of Hamlet and of Faust.

The representation of such a man's feelings must be interesting, if consistently drawn. We all naturally take pleasure, says

Aristotle, in any imitation or representation whatever: this is the basis of our love of poetry; and we take pleasure in them, he adds, because all knowledge is naturally agreeable to us; not to the philosopher only, but to mankind at large. Every representation, therefore, which is consistently drawn may be supposed to be interesting, inasmuch as it gratifies this natural interest in knowledge of all kinds. What is *not* interesting, is that which does not add to our knowledge of any kind; that which is vaguely conceived and loosely drawn; a representation which is general, indeterminate, and faint, instead of being particular, precise, and firm.

Any accurate representation may therefore be expected to be interesting; but, if the representation be a poetical one, more than this is demanded. It is demanded, not only that it shall interest, but also that it shall inspirit and rejoice the reader; that it shall convey a charm, and infuse delight. For the Muses, as Hesiod says, were born that they might be 'a forgetfulness of evils, and a truce from cares:' and it is not enough that the poet should add to the knowledge of men, it is required of him also that he should add to their happiness. 'All art,' says Schiller, 'is dedicated to Joy, and there is no higher and no more serious problem, than how to make men happy. The right art is that alone, which creates the highest enjoyment.'

A poetical work, therefore, is not yet justified when it has been shown to be an accurate, and therefore interesting representation; it has to be shown also that it is a representation from which men can derive enjoyment. In presence of the most tragic circumstances, represented in a work of art, the feeling of enjoyment, as is well known, may still subsist; the representation of the most utter calamity, of the liveliest anguish, is not sufficient to destroy it; the more tragic the situation, the deeper becomes the enjoyment; and the situation is more tragic in proportion as it becomes more terrible.

What then are the situations, from the representation of which, though accurate, no poetical enjoyment can be derived? They are those in which the suffering finds no vent in action; in which a continuous state of mental distress is prolonged, unrelieved by incident, hope, or resistance; in which there is everything to be endured, nothing to be done. In such situations there is inevitably something morbid, in the description of them something monotonous. When they occur in actual life, they are painful, not tragic; the representation of them in poetry is painful also.

To this class of situations, poetically faulty as it appears to me, that of Empedocles, as I have endeavoured to represent him, belongs; and I have therefore excluded the poem from the present collection.

And why, it may be asked, have I entered into this explanation respecting a matter so unimportant as the admission or exclusion of the poem in question? I have done so, because I was anxious to avow that the sole reason for its exclusion was that which has been stated above; and that it has not been excluded in deference to the opinion which many critics of the present day appear to entertain against subjects chosen from distant times and countries: against the choice, in short, of any subjects but modern ones.

'The poet,' it is said,[1] and by an intelligent critic, 'the poet who would really fix the public attention must leave the exhausted past, and draw his subjects from matters of present import, and *therefore* both of interest and novelty.'

Now this view I believe to be completely false. It is worth examining, inasmuch as it is a fair sample of a class of critical dicta everywhere current at the present day, having a philosophical form and air, but no real basis in fact; and which are calculated to vitiate the judgment of readers of poetry, while they exert, so far as they are adopted, a misleading influence on the practice of those who make it.

What are the eternal objects of poetry, among all nations, and at all times? They are actions; human actions; possessing an inherent interest in themselves, and which are to be communicated in an interesting manner by the art of the poet. Vainly will the latter imagine that he has everything in his own power; that he can make an intrinsically inferior action

[1] In the *Spectator* of April 2, 1853. The words quoted were not used with reference to poems of mine.

equally delightful with a more excellent one by his treatment of it. He may indeed compel us to admire his skill, but his work will possess, within itself, an incurable defect.

The poet, then, has in the first place to select an excellent action; and what actions are the most excellent? Those, certainly, which most powerfully appeal to the great primary human affections: to those elementary feelings which subsist permanently in the race, and which are independent of time. These feelings are permanent and the same; that which interests them is permanent and the same also. The modernness or antiquity of an action, therefore, has nothing to do with its fitness for poetical representation; this depends upon its inherent qualities. To the elementary part of our nature, to our passions, that which is great and passionate is eternally interesting; and interesting solely in proportion to its greatness and to its passion. A great human action of a thousand years ago is more interesting to it than a smaller human action of to-day, even though upon the representation of this last the most consummate skill may have been expended, and though it has the advantage of appealing by its modern language, familiar manners, and contemporary allusions, to all our transient feelings and interests. These, however, have no right to demand of a poetical work that it shall satisfy them; their claims are to be directed elsewhere. Poetical works belong to the domain of our permanent passions; let them interest these, and the voice of all subordinate claims upon them is at once silenced.

Achilles, Prometheus, Clytemnestra, Dido,—what modern poem presents personages as interesting, even to us moderns, as these personages of an 'exhausted past'? We have the domestic epic dealing with the details of modern life which pass daily under our eyes; we have poems representing modern personages in contact with the problems of modern life, moral, intellectual, and social; these works have been produced by poets the most distinguished of their nation and time; yet I fearlessly assert that *Hermann and Dorothea*, *Childe Harold*, *Jocelyn*, *The Excursion*, leave the reader cold in comparison with the effect produced upon him by the latter books of the *Iliad*, by the *Oresteia*, or by the episode of Dido. And why is this? Simply because in the three last-named cases the action is greater, the personages nobler, the situations more intense: and this is the true basis of the interest in a poetical work, and this alone.

It may be urged, however, that past actions may be interesting in themselves, but that they are not to be adopted by the modern poet, because it is impossible for him to have them clearly present to his own mind, and he cannot therefore feel them deeply, nor represent them forcibly. But this is not necessarily the case. The externals of a past action, indeed, he cannot know with the precision of a contemporary; but his business is with its essentials. The outward man of Œdipus or of Macbeth, the houses in which they lived, the ceremonies of their courts, he cannot accurately figure to himself; but neither do they essentially concern him. His business is with their inward man; with their feelings and behaviour in certain tragic situations, which engage their passions as men; these have in them nothing local and casual; they are as accessible to the modern poet as to a contemporary.

The date of an action, then, signifies nothing: the action itself, its selection and construction, this is what is all-important. This the Greeks understood far more clearly than we do. The radical difference between their poetical theory and ours consists, as it appears to me, in this: that, with them, the poetical character of the action in itself, and the conduct of it, was the first consideration; with us, attention is fixed mainly on the value of the separate thoughts and images which occur in the treatment of an action. They regarded the whole; we regard the parts. With them, the action predominated over the expression of it; with us, the expression predominates over the action. Not that they failed in expression, or were inattentive to it; on the contrary, they are the highest models of expression, the unapproached masters of the *grand style*. But their expression is so excellent because it is so admirably kept in its right degree of prominence; because it is so simple and so well subordinated; because it draws its force directly from the pregnancy of the matter which it conveys. For what reason was the Greek tragic poet confined to so limited a range of subjects? Because there are so few actions which unite in themselves, in the highest degree, the conditions of excellence: and it was not thought that on any but an excellent subject could an excellent poem be constructed. A few actions, therefore, eminently adapted for tragedy, maintained almost exclusive possession of the Greek tragic stage. Their significance appeared inexhaustible; they were as permanent problems, perpetually offered to the genius of every fresh poet. This too is the reason of what appears to us moderns a certain baldness of expression in Greek tragedy; of the triviality with which we often reproach the remarks of the chorus, where it takes part in the dialogue: that the action itself, the situation of Orestes, or Merope, or Alcmæon, was to stand the central point of interest, unforgotten, absorbing, principal; that no accessories were for a moment to distract the spectator's attention from this; that the tone of the parts was to be perpetually kept down, in order not to impair the grandiose effect of the whole. The terrible old mythic story on which the drama was founded stood, before he entered the theatre, traced in its bare outlines upon the spectator's mind; it stood in his memory, as a group of statuary, faintly seen, at the end of a long and dark vista: then came the poet, embodying outlines, developing situations, not a word wasted, not a sentiment capriciously thrown in: stroke upon stroke, the drama proceeded: the light deepened upon the group; more and more it revealed itself to the riveted gaze of the spectator: until at last, when the final words were spoken, it stood before him in broad sunlight, a model of immortal beauty.

This was what a Greek critic demanded; this was what a Greek poet endeavoured to effect. It signified nothing to what time an action belonged. We do not find that the *Persæ* occupied a particularly high rank among the dramas of Æschylus, because it represented a matter of contemporary interest; this was not what a cultivated Athenian required. He required that the permanent elements of his nature should be moved; and dramas of which the action, though taken from a long-distant mythic time, yet was calculated to accomplish this in a higher degree than that of the *Persæ*, stood higher in his estimation accordingly. The Greeks felt, no doubt, with their exquisite sagacity of taste, that an action of present times was too near them, too much mixed up with what was accidental and passing, to form a sufficiently grand, detached, and self-subsistent object for a tragic poem. Such objects belonged to 5 the domain of the comic poet, and of the lighter kinds of poetry. For the more serious kinds, for *pragmatic* poetry, to use an excellent expression of Polybius, they were more difficult and severe in the range of subjects which they permitted. Their theory and practice alike, the admirable treatise of 10 Aristotle, and the unrivalled works of their poets, exclaim with a thousand tongues—'All depends upon the subject; choose a fitting action, penetrate yourself with the feeling of its situations; this done, everything else will follow.'

But for all kinds of poetry alike there was one point on 15 which they were rigidly exacting: the adaptability of the subject to the kind of poetry selected, and the careful construction of the poem.

How different a way of thinking from this is ours! We can hardly at the present day understand what Menander meant, 20 when he told a man who enquired as to the progress of his comedy that he had finished it, not having yet written a single line, because he had constructed the action of it in his mind. A modern critic would have assured him that the merit of his piece depended on the brilliant things which arose 25 under his pen as he went along. We have poems which seem to exist merely for the sake of single lines and passages; not for the sake of producing any total impression. We have critics who seem to direct their attention merely to detached expressions, to the language about the action, not to the action itself. 30 I verily think that the majority of them do not in their hearts believe that there is such a thing as a total impression to be derived from a poem at all, or to be demanded from a poet; they think the term a commonplace of metaphysical criticism. They will permit the poet to select any action he pleases, and 35 to suffer that action to go as it will, provided he gratifies them with occasional bursts of fine writing, and with a shower of isolated thoughts and images. That is, they permit him to leave their poetical sense ungratified, provided that he gratifies their rhetorical sense and their curiosity. Of his neglecting to gratify these, there is little danger. He needs rather to be warned against the danger of attempting to gratify these alone; he needs rather to be perpetually reminded to prefer his action to everything else; so to treat this, as to permit its inherent excellences to develop themselves, without interruption from the intrusion of his personal peculiarities; most fortunate, when he most entirely succeeds in effacing himself, and in enabling a noble action to subsist as it did in nature.

But the modern critic not only permits a false practice; he absolutely prescribes false aims.—'A true allegory of the state of one's own mind in a representative history,' the poet is told, 'is perhaps the highest thing that one can attempt in the way of poetry.' And accordingly he attempts it. An allegory of the state of one's own mind, the highest problem of an art which imitates actions! No assuredly, it is not, it never can be so: no great poetical work has ever been produced with such an aim. *Faust* itself, in which something of the kind is attempted, wonderful passages as it contains, and in spite of the unsurpassed beauty of the scenes which relate to Margaret, *Faust* itself, judged as a whole, and judged strictly as a poetical work, is defective: its illustrious author, the greatest poet of modern times, the greatest critic of all times, would have been the first to acknowledge it; he only defended his work, indeed, by asserting it to be 'something incommensurable.'

The confusion of the present times is great, the multitude of voices counselling different things bewildering, the number of existing works capable of attracting a young writer's attention and of becoming his models, immense. What he wants is a hand to guide him through the confusion, a voice to prescribe to him the aim which he should keep in view, and to explain to him that the value of the literary works which offer themselves to his attention is relative to their power of helping him forward on his road towards this aim. Such a guide the English writer at the present day will nowhere find. Failing this, all that can be looked for, all indeed that can be desired, is, that his attention should be fixed on excellent models; that he may reproduce, at any rate, something of their excellence, by penetrating himself with their works and by catching their spirit, if he cannot be taught to produce what is excellent independently.

Foremost among these models for the English writer stands Shakespeare: a name the greatest perhaps of all poetical names; a name never to be mentioned without reverence. I will venture, however, to express a doubt, whether the influence of his works, excellent and fruitful for the readers of poetry, for the great majority, has been of unmixed advantage to the writers of it. Shakespeare indeed chose excellent subjects; the world could afford no better than Macbeth, or Romeo and Juliet, or Othello; he had no theory respecting the necessity of choosing subjects of present import, or the paramount interest attaching to allegories of the state of one's own mind; like all great poets, he knew well what constituted a poetical action; like them, wherever he found such an action, he took it; like them, too, he found his best in past times. But to these general characteristics of all great poets he added a special one of his own; a gift, namely, of happy, abundant, and ingenious expression, eminent and unrivalled: so eminent as irresistibly to strike the attention first in him, and even to throw into comparative shade his other excellences as a poet. Here has been the mischief. These other excellences were his fundamental excellences *as a poet;* what distinguishes the artist from the mere amateur, says Goethe, is *Architectonicè* in the highest sense; that power of execution, which creates, forms, and constitutes: not the profoundness of single thoughts, not the richness of imagery, not the abundance of illustration. But these attractive accessories of a poetical work being more easily seized than the spirit of the whole, and these accessories being possessed by Shakespeare in an unequalled degree, a young writer having recourse to Shakespeare as his model runs great risk of being vanquished and absorbed by them, and, in consequence, of reproducing, according to the measure of his power, these, and these alone. Of this preponderating quality of Shakespeare's genius, accordingly, almost the whole of modern English poetry has, it appears to me, felt the influence. To the exclusive attention on the part of his imitators to this it is in a great degree owing, that of the majority of modern poetical works the details alone are valuable, the composition worthless. In reading them one is perpetually reminded of that terrible sentence on a modern French poet:—*Il dit tout ce qu'il veut, mais malheureusement il n'a rien à dire.*

Let me give an instance of what I mean. I will take it from the works of the very chief among those who seem to have been formed in the school of Shakespeare: of one whose exquisite genius and pathetic death render him for ever interesting. I will take the poem of *Isabella, or the Pot of Basil*, by Keats. I choose this rather than the *Endymion*, because the latter work (which a modern critic has classed with the *Fairy Queen!*), although undoubtedly there blows through it the breath of genius, is yet as a whole so utterly incoherent, as not strictly to merit the name of a poem at all. The poem of *Isabella*, then, is a perfect treasure-house of graceful and felicitous words and images: almost in every stanza there occurs one of those vivid and picturesque turns of expression, by which the object is made to flash upon the eye of the mind, and which thrill the reader with a sudden delight. This one short poem contains, perhaps, a greater number of happy single expressions which one could quote than all the extant tragedies of Sophocles. But the action, the story? The action in itself is an excellent one; but so feebly is it conceived by the poet, so loosely constructed, that the effect produced by it, in and for itself, is absolutely null. Let the reader, after he has finished the poem of Keats, turn to the same story in the *Decameron:* he will then feel how pregnant and interesting the same action has become in the hands of a great artist, who above all things delineates his object; who subordinates expression to that which it is designed to express.

I have said that the imitators of Shakespeare, fixing their attention on his wonderful gift of expression, have directed their imitation to this, neglecting his other excellences. These excellences, the fundamental excellences of poetical art, Shakespeare no doubt possessed them,—possessed many of them in a splendid degree; but it may perhaps be doubted whether even he himself did not sometimes give scope to his faculty of expression to the prejudice of a higher poetical duty. For we must never forget that Shakespeare is the great poet he is from his skill in discerning and firmly conceiving an excellent action, from his power of intensely feeling a situation, of intimately associating himself with a character; not from his gift of expression, which rather even leads him astray, degenerating sometimes into a fondness for curiosity of expression, into an irritability of fancy, which seems to make it impossible for him to say a thing plainly, even when the press of the action demands the very directest language, or its level character the very simplest. Mr. Hallam, than whom it is impossible to find a saner and more judicious critic, has had the courage (for at the present day it needs courage) to remark, how extremely and faultily difficult Shakespeare's language often is. It is so: you may find main scenes in some of his greatest tragedies, *King Lear* for instance, where the language is so artificial, so curiously tortured, and so difficult, that every speech has to be read two or three times before its meaning can be comprehended. This over-curiousness of expression is indeed but the excessive employment of a wonderful gift,—of the power of saying a thing in a happier way than any other man; nevertheless, it is carried so far that one understands what M. Guizot meant, when he said that Shakespeare appears in his language to have tried all styles except that of simplicity. He has not the severe and scrupulous self-restraint of the ancients, partly, no doubt, because he had a far less cultivated and exacting audience. He has indeed a far wider range than they had, a far richer fertility of thought; in this respect he rises above them. In his strong conception of his subject, in the genuine way in which he is penetrated with it, he resembles them, and is unlike the moderns. But in the accurate limitation of it, the conscientious rejection of superfluities, the simple and rigorous development of it from the first line of his work to the last, he falls below them, and comes nearer to the moderns. In his chief works, besides what he has of his own, he has the elementary soundness of the ancients; he has their important action and their large and broad manner; but he has not their purity of method. He is therefore a less safe model; for what he has of his own is personal, and inseparable from his own rich nature; it may be imitated and exaggerated, it cannot be learned or applied as an art. He is above all suggestive; more valuable, therefore, to young writers as men than as artists. But clearness of arrangement, rigour of development, simplicity of style,—these may to a certain extent be learned; and these may, I am convinced, be learned best from the ancients, who, although infinitely less suggestive than Shakespeare, are thus, to the artist, more instructive.

What then, it will be asked, are the ancients to be our sole models? the ancients with their comparatively narrow range of experience, and their widely different circumstances? Not, certainly, that which is narrow in the ancients, nor that in which we can no longer sympathise. An action like the action of the *Antigone* of Sophocles, which turns upon the conflict between the heroine's duty to her brother's corpse and that to the laws of her country, is no longer one in which it is possible that we should feel a deep interest. I am speaking too, it will be remembered, not of the best sources of intellectual stimulus for the general reader, but of the best models of instruction for the individual writer. This last may certainly learn of the ancients, better than anywhere else, three things which it is vitally important for him to know:—the all-importance of the choice of a subject; the necessity of accurate construction; and the subordinate character of expression. He will learn from them how unspeakably superior is the effect of the one moral impression left by a great action treated as a whole, to the effect produced by the most striking single thought or by the happiest image. As he penetrates into the spirit of the great classical works, as he becomes gradually aware of their intense significance, their noble simplicity, and their calm pathos, he will be convinced that it is this effect, unity and profoundness of moral impression, at which the ancient poets aimed; that it is this which constitutes the grandeur of their works, and which makes them immortal. He will desire to direct his own efforts towards producing the same effect.

Above all, he will deliver himself from the jargon of modern criticism, and escape the danger of producing poetical works conceived in the spirit of the passing time, and which partake of its transitoriness.

The present age makes great claims upon us: we owe it service, it will not be satisfied without our admiration. I know not how it is, but their commerce with the ancients appears to me to produce, in those who constantly practise it, a steadying and composing effect upon their judgment, not of literary works only, but of men and events in general. They are like persons who have had a very weighty and impressive experience: they are more truly than others under the empire of facts, and more independent of the language current among those with whom they live. They wish neither to applaud nor to revile their age; they wish to know what it is, what it can give them, and whether this is what they want. What they want, they know very well; they want to educe and cultivate what is best and noblest in themselves; they know, too, that this is no easy task—χαλεπὸν, as Pittacus said, χαλεπὸν ἐσθλὸν ἔμμεναι—and they ask themselves sincerely whether their age and its literature can assist them in the attempt. If they are endeavouring to practise any art, they remember the plain and simple proceedings of the old artists, who attained their grand results by penetrating themselves with some noble and significant action, not by inflating themselves with a belief in the pre-eminent importance and greatness of their own times. They do not talk of their mission, nor of interpreting their age, nor of the coming poet; all this, they know, is the mere delirium of vanity; their business is not to praise their age, but to afford to the men who live in it the highest pleasure which they are capable of feeling. If asked to afford this by means of subjects drawn from the age itself, they ask what special fitness the present age has for supplying them. They are told that it is an era of progress, an age commissioned to carry out the great ideas of industrial development and social amelioration. They reply that with all this they can do nothing; that the elements they need for the exercise of their art are great actions, calculated powerfully and delightfully to affect what is permanent in the human soul; that so far as the present age can supply such actions, they will gladly make use of them; but that an age wanting in moral grandeur can with difficulty supply such, and an age of spiritual discomfort with difficulty be powerfully and delightfully affected by them.

A host of voices will indignantly rejoin that the present age is inferior to the past neither in moral grandeur nor in spiritual health. He who possesses the discipline I speak of will content himself with remembering the judgments passed upon the present age, in this respect, by the men of strongest head and widest culture whom it has produced; by Goethe and by Niebuhr. It will be sufficient for him that he knows the opinions held by these two great men respecting the present age and its literature; and that he feels assured in his own mind that their aims and demands upon life were such as he would wish, at any rate, his own to be; and their judgment as to what is impeding and disabling such as he may safely follow. He will not, however, maintain a hostile attitude towards the false pretensions of his age: he will content himself with not being overwhelmed by them. He will esteem himself fortunate if he can succeed in banishing from his mind all feelings of contradiction, and irritation, and impatience; in order to delight himself with the contemplation of some noble action of a heroic time, and to enable others, through his representation of it, to delight in it also.

I am far indeed from making any claim, for myself, that I possess this discipline; or for the following poems, that they breathe its spirit. But I say, that in the sincere endeavour to learn and practise, amid the bewildering confusion of our times, what is sound and true in poetical art, I seemed to myself to find the only sure guidance, the only solid footing, among the ancients. They, at any rate, knew what they wanted in art, and we do not. It is this uncertainty which is disheartening, and not hostile criticism. How often have I felt this when reading words of disparagement or of cavil: that it is the uncertainty as to what is really to be aimed at which makes our difficulty, not the dissatisfaction of the critic, who himself suffers from the same uncertainty! *Non me tua fervida terrent Dicta; . . . Dii me terrent, et Jupiter hostis.*

Two kinds of *dilettanti*, says Goethe, there are in poetry: he who neglects the indispensable mechanical part, and thinks he has done enough if he shows spirituality and feeling; and 5 he who seeks to arrive at poetry merely by mechanism, in which he can acquire an artisan's readiness, and is without soul and matter. And he adds, that the first does most harm to art, and the last to himself. If we must be *dilettanti:* if it is impossible for us, under the circumstances amidst which we live, to think 10 clearly, to feel nobly, and to delineate firmly: if we cannot attain to the mastery of the great artists;—let us, at least, have so much respect for our art as to prefer it to ourselves. Let us not bewilder our successors; let us transmit to them the practice of poetry, with its boundaries and wholesome regula- 15 tive laws, under which excellent works may again, perhaps, at some future time, be produced, not yet fallen into oblivion through our neglect, not yet condemned and cancelled by the influence of their eternal enemy, caprice.

Preface to Second Edition of *Poems*

(1854)

I have allowed the Preface to the former edition of these Poems to stand almost without change, because I still believe it to be, in the main, true. I must not, however, be supposed insensible to the force of much that has been alleged against portions of it, or unaware that it contains many things incompletely stated, many things which need limitation. It leaves, too, untouched the question, how far and in what manner the opinions there expressed respecting the choice of subjects apply to lyric poetry,—that region of the poetical field which is chiefly cultivated at present. But neither do I propose at the present time to supply these deficiencies, nor, indeed, would this be the proper place for attempting it. On one or two points alone I wish to offer, in the briefest possible way, some explanation.

An objection has been warmly urged to the classing together, as subjects equally belonging to a past time, Œdipus and Macbeth. And it is no doubt true that to Shakespeare, standing on the verge of the middle ages, the epoch of Macbeth was more familiar than that of Œdipus. But I was speaking of actions as they presented themselves to us moderns: and it will hardly be said that the European mind, in our day, has much more affinity with the times of Macbeth than with those of Œdipus. As moderns, it seems to me, we have no longer any direct affinity with the circumstances and feelings of either. As individuals, we are attracted towards this or that personage, we have a capacity for imagining him, irrespective of his times, solely according to a law of personal sympathy; and those subjects for which we feel this personal attraction most strongly, we may hope to treat successfully. Prometheus or Joan of Arc, Charlemagne or Agamemnon,—one of these is not really nearer to us now than another. Each can be made present only by an act of poetic imagination; but this man's imagination has an affinity for one of them, and that man's for another. 5

It has been said that I wish to limit the poet, in his choice of subjects, to the period of Greek and Roman antiquity; but it is not so. I only counsel him to choose for his subjects great actions, without regarding to what time they belong. Nor do I deny that the poetic faculty can and does manifest itself in 10 treating the most trifling action, the most hopeless subject. But it is a pity that power should be wasted; and that the poet should be compelled to impart interest and force to his subject, instead of receiving them from it, and thereby doubling his impressiveness. There is, it has been excellently said, an 15 immortal strength in the stories of great actions; the most gifted poet, then, may well be glad to supplement with it that mortal weakness, which, in presence of the vast spectacle of life and the world, he must for ever feel to be his individual portion.

Again, with respect to the study of the classical writers of 20 antiquity: it has been said that we should emulate rather than imitate them. I make no objection; all I say is, let us study them. They can help to cure us of what is, it seems to me, the great vice of our intellect, manifesting itself in our incredible vagaries in literature, in art, in religion, in morals: namely, that 25 it is *fantastic*, and wants *sanity*. Sanity,—that is the great virtue of the ancient literature; the want of that is the great defect of the modern, in spite of all its variety and power. It is impossible to read carefully the great ancients, without losing something of our caprice and eccentricity; and to emulate 30 them we must at least read them.

On the Modern Element in Literature

[What follows was delivered as an inaugural lecture in the Poetry Chair at Oxford. It was never printed, but there appeared at the time several comments on it from critics who had either heard it, or heard reports about it. It was meant to be followed and completed by a course of lectures developing the subject entirely, and some of these were given. But the course was broken off because I found my knowledge insufficient for treating in a solid way many portions of the subject chosen. The inaugural lecture, however, treating a portion of the subject where my knowledge was perhaps less insufficient, and where besides my hearers were better able to help themselves out from their own knowledge, is here printed. No one feels the imperfection of this sketchy and generalizing mode of treatment more than I do; and not only is this mode of treatment less to my taste now than it was eleven years ago, but the style too, which is that of the doctor rather than the explorer, is a style which I have long since learnt to abandon. Nevertheless, having written much of late about Hellenism and Hebraism, and Hellenism being to many people almost an empty name compared with Hebraism, I print this lecture with the hope that it may serve, in the absence of other and fuller illustrations, to give some notion of the Hellenic spirit and its works, and of their significance in the history of the evolution of the human spirit in general.

M. A.]

It is related in one of those legends which illustrate the history of Buddhism, that a certain disciple once presented himself before his master, Buddha, with the desire to be permitted to undertake a mission of peculiar difficulty. The compassionate teacher represented to him the obstacles to be surmounted and the risks to be run. Pourna—so the disciple was called—insisted, and replied, with equal humility and adroitness, to the successive objections of his adviser. Satisfied at last by his answers of the fitness of his disciple, Buddha accorded to him the desired permission; and dismissed him to his task with these remarkable words, nearly identical with those in which he himself is said to have been admonished by a divinity at the outset of his own career:—"Go then, O Pourna," are his words; "having been delivered, deliver; having been consoled, console; being arrived thyself at the farther bank, enable others to arrive there also."

It was a moral deliverance, eminently, of which the great Oriental reformer spoke; it was a deliverance from the pride, the sloth, the anger, the selfishness, which impair the moral activity of man—a deliverance which is demanded of all individuals and in all ages. But there is another deliverance for the human race, hardly less important, indeed, than the first—for in the enjoyment of both united consists man's true freedom—but demanded far less universally, and even more rarely and imperfectly obtained; a deliverance neglected, apparently hardly conceived, in some ages, while it has been pursued with earnestness in others, which derive from that very pursuit their peculiar character. This deliverance is an intellectual deliverance.

An intellectual deliverance is the peculiar demand of those ages which are called modern; and those nations are said to be imbued with the modern spirit most eminently in which the demand for such a deliverance has been made with most zeal, and satisfied with most completeness. Such a deliverance is emphatically, whether we will or no, the demand of the age in which we ourselves live. All intellectual pursuits our age judges according to their power of helping to satisfy this demand; of all studies it asks, above all, the question, how far they can contribute to this deliverance.

I propose, on this my first occasion of speaking here, to attempt such a general survey of ancient classical literature and history as may afford us the conviction—in presence of the doubts so often expressed of the profitableness, in the present day, of our study of this literature—that, even admitting to their fullest extent the legitimate demands of our age, the literature of ancient Greece is, even for modern times, a mighty agent of intellectual deliverance; even for modern times, therefore, an object of indestructible interest.

But first let us ask ourselves why the demand for an intellectual deliverance arises in such an age as the present, and in what the deliverance itself consists? The demand arises, because our present age has around it a copious and complex present, and behind it a copious and complex past; it arises, because the present age exhibits to the individual man who contemplates it the spectacle of a vast multitude of facts awaiting and inviting his comprehension. The deliverance consists in man's comprehension of this present and past. It begins when our mind begins to enter into possession of the general ideas which are the law of this vast multitude of facts. It is perfect when we have acquired that harmonious acquiescence of mind which we feel in contemplating a grand spectacle that is intelligible to us; when we have lost that impatient irritation of mind which we feel in presence of an immense, moving, confused spectacle which, while it perpetually excites our curiosity, perpetually baffles our comprehension.

This, then, is what distinguishes certain epochs in the history of the human race, and our own amongst the number;—on the one hand, the presence of a significant spectacle to contemplate; on the other hand, the desire to find the true point of view from which to contemplate this spectacle. He who has found that point of view, he who adequately comprehends this spectacle, has risen to the comprehension of his age: he who communicates that point of view to his age, he who interprets to it that spectacle, is one of his age's intellectual deliverers.

The spectacle, the facts, presented for the comprehension of the present age, are indeed immense. The facts consist of the events, the institutions, the sciences, the arts, the literatures, in which human life has manifested itself up to the present time: the spectacle is the collective life of humanity. And everywhere there is connexion, everywhere there is illustration: no single event, no single literature, is adequately comprehended except in its relation to other events, to other literatures. The literature of ancient Greece, the literature of the Christian Middle Age, so long as they are regarded as two isolated literatures, two isolated growths of the human spirit, are not adequately comprehended; and it is adequate comprehension which is the demand of the present age. "We must compare," —the illustrious Chancellor of Cambridge [1] said the other day to his hearers at Manchester,—"we must compare the works of other ages with those of our own age and country; that, while we feel proud of the immense development of knowledge and power of production which we possess, we may learn humility in contemplating the refinement of feeling and intensity of thought manifested in the works of the older schools." To know how others stand, that we may know how we ourselves stand; and to know how we ourselves stand, that we may correct our mistakes and achieve our deliverance—that is our problem.

But all facts, all the elements of the spectacle before us, have not an equal value—do not merit a like attention: and it is well that they do not, for no man would be adequate to the task of thoroughly mastering them all. Some have more significance for us, others have less; some merit our utmost attention in all their details, others it is sufficient to comprehend in their general character, and then they may be dismissed.

What facts, then, let us ask ourselves, what elements of the spectacle before us, will naturally be most interesting to a highly developed age like our own, to an age making the demand which we have described for an intellectual deliverance by means of the complete intelligence of its own situation? Evidently, the other ages similarly developed, and making the same demand. And what past literature will naturally be most interesting to such an age as our own? Evidently, the literatures which have most successfully solved for *their* ages the problem which occupies ours: the literatures which in their day and for their own nation have adequately comprehended, have adequately represented, the spectacle before them. A signifi-

[1] The late Prince Consort.

cant, a highly-developed, a culminating epoch, on the one hand,—a comprehensive, a commensurate, an adequate literature, on the other,—these will naturally be the objects of deepest interest to our modern age. Such an epoch and such a literature are, in fact, *modern,* in the same sense in which our own age and literature are modern; they are founded upon a rich past and upon an instructive fulness of experience.

It may, however, happen that a great epoch is without a perfectly adequate literature; it may happen that a great age, a great nation, has attained a remarkable fulness of political and social development, without intellectually taking the complete measure of itself, without adequately representing that development in its literature. In this case, the *epoch,* the *nation* itself, will still be an object of the greatest interest to us; but the *literature* will be an object of less interest to us: the facts, the material spectacle, are there; but the contemporary view of the facts, the intellectual interpretation, are inferior and inadequate.

It may happen, on the other hand, that great authors, that a powerful literature, are found in an age and nation less great and powerful than themselves; it may happen that a literature, that a man of genius, may arise adequate to the representation of a greater, a more highly developed age than that in which they appear; it may happen that a literature completely interprets its epoch, and yet has something over; that it has a force, a richness, a geniality, a power of view which the materials at its disposition are insufficient adequately to employ. In such a case, the literature will be more interesting to us than the epoch. The interpreting power, the illuminating and revealing intellect, are there; but the spectacle on which they throw their light is not fully worthy of them.

And I shall not, I hope, be thought to magnify too much my office if I add, that it is to the poetical literature of an age that we must, in general, look for the most perfect, the most adequate interpretation of that age,—for the performance of a work which demands the most energetic and harmonious activity of all the powers of the human mind. Because that activity of the whole mind, that genius, as Johnson nobly describes it, "without which judgment is cold and knowledge is inert; that energy which collects, combines, amplifies, and animates," is in poetry at its highest stretch and in its most energetic exertion.

What we seek, therefore, what will most enlighten us, most contribute to our intellectual deliverance, is the union of two things; it is the coexistence, the simultaneous appearance, of a great epoch and a great literature.

Now the culminating age in the life of ancient Greece I call, beyond question, a great epoch; the life of Athens in the fifth century before our era I call one of the highly developed, one of the marking, one of the modern periods in the life of the whole human race. It has been said that the "Athens of Pericles was a vigorous man, at the summit of his bodily strength and mental energy." There was the utmost energy of life there, public and private; the most entire freedom, the most unprejudiced and intelligent observation of human affairs. Let us rapidly examine some of the characteristics which distinguish modern epochs; let us see how far the culminating century of ancient Greece exhibits them; let us compare it, in respect of them, with a much later, a celebrated century; let us compare it with the age of Elizabeth in our own country.

To begin with what is exterior. One of the most characteristic outward features of a *modern* age, of an age of advanced civilization, is the banishment of the ensigns of war and bloodshed from the intercourse of civil life. Crime still exists, and wars are still carried on; but within the limits of civil life a circle has been formed within which man can move securely, and develop the arts of peace uninterruptedly. The private man does not go forth to his daily occupation prepared to assail the life of his neighbour or to have to defend his own. With the disappearance of the constant means of offence the occasions of offence diminish; society at last acquires repose, confidence, and free activity. An important inward characteristic, again, is the growth of a tolerant spirit; that spirit which is the offspring of an enlarged knowledge; a spirit patient of the diversities of habits and opinions. Other characteristics are the multiplication of the conveniences of life, the formation of taste, the capacity for refined pursuits. And this leads us to the supreme characteristic of all: the intellectual maturity of man himself; the tendency to observe facts with a critical spirit; to search for their law, not to wander among them at random; to judge by the rule of reason, not by the impulse of prejudice or caprice.

Well, now, with respect to the presence of all these characteristics in the age of Pericles, we possess the explicit testimony of an immortal work,—of the history of Thucydides. "The Athenians first," he says—speaking of the gradual development of Grecian society up to the period when the Peloponnesian war commenced—"the Athenians first left off the habit of wearing arms:" that is, this mark of superior civilization had, in the age of Pericles, become general in Greece, had long been visible at Athens. In the time of Elizabeth, on the other hand, the wearing of arms was universal in England and throughout Europe. Again, the conveniences, the ornaments, the luxuries of life, had become common at Athens at the time of which we are speaking. But there had been an advance even beyond this; there had been an advance to that perfection, that propriety of taste which proscribes the excess of ornament, the extravagance of luxury. The Athenians had given up, Thucydides says, had given up, although not very long before, an extravagance of dress and an excess of personal ornament which, in the first flush of newly-discovered luxury, had been adopted by some of the richer classes. The height of civilization in this respect seems to have been attained; there was general elegance and refinement of life, and there was simplicity. What was the case in this respect in the Elizabethan age? The scholar Casaubon, who settled in England in the reign of James I., bears evidence to the want here, even at that time, of conveniences of life which were already to be met with on the continent of Europe. On the other hand, the taste for fantastic, for excessive personal adornment, to which the portraits of the time bear testimony, is admirably set forth in the work of a great novelist, who was also a very truthful antiquarian—in the "Kenilworth" of Sir Walter Scott. We all remember the description, in the thirteenth and fourteenth chapters of the second volume of "Kenilworth," of the barbarous magnificence, the "fierce vanities," of the dress of the period.

Pericles praises the Athenians that they had discovered sources of recreation for the spirit to counterbalance the labours of the body: compare these, compare the pleasures which charmed the whole body of the Athenian people through the yearly round of their festivals with the popular shows and pastimes in "Kenilworth." "We have freedom," says Pericles, "for individual diversities of opinion and character; we do not take offence at the tastes and habits of our neighbour if they differ from our own." Yes, in Greece, in the Athens of Pericles, there is toleration; but in England, in the England of the sixteenth century?—the Puritans are then in full growth. So that with regard to these characteristics of civilization of a modern spirit which we have hitherto enumerated, the superiority, it will be admitted, rests with the age of Pericles.

Let us pass to what we said was the supreme characteristic of a highly developed, a modern age—the manifestation of a critical spirit, the endeavour after a rational arrangement and appreciation of facts. Let us consider one or two of the passages in the masterly introduction which Thucydides, the contemporary of Pericles, has prefixed to his history. What was his motive in choosing the Peloponnesian War for his subject? Because it was, in his opinion, the most important, the most instructive event which had, up to that time, happened in the history of mankind. What is his effort in the first twenty-three chapters of his history? To place in their correct point of view all the facts which had brought Grecian society to the point at which that dominant event found it; to strip these facts of their exaggeration, to examine them critically. The enterprises undertaken in the early times of Greece were on a much smaller scale than had been commonly supposed. The Greek chiefs were induced to combine in the expedition against Troy, not by their respect for an oath taken by them all when suitors to Helen, but by their respect for the preponderating influence of Agamemnon; the siege of Troy had been protracted not so much by the valour of the besieged as by the inadequate mode of warfare necessitated by the want of funds of the besiegers. No doubt Thucydides' criticism of the Trojan war is not perfect; but observe how in these and many other points he labours to correct popular errors, to assign their true character to facts, complaining, as he does so, of men's habit of *uncritical* reception of current stories. "So little a matter of care to most men," he says, "is the search after truth, and so inclined are they to take up any story which is ready to their hand." "He himself," he continues, "has endeavoured to give a true picture, and believes that in the main he has done so. For some readers his history may want the charm of the uncritical, half-fabulous narratives of earlier writers; but for such as desire to gain a clear knowledge of the past, and thereby of the future also, which will surely, after the course of human things, represent again hereafter, if not the very image, yet the near resemblance of the past—if such shall judge my work to be profitable, I shall be well content."

What language shall we properly call this? It is *modern* language; it is the language of a thoughtful philosophic man of our own days; it is the language of Burke or Niebuhr assigning the true aim of history. And yet Thucydides is no mere literary man; no isolated thinker, speaking far over the heads of his hearers to a future age—no: he was a man of action, a man of the world, a man of his time. He represents, at its best indeed, but he represents, the general intelligence of his age and nation; of a nation the meanest citizens of which could follow with comprehension the profoundly thoughtful speeches of Pericles.

Let us now turn for a contrast to a historian of the Elizabethan age, also a man of great mark and ability, also a man of action, also a man of the world, Sir Walter Ralegh. Sir Walter Ralegh writes the "History of the World," as Thucydides has written the "History of the Peloponnesian War;" let us hear his language; let us mark his point of view; let us see what problems occur to him for solution. "Seeing," he says, "that we digress in all the ways of our lives—yea, "seeing the life of man is nothing else but digression—I may "be the better excused in writing their lives and actions." What are the preliminary facts which he discusses, as Thucydides discusses the Trojan War and the early naval power of Crete, and which are to lead up to his main inquiry? Open the table of contents of his first volume. You will find:—"Of the firma- "ment, and of the waters above the firmament, and whether "there be any crystalline Heaven, or any primum mobile." You will then find:—"Of Fate, and that the stars have great "influence, and that their operations may diversely be pre- "vented or furthered." Then you come to two entire chapters on the place of Paradise, and on the two chief trees in the garden of Paradise. And in what style, with what power of criticism, does Ralegh treat the subjects so selected? I turn to the 7th section of the third chapter of his first book, which treats "Of their opinion which make Paradise as high as the "moon, and of others which make it higher than the middle "region of the air." Thus he begins the discussion of this opinion:—"Whereas Beda saith, and as the schoolmen affirm "Paradise to be a place altogether removed from the knowledge "of men ('locus a cognitione hominum remotissimus'), and "Barcephas conceived that Paradise was far in the east, but "mounted above the ocean and all the earth, and near the "orb of the moon (which opinion, though the schoolmen "charge Beda withal, yet Pererius lays it off from Beda, upon "Strabus, and his master Rabanus); and whereas Rupertus in his "geography of Paradise doth not much differ from the rest, but "finds it seated next or nearest Heaven—" So he states the error, and now for his own criticism of it. "First, such a place cannot "be commodious to live in, for being set so near the moon it had "been too near the sun and other heavenly bodies. Secondly, "it must have been too joint a neighbour to the element of "fire. Thirdly, the air in that region is so violently moved and "carried about with such swiftness as nothing in that place can "consist or have abiding. Fourthly,"—but what has been quoted is surely enough, and there is no use in continuing.

Which is the ancient here, and which is the modern? Which uses the language of an intelligent man of our own days? which a language wholly obsolete and unfamiliar to us? Which has the rational appreciation and control of his facts? which wanders among them helplessly and without a clue? Is it our own countryman, or is it the Greek? And the language of Ralegh affords a fair sample of the critical power, of the point of view, possessed by the majority of intelligent men of his day; as the language of Thucydides affords us a fair sample of the critical power of the majority of intelligent men in the age of Pericles.

Well, then, in the age of Pericles we have, in spite of its antiquity, a highly-developed, a modern, a deeply interesting epoch. Next comes the question: Is this epoch adequately interpreted by its highest literature? Now, the peculiar characteristic of the highest literature—the poetry—of the fifth century in Greece before the Christian era, is its *adequacy;* the peculiar characteristic of the poetry of Sophocles is its consummate, its unrivalled *adequacy;* that it represents the highly developed human nature of that age—human nature developed in a number of directions, politically, socially, religiously, morally developed—in its completest and most harmonious development in all these directions; while there is shed over this poetry the charm of that noble serenity which always accompanies true insight. If in the body of Athenians of that time there was, as we have said, the utmost energy of mature manhood, public and private; the most entire freedom, the most unprejudiced and intelligent observation of human affairs—in Sophocles there is the same energy, the same maturity, the same freedom, the same intelligent observation; but all these idealized and glorified by the grace and light shed over them from the noblest poetical feeling. And therefore I have ventured to say of Sophocles, that he "saw life steadily, and saw it whole." Well may we understand how Pericles—how the great statesman whose aim was, it has been said, "to realize in Athens the idea which he had conceived of human greatness," and who partly succeeded in his aim—should have been drawn to the great poet whose works are the noblest reflection of his success.

I assert, therefore, though the detailed proof of the assertion must be reserved for other opportunities, that, if the fifth century in Greece before our era is a significant and modern epoch, the poetry of that epoch—the poetry of Pindar, Æschylus, and Sophocles—is an adequate representation and interpretation of it.

The poetry of Aristophanes is an adequate representation of it also. True, this poetry regards humanity from the comic side; but there is a comic side from which to regard humanity as well as a tragic one; and the distinction of Aristophanes is to have regarded it from the true point of view on the comic side. He too, like Sophocles, regards the human nature of his time in its fullest development; the boldest creations of a riotous imagination are in Aristophanes, as has been justly said, based always upon the foundation of a serious thought: politics, education, social life, literature—all the great modes in which the human life of his day manifested itself—are the subjects of his thoughts, and of his penetrating comment. There is shed, therefore, over his poetry the charm, the vital freshness, which is felt when man and his relations are from any side adequately, and therefore genially, regarded. Here is the true difference between Aristophanes and Menander. There has been preserved an epitome of a comparison by Plutarch between Aristophanes and Menander, in which the grossness of the former, the exquisite truth to life and felicity of observation of the latter, are strongly insisted upon; and the preference of the refined, the learned, the intelligent men of a later period for Menander loudly proclaimed. "What should take a man of refinement to "the theatre," asks Plutarch, "except to see one of Menander's "plays? When do you see the theatre filled with cultivated "persons, except when Menander is acted? and he is the "favourite refreshment," he continues, "to the overstrained "mind of the laborious philosopher." And every one knows the famous line of tribute to this poet by an enthusiastic admirer in antiquity:—"O Life and Menander, which of you painted the other?" We remember, too, how a great English statesman is said to have declared that there was no lost work of antiquity which he so ardently desired to recover as a play of Menander. Yet Menander has perished, and Aristophanes has survived. And to what is this to be attributed? To the instinct of self-preservation in humanity. The human race has the strongest, the most invincible tendency to *live*, to *develop* itself. It retains, it clings to what fosters its life, what favours its development, to the literature which exhibits it in its vigour; it rejects, it abandons what does not foster its development, the literature which exhibits it arrested and decayed. Now, between the times of Sophocles and Menander a great check had befallen the development of Greece;—the failure of the Athenian expedition to Syracuse, and the consequent termination of the Peloponnesian War in a result unfavourable to Athens. The free expansion of her growth was checked; one of the noblest channels of Athenian life, that of political activity, had begun to narrow and to dry up. That was the true catastrophe of the ancient world; it was then that the oracles of the ancient world should have become silent, and that its gods should have forsaken their temples; for from that date the intellectual and spiritual life of Greece was left without an adequate material basis of political and practical life; and both began inevitably to decay. The opportunity of the ancient world was then lost, never to return; for neither the Macedonian nor the Roman world, which possessed an adequate material basis, possessed, like the Athens of earlier times, an adequate intellect and soul to inform and inspire them; and there was left of the ancient world, when Christianity arrived, of Greece only a head without a body, and of Rome only a body without a soul.

It is Athens after this check, after this diminution of vitality,—it is man with part of his life shorn away, refined and intelligent indeed, but sceptical, frivolous, and dissolute,—which the poetry of Menander represented. The cultivated, the accomplished might applaud the dexterity, the perfection of the representation—might prefer it to the free genial delineation of a more living time with which they were no longer in sympathy. But the instinct of humanity taught it, that in the one poetry there was the seed of life, in the other poetry the seed of death; and it has rescued Aristophanes, while it has left Menander to his fate.

In the flowering period of the life of Greece, therefore, we have a culminating age, one of the flowering periods of the life of the human race: in the poetry of that age we have a literature commensurate with its epoch. It is most perfectly commensurate in the poetry of Pindar, Æschylus, Sophocles, Aristophanes; these, therefore, will be the supremely interesting objects in this literature; but the stages in literature which led up to this point of perfection, the stages in literature which led downward from it, will be deeply interesting also. A distinguished person,[1] who has lately been occupying himself with Homer, has remarked that an undue preference is given, in the studies of Oxford, to these poets over Homer. The justification of such a preference, even if we put aside all philological considerations, lies, perhaps, in what I have said. Homer himself is eternally interesting; he is a greater poetical power than even Sophocles or Æschylus; but his age is less interesting than himself. Æschylus and Sophocles represent an age as interesting as themselves; the names, indeed, in their dramas are the names of the old heroic world, from which they were far separated; but these names are taken, because the use of them permits to the poet that free and ideal treatment of his characters which the highest tragedy demands; and into these figures of the old world is poured all the fulness of life and of thought which the new world had accumulated. This new world in its maturity of reason resembles our own; and the advantage over Homer in their greater significance for *us*, which Æschylus and Sophocles gain by belonging to this new world, more than compensates for their poetical inferiority to him.

Let us now pass to the Roman world. There is no necessity to accumulate proofs that the culminating period of Roman history is to be classed among the leading, the significant, the modern periods of the world. There is universally current, I think, a pretty correct appreciation of the high development of the Rome of Cicero and Augustus; no one doubts that material civilization and the refinements of life were largely diffused in it; no one doubts that cultivation of mind and intelligence were widely diffused in it. Therefore, I will not occupy time by showing that Cicero corresponded with his friends in the

[1] Mr. Gladstone.

style of the most accomplished, the most easy letter-writers of modern times; that Cæsar did not write history like Sir Walter Ralegh. The great period of Rome is, perhaps, on the whole, the greatest, the fullest, the most significant period on record; it is certainly a greater, a fuller period than the age of Pericles. It is an infinitely larger school for the men reared in it; the relations of life are immeasurably multiplied, the events which happen are on an immeasurably grander scale. The facts, the spectacle of this Roman world, then, are immense: let us see how far the literature, the interpretation of the facts, has been adequate.

Let us begin with a great poet, a great philosopher, Lucretius. In the case of Thucydides I called attention to the fact that his habit of mind, his mode of dealing with questions, were modern; that they were those of an enlightened, reflecting man among ourselves. Let me call attention to the exhibition in Lucretius of a modern *feeling* not less remarkable than the modern *thought* in Thucydides. The predominance of thought, of reflection, in modern epochs is not without its penalties; in the unsound, in the over-tasked, in the over-sensitive, it has produced the most painful, the most lamentable results; it has produced a state of feeling unknown to less enlightened but perhaps healthier epochs—the feeling of depression, the feeling of *ennui*. Depression and *ennui;* these are the characteristics stamped on how many of the representative works of modern times! they are also the characteristics stamped on the poem of Lucretius. One of the most powerful, the most solemn passages of the work of Lucretius, one of the most powerful, the most solemn passages in the literature of the whole world, is the well-known conclusion of the third book. With masterly touches he exhibits the lassitude, the incurable tedium which pursue men in their amusements; with indignant irony he upbraids them for the cowardice with which they cling to a life which for most is miserable; to a life which contains, for the most fortunate, nothing but the old dull round of the same unsatisfying objects for ever presented. "A "man rushes abroad," he says, "because he is sick of being "at home; and suddenly comes home again because he finds "himself no whit easier abroad. He posts as fast as his horses "can take him to his country-seat: when he has got there he "hesitates what to do; or he throws himself down moodily to "sleep, and seeks forgetfulness in that; or he makes the best of "his way back to town again with the same speed as he fled 5 "from it. Thus every one flies from himself." What a picture of *ennui!* of the disease of the most modern societies, the most advanced civilizations! "O man," he exclaims again, "the lights "of the world, Scipio, Homer, Epicurus, are dead; wilt thou "hesitate and fret at dying, whose life is well-nigh dead whilst 10 "thou art yet alive; who consumest in sleep the greater part "of thy span, and when awake dronest and ceasest not to "dream; and carriest about a mind troubled with baseless fear, "and canst not find what it is that aileth thee when thou "staggerest like a drunken wretch in the press of thy cares, 15 "and welterest hither and thither in the unsteady wandering "of thy spirit!" And again: "I have nothing more than you "have already seen," he makes Nature say to man, "to invent "for your amusement; *eadem sunt omnia semper*—all things "continue the same for ever." 20

Yes, Lucretius is modern; but is he adequate? And how can a man adequately interpret the activity of his age when he is not in sympathy with it? Think of the varied, the abundant, the wide spectacle of the Roman life of his day; think of its fulness of occupation, its energy of effort. From these Lu- 25 cretius withdraws himself, and bids his disciples to withdraw themselves; he bids them to leave the business of the world, and to apply themselves "*naturam cognoscere rerum*—to learn the nature of things;" but there is no peace, no cheerfulness for him either in the world from which he comes, or in the 30 solitude to which he goes. With stern effort, with gloomy despair, he seems to rivet his eyes on the elementary reality, the naked framework of the world, because the world in its fulness and movement is too exciting a spectacle for his dis- composed brain. He seems to feel the spectacle of it at once 35 terrifying and alluring; and to deliver himself from it he has to keep perpetually repeating his formula of disenchantment and annihilation. In reading him, you understand the tradition which represents him as having been driven mad by a poison administered as a love-charm by his mistress, and as having composed his great work in the intervals of his madness. Lucretius is, therefore, overstrained, gloom-weighted, morbid; and he who is morbid is no adequate interpreter of his age.

I pass to Virgil; to the poetical name which of all poetical names has perhaps had the most prodigious fortune; the name which for Dante, for the Middle Age, represented the perfection of classical antiquity. The perfection of classical antiquity Virgil does not represent; but far be it from me to add my voice to those which have decried his genius; nothing that I shall say is, or can ever be, inconsistent with a profound, an almost affectionate veneration for him. But with respect to him, as with respect to Lucretius, I shall freely ask the question, *Is he adequate?* Does he represent the epoch in which he lived, the mighty Roman world of his time, as the great poets of the great epoch of Greek life represented theirs, in all its fulness, in all its significance?

From the very form itself of his great poem, the Æneid, one would be led to augur that this was impossible. The epic form, as a form for representing contemporary or nearly contemporary events, has attained, in the poems of Homer, an unmatched, an immortal success; the epic form as employed by learned poets for the reproduction of the events of a past age has attained a very considerable success. But for *this* purpose, for the poetic treatment of the events of a *past* age, the epic form is a less vital form than the dramatic form. The great poets of the modern period of Greece are accordingly, as we have seen, the *dramatic* poets. The chief of these—Æschylus, Sophocles, Euripides, Aristophanes—have survived: the distinguished epic poets of the same period—Panyasis, Chœrilus, Antimachus—though praised by the Alexandrian critics, have perished in a common destruction with the undistinguished. And what is the reason of this? It is, that the dramatic form exhibits, above all, *the actions of man as strictly determined by his thoughts and feelings;* it exhibits, therefore, what may be always accessible, always intelligible, always interesting. But the epic form takes a wider range; it represents not only the thought and passion of man, that which is universal and eternal, but also the forms of outward life, the fashion of manners, the aspects of nature, that which is local or transient. To exhibit adequately what is local and transient, only a witness, a contemporary, can suffice. In the *reconstruction*, by learning and antiquarian ingenuity, of the local and transient features of a past age, in their representation by one who is not a witness or contemporary, it is impossible to feel the liveliest kind of interest. What, for instance, is the most interesting portion of the Æneid,—the portion where Virgil seems to be moving most freely, and therefore to be most animated, most forcible? Precisely that portion which has most a *dramatic* character; the episode of Dido; that portion where locality and manners are nothing—where persons and characters are everything. We might presume beforehand, therefore, that if Virgil, at a time when contemporary epic poetry was no longer possible, had been inspired to represent human life in its fullest significance, he would not have selected the epic form. Accordingly, what is, in fact, the character of the poem, the frame of mind of the poet? Has the poem the depth, the completeness of the poems of Æschylus or Sophocles, of those adequate and consummate representations of human life? Has the poet the serious cheerfulness of Sophocles, of a man who has mastered the problem of human life, who knows its gravity, and is therefore serious, but who knows that he comprehends it, and is therefore cheerful? Over the whole of the great poem of Virgil, over the whole Æneid, there rests an ineffable melancholy: not a rigid, a moody gloom, like the melancholy of Lucretius; no, a sweet, a touching sadness, but still a sadness; a melancholy which is at once a source of charm in the poem, and a testimony to its incompleteness. Virgil, as Niebuhr has well said, expressed no affected self-disparagement, but the haunting, the irresistible self-dissatisfaction of his heart, when he desired on his deathbed that his poem might be destroyed. A man of the most delicate genius, the most rich learning, but of weak health, of the most sensitive nature, in a great and overwhelming world; conscious, at heart, of his inadequacy for the thorough spiritual mastery of that world and its inter-

period of Greece; but we have not a commensurate literature. In Greece we have seen a highly modern, a most significant and interesting period, although on a scale of less magnitude and importance than the great period of Rome; but then, co-existing with the great epoch of Greece there is what is wanting to that of Rome, a commensurate, an interesting literature.

The intellectual history of our race cannot be clearly understood without applying to other ages, nations, and literatures the same method of inquiry which we have been here imperfectly applying to what is called classical antiquity. But enough has at least been said, perhaps, to establish the absolute, the enduring interest of Greek literature, and, above all, of Greek poetry.

Preface to *Merope*

I am not about to defend myself for having taken the story of the following tragedy from classical antiquity. On this subject I have already said all which appears to me to be necessary. For those readers to whom my tragedy will give pleasure, no argument on such a matter is required: one critic, whose fine intelligence it would have been an honour to convince, lives, alas! no longer: there are others, upon whom no arguments which I could possibly use would produce any impression. The Athenians fined Phrynichus for representing to them their own sufferings: there are critics who would fine us for representing to them anything else.

But, as often as it has happened to me to be blamed or praised for my supposed addiction to the classical school in poetry, I have thought, with real humiliation, how little any works of mine were entitled to rank among the genuine works of that school; how little they were calculated to give, to readers unacquainted with the great creations of classical antiquity, any adequate impression of their form or of their spirit. And yet, whatever the critics may say, there exists, I am convinced, even in England, even in this stronghold of the romantic school, a wide though an ill-informed curiosity on the subject of the so-called classical school, meriting a more complete satisfaction than it has hitherto obtained. Greek art—the antique—classical beauty—a nameless hope and interest attaches, I can often see, to these words, even in the minds of those who have been brought up among the productions of the romantic school; of those who have been taught to consider classicalism as inseparable from coldness, and the antique as another phrase for the unreal. So immortal, so indestructible is the power of true beauty, of consummate form: it may be submerged, but the tradition of it survives: nations arise which know it not, which hardly believe in the report of it; but they, too, are haunted with an indefinable interest in its name, with an inexplicable curiosity as to its nature. 5

But however the case may be with regard to the curiosity of the public, I have long had the strongest desire to attempt, for my own satisfaction, to come to closer quarters with the form which produces such grand effects in the hands of the Greek masters; to try to obtain, through the medium of a living, familiar language, a fuller and more intense feeling of that beauty, which, even when apprehended through the medium of a dead language, so powerfully affected me. In his delightful *Life of Goethe*, Mr. Lewes has most truly observed that Goethe's *Iphigeneia* enjoys an inestimable advantage in being written in a language which, being a modern language, is in some sort our own. Not only is it vain to expect that the vast majority of mankind will ever undertake the toil of mastering a dead language, above all, a dead language so difficult as the Greek; but it may be doubted whether even those, whose enthusiasm shrinks from no toil, can ever so thoroughly press into the intimate feeling of works composed in a dead language as their enthusiasm would desire. 10 15 20

I desired to try, therefore, how much of the effectiveness of the Greek poetical forms I could retain in an English poem constructed under the conditions of those forms; of those forms, too, in their severest and most definite expression, in their application to dramatic poetry. 25

I thought at first that I might accomplish my object by a translation of one of the great works of Æschylus or Sophocles. But a translation is a work not only inferior to the original by the whole difference of talent between the first composer and his translator: it is even inferior to the best which the translator could do under more inspiring circumstances. No man can do his best with a subject which does not penetrate him: 30 35 no man can be penetrated by a subject which he does not conceive independently.

Should I take some subject on which we have an extant work by one of the great Greek poets, and treat it independently? Something was to be said for such a course: in antiquity, the same tragic stories were handled by all the tragic poets: Voltaire says truly that to see the same materials differently treated by different poets is most interesting; accordingly, we have an *Œdipus* of Corneille, an *Œdipus* of Voltaire: innumerable are the *Agamemnons*, the *Electras*, the *Antigones*, of the French and Italian poets from the sixteenth to the nineteenth century. But the same disadvantage which we have in translating clings to us in our attempt to treat these subjects independently: their treatment by the ancient masters is so overwhelmingly great and powerful that we can henceforth conceive them only as they are there treated: an independent conception of them has become impossible for us: in working upon them we are still, therefore, subject to conditions under which no man can do his best.

It remained to select a subject from among those which had been considered to possess the true requisites of good tragic subjects; on which great works had been composed, but had not survived to chill emulation by their grandeur. Of such subjects there is, fortunately, no lack. In the writings of Hyginus, a Latin mythographer of uncertain date, we possess a large stock of them. The heroic stories in Hyginus, Maffei, the reformer of the Italian theatre, imagined rightly or wrongly to be the actual summaries of lost Greek dramas: they are, at any rate, subjects on which lost dramas were founded. Maffei counsels the poets of his nation to turn from the inferior subjects on which they were employing themselves, to this "*miniera di tragici argomenti*," this rich mine of subjects for tragedy. Lessing, the great German critic, echoes Maffei's counsel, but adds a warning. "Yes," he cries, "the great subjects are there, but they await an intelligent eye to regard them: they can be handled, not by the great majority of poets, but only by the small minority."

Among these subjects presented in the collection of Hyginus, there is one which has long attracted my interest, from the testimony of the ancients to its excellence, and from the results which that testimony has called forth from the emulation of the moderns. That subject is the story of Merope. To the effectiveness of the situations which this story offered, Aristotle and Plutarch have borne witness: a celebrated tragedy upon it, probably by Euripides, existed in antiquity. "The *Cresphontes* of Euripides is lost," exclaims the reviewer of Voltaire's *Merope*, a jesuit, and not unwilling to conciliate the terrible pupil of his order; "the *Cresphontes* of Euripides is lost: M. de Voltaire has restored it to us." "Aristotle," says Voltaire, "Aristotle, in his immortal work on Poetry, does not hesitate to affirm that the recognition between Merope and her son was the most interesting moment of the Greek stage." Aristotle affirms no such thing; but he *does* say that the story of Merope, like the stories of Iphigeneia and Antiope, supplies an example of a recognition of the most affecting kind. And Plutarch says: "Look at Merope in the tragedy, lifting up the axe against her own son as being the murderer of her own son, and crying—

> ὁσιωτέραν δὴ τήνδ' ἐγὼ δίδωμί σοι
> πληγήν ——

> A more just stroke than that thou gav'st my son,
> Take——

What an agitation she makes in the theatre! how she fills the spectators with terror lest she should be too quick for the old man who is trying to stop her, and should strike the lad!"

It is singular that neither Aristotle nor Plutarch names the author of the tragedy: scholiasts and other late writers quote from it as from a work of Euripides; but the only writer of authority who names him as its author is Cicero. About fifty lines of it have come down to us: the most important of these remains are the passage just quoted, and a choral address to Peace; of these I have made use in my tragedy, translating the former, and of the latter adopting the general thought, that of rejoicing at the return of peace: the other fragments consist chiefly of detached moral sentences, of which I have not made any use.

It may be interesting to give some account of the more celebrated of those modern works which have been founded upon this subject. But before I proceed to do this, I will state what accounts we have of the story itself.

These proceed from three sources—Apollodorus, Pausanias, and Hyginus. Of their accounts that of Apollodorus is the most ancient, that of Pausanias the most historically valuable, and that of Hyginus the fullest. I will begin with the last-named writer.

Hyginus says:—

"Merope sent away and concealed her infant son. Polyphontes sought for him everywhere, and promised gold to whoever should slay him. He, when he grew up, laid a plan to avenge the murder of his father and brothers. In pursuance of this plan he came to king Polyphontes and asked for the promised gold, saying that he had slain the son of Cresphontes and Merope. The king ordered him to be hospitably entertained, intending to inquire further of him. He, being very tired, went to sleep, and an old man, who was the channel through whom the mother and son used to communicate, arrives at this moment in tears, bringing word to Merope that her son had disappeared from his protector's house. Merope, believing that the sleeping stranger is the murderer of her son, comes into the guest-chamber with an axe, not knowing that he whom she would slay was her son: the old man recognised him, and withheld Merope from slaying him. After the recognition had taken place, Merope, to prepare the way for her vengeance, affected to be reconciled with Polyphontes. The king, overjoyed, celebrated a sacrifice: his guest, pretending to strike the sacrificial victim, slew the king, and so got back his father's kingdom."

Apollodorus says:—

"Cresphontes had not reigned long in Messenia when he was murdered together with two of his sons. And Polyphontes reigned in his stead, he, too, being of the family of Hercules;

and he had for his wife, against her will, Merope, the widow of the murdered king. But Merope had borne to Cresphontes a third son, called Æpytus: him she gave to her own father to bring up. He, when he came to man's estate, returned secretly to Messenia, and slew Polyphontes and the other 5 murderers of his father."

Pausanias adds nothing to the facts told by Apollodorus, except that he records the proceedings of Cresphontes which had provoked the resentment of his Dorian nobles, and led to his murder. His statements on this point will be found in 10 the Historical Introduction which follows this Preface.

The account of the modern fortunes of the story of Merope is a curious chapter in literary history. In the early age of the French theatre this subject attracted the notice of a great man, if not a great poet, the cardinal Richelieu. At his theatre, 15 in the Palais Royal, was brought out, in 1641, a tragedy under the title of *Téléphonte*, the name given by Hyginus to the surviving son of Merope. This piece is said by Voltaire to have contained about a hundred lines by the great cardinal, who had, as is well known, more bent than genius for dramatic 20 composition. There his vein appears to have dried up, and the rest is by an undistinguished hand. This tragedy was followed by another on the same subject from the resident minister, at Paris, of the celebrated Christina of Sweden. Two pieces with the title of *Merope*, besides others on the same 25 story, but with different names, were brought out at Paris before the *Merope* of Voltaire appeared. It seems that none of them created any memorable impression.

The first eminent success was in Italy. There too, as in France, more than one *Merope* was early produced: one of 30 them in the sixteenth century, by a Count Torelli, composed with choruses: but the first success was achieved by Maffei. Scipio Maffei, called by Voltaire the Sophocles and Varro of Verona, was a noble and cultivated person. He became in middle life the historian of his native place, Verona; and may 35 claim the honour of having partly anticipated Niebuhr in his famous discovery, in the Capitular library of that city, of the lost works of Gaius, the Roman lawyer. He visited France and England, and received an honorary degree at Oxford. But in earlier life he signalised himself as the reviver of the study of Greek literature in Italy; and with the aim to promote that study, and to rescue the Italian theatre from the debasement into which it had fallen, he brought out at Modena, in 1713, his tragedy of *Merope.*

The effect was immense. "Let the Greek and Roman writers give place: here is a greater production than the *Œdipus!*" wrote, in Latin verse, an enthusiastic admirer. In the winter following its appearance, the tragedy kept constant possession of the stage in Italy; and its reputation travelled into France and England. In England a play was produced in 1731, by a writer called Jeffreys, professedly taken from the *Merope* of Maffei. But at this period a love-intrigue was considered indispensable in a tragedy: Voltaire was even compelled by the actors to introduce one in his *Œdipus:* and although in Maffei's work there is no love-intrigue, the English adapter felt himself bound to supply the deficiency. Accordingly he makes, if we may trust Voltaire, the unknown son of Merope in love with one of her maids of honour: he is brought before his mother as his own supposed murderer: she gives him the choice of death by the dagger or by poison: he chooses the latter, drinks off the poison and falls insensible: but reappears at the end of the tragedy safe and sound, a friend of the maid of honour having substituted a sleeping-draught for the poison. Such is Voltaire's account of this English *Merope*, of which I have not been able to obtain sight. Voltaire is apt to exaggerate; but the work was, without doubt, sufficiently absurd. A better English translation, by Ayre, appeared in 1740. I have taken from Maffei a line in my tragedy—

"Tyrants think, him they murder not, they spare."

Maffei has—

"Ecco il don dei tiranni: a lor rassembra,
Morte non dando altrui, di dar la vita."

Maffei makes some important changes in the story as told by its ancient relaters. In his tragedy the unknown prince,

Merope's son, is called Egisto: Merope herself is not, as the ancients represented her, at the time of her son's return the wife of Polyphontes, but is repelling the importunate offer of his hand by her husband's murderer: Egisto does not, like Orestes, know his own parentage, and return secretly to his own home in order to wreak vengeance, in concert with his mother, upon his father's murderer: he imagines himself the son of Messenian parents, but of a rank not royal, intrusted to an old man, Polidoro, to be brought up; and is driven by curiosity to quit his protector and visit his native land. He enters Messenia, and is attacked by a robber, whom he kills. The blood upon his dress attracts the notice of some soldiers of Polyphontes whom he falls in with; he is seized and brought to the royal palace. On hearing his story, a suspicion seizes Merope, who has heard from Polidoro that her son has quitted him, that the slain person must have been her own son. The suspicion is confirmed by the sight of a ring on the finger of Egisto, which had belonged to Cresphontes, and which Merope supposes the unknown stranger to have taken from her murdered son: she twice attempts his life: the arrival of Polidoro at last clears up the mystery for her; but at the very moment when she recognises Egisto, they are separated, and no interview of recognition takes place between the mother and son. Finally, the prince is made acquainted with his origin, and kills Polyphontes in the manner described by Hyginus.

This is an outline of the story as arranged by Maffei. This arrangement has been followed, in the main, by all his successors. His treatment of the subject has, I think, some grave defects, which I shall presently notice: but his work has much nobleness and feeling; it seems to me to possess, on the whole, more merit of a strictly poetical kind than any of the subsequent works upon the same subject.

Voltaire's curiosity, which never slumbered, was attracted by the success of Maffei. It was not until 1736, however, when his interest in Maffei's tragedy had been increased by a personal acquaintance with its author, that his own *Merope* was composed. It was not brought out upon the stage until 1743.

It was received, like its Italian predecessor, with an enthusiasm which, assuredly, the English *Merope* will not excite. From its exhibition dates the practice of calling for a successful author to appear at the close of his piece: the audience were so much enchanted with Voltaire's tragedy, that they insisted on seeing the man who had given them such delight. To Corneille had been paid the honour of reserving for him the same seat in the theatre at all representations; but neither he nor Racine were ever "called for."

Voltaire, in a long complimentary letter, dedicated his tragedy to Maffei. He had at first intended, he says, merely to translate the *Merope* of his predecessor, which he so greatly admired: he still admired it; above all, he admired it because it possessed *simplicity;* that simplicity which is, he says, his own idol. But he has to deal with a Parisian audience, with an audience who have been glutted with masterpieces until their delicacy has become excessive; until they can no longer support the simple and rustic air, the details of country life, which Maffei had imitated from the Greek theatre. The audience of Paris, of that city in which some thirty thousand spectators daily witnessed theatrical performances, and thus acquired, by constant practice, a severity of taste, to which the ten thousand Athenians who saw tragedies but four times a year could not pretend—of that terrible city, in which

"Et pueri nasum rhinocerotis habent:"

this audience loved simplicity, indeed, but not the same simplicity which was loved at Athens and imitated by Maffei. "I regret this," says Voltaire, "for how fond I am of simple nature! but, *il faut se plier au goût d'une nation,* one must accommodate oneself to the taste of one's countrymen."

He does himself less than justice. When he objects, indeed, to that in Maffei's work which is truly "naïf et rustique," to that which is truly in a Greek spirit, he is wrong. His objection, for instance, to the passage in which the old retainer of Cresphontes describes, in the language of a man of his class, the rejoicings which celebrated his master's accession, is, in my opinion, perfectly groundless. But the wonderful penetration and clear sense of Voltaire seizes, in general, upon really weak points in Maffei's work: upon points which, to an Athenian, would have seemed as weak as they seemed to Voltaire. A French audience, he says, would not have borne to witness Polyphontes making love to Merope, whose husband he had murdered: neither would an Athenian audience have borne it. To hear Polyphontes say to Merope "*Io t'amo*," even though he is but feigning, for state purposes, a love which he has not really, shocks the natural feeling of mankind. Our usages, says Voltaire, would not permit that Merope should twice rush upon her son to slay him, once with a javelin, the next time with an axe. The French dramatic usages, then, would on this point have perfectly agreed with the laws of reason and good taste: this repetition of the same incident is tasteless and unmeaning. It is a grave fault of art, says Voltaire, that, at the critical moment of recognition, not a word passes between Merope and her son. He is right; a noble opportunity is thus thrown away. He objects to Maffei's excessive introduction of conversations between subaltern personages: these conversations are, no doubt, tiresome. Other points there are, with respect to which we may say that Voltaire's objections would have been perfectly sound had Maffei really done what is imputed to him: but he has not. Voltaire has a talent for misrepresentation, and he often uses it unscrupulously.

He never used it more unscrupulously than on this occasion. The French public, it appears, took Voltaire's expressions of obligation to Maffei somewhat more literally than Voltaire liked: they imagined that the French *Merope* was rather a successful adaptation of the Italian *Merope* than an original work. It was necessary to undeceive them. A letter appeared, addressed by a M. de La Lindelle to Voltaire, in which Voltaire is reproached for his excessive praises of Maffei's tragedy, in which that work is rigorously analysed, its faults remorselessly displayed. No merit is allowed to it: it is a thoroughly bad piece on a thoroughly good subject. Lessing, who, in 1768, in his *Hamburgische Dramaturgie*, reviewed Voltaire's *Merope* at great length, evidently has divined, what is the truth, that M. de La Lindelle and Voltaire are one and the same person. It required indeed but little of the great Lessing's sagacity to divine that. An unknown M. de La Lindelle does not write one letter in that style of unmatched incisiveness and animation, that style compared to which the style of Lord Macaulay is tame, and the style of Isocrates is obscure, and then pass for ever from the human stage. M. de La Lindelle *is* Voltaire; but that does not hinder Voltaire from replying to him with perfect gravity. "You terrify me!" he exclaims to his correspondent—that is, to himself: "you terrify me! you are as hypercritical as Scaliger. Why not fix your attention rather on the beauties of M. Maffei's work, than on its undoubted defects? It is my sincere opinion that, in some points, M. Maffei's *Merope* is superior to my own." The transaction is one of the most signal instances of literary sharp practice on record. To this day, in the ordinary editions of Voltaire, M. de La Lindelle's letter figures, in the correspondence prefixed to the tragedy of *Merope*, as the letter of an authentic person; although the true history of the proceeding has long been well known, and Voltaire's conduct in it was severely blamed by La Harpe.

Voltaire had said that his *Merope* was occasioned by that of Maffei. "*Occasioned*," says Lessing, "is too weak a word: M. de Voltaire's tragedy owes *everything* to that of M. Maffei." This is not just. We have seen the faults in Maffei's work pointed out by Voltaire. Some of these faults he avoids: at the same time he discerns, with masterly clearness, the true difficulties of the subject. "Comment se prendre," he says, "pour faire penser à Mérope que son fils est l'assassin de son fils même?" That is one problem; here is another: "Comment trouver des motifs nécessaires pour que Polyphonte veuille épouser Mérope?" Let us see which of Maffei's faults Voltaire avoids: let us see how far he solves the problems which he himself has enunciated.

The story, in its main outline, is the same with Voltaire as with Maffei; but in some particulars it is altered, so as to have more probability. Like Maffei's Egisto, Voltaire's Égisthe does not know his own origin: like him, youthful curiosity drives him to quit his aged protector, and to re-enter Messenia. Like him he has an encounter with a stranger, whom he slays, and whose blood, staining his clothes, leads to his apprehension. But this stranger is an emissary of Polyphontes, sent to effect the young prince's murder. This is an improvement upon the robber of Maffei, who has no connexion whatever with the action of the piece. Suspicion falls upon Égisthe on the same grounds as those on which it fell upon Egisto. The suspicion is confirmed in Égisthe's case by the appearance of a coat of armour, as, in Egisto's case, it was confirmed by the appearance of a ring. In neither case does Merope seem to have sufficient cause to believe the unknown youth to be her son's murderer. In Voltaire's tragedy, Merope is ignorant until the end of the third act that Polyphontes is her husband's murderer; nay, she believes that Cresphontes, murdered by the brigands of Pylos, has been avenged by Polyphontes, who claims her gratitude on that ground. He desires to marry her in order to strengthen his position. "Of interests in the state," he says,

> "Il ne reste aujourd'hui que le vôtre et le mien:
> Nous devons l'un à l'autre un mutuel soutien."

Voltaire thus departs widely from the tradition; but he can represent Merope as entertaining and discussing the tyrant's offer of marriage without shocking our feelings. The style, however, in which Voltaire makes Polyphontes urge his addresses, would sometimes, I think, have wounded a Greek's taste as much as Maffei's *Io t'amo*—

> "Je sais que vos appas, encore dans le printemps,
> Pourraient s'effaroucher de l'hiver de mes ans."

What an address from a stern, care-haunted ruler to a widowed queen, the mother of a grown-up son! The tragedy proceeds; and Merope is about to slay her son, when his aged guardian arrives and makes known to her who the youth is. This is as in Maffei's piece; but Voltaire avoids the absurdity of the double attempt by Merope on her son's life. Yet he, too, permits Égisthe to leave the stage without exchanging a word with his mother: the very fault which he justly censures in Maffei. Égisthe, indeed, does not even learn, on this occasion, that Merope is his mother: the recognition is thus cut in half. The second half of it comes afterwards, in the presence of Polyphontes; and his presence imposes, of course, a restraint upon the mother and son. Merope is driven, by fear for her son's safety, to consent to marry Polyphontes, although his full guilt is now revealed to her; but she is saved by her son, who slays the tyrant in the manner told in the tradition and followed by Maffei.

What is the real merit of Voltaire's tragedy? We must forget the rhymed Alexandrines; that metre, faulty not so much because it is disagreeable in itself, as because it has in it something which is essentially unsuited to perfect tragedy; that metre which is so indefensible, and which Voltaire has so ingeniously laboured to defend. He takes a noble passage from Racine's *Phédre*, alters words so as to remove the rhyme, and asks if the passage now produces as good an effect as before. But a fine passage which we are used to we like in the form in which we are used to it, with all its faults. Prose is, undoubtedly, a less noble vehicle for tragedy than verse; yet we should not like the fine passages in Goethe's prose tragedy of *Egmont* the better for having them turned into verse. Besides, it is not clear that the unrhymed Alexandrine is a better tragic metre than the rhymed. Voltaire says that usage has now established the metre in France, and that the dramatic poet has no escape from it. For him and his contemporaries this is a valid plea; but how much one regrets that the poetical feeling of the French nation did not, at a period when such an alteration was still possible, change for a better this unsuitable tragic metre, as the Greeks, in the early period of their tragic art, changed for the more fitting iambus their trochaic tetrameter.

To return to Voltaire's *Merope*. It is admirably constructed, and must have been most effective on the stage. One feels, as one reads it, that a poet gains something by living amongst a population who have the nose of the rhinoceros: his ingenuity becomes sharpened. This work has, besides, that stamp of a prodigious talent which none of Voltaire's works are without; it has vigour, clearness, rapid movement; it has lines which are models of terse observation—

> "Le premier qui fut roi fut un soldat heureux:
> Qui sert bien son pays n'a pas besoin d'aieux." 5

It has lines which are models of powerful, animated, rhetoric—

> MÉROPE.
> "Courons à Polyphonte—implorons son appui."
>
> NARBAS.
> "N'implorez que les dieux, et ne craignez que lui." 10

What it wants is a charm of poetical feeling, which Racine's tragedies possess, and which has given to them the decisive superiority over those of Voltaire. He has managed his story with great adroitness; but he has departed from the original tradition yet further than Maffei. He has avoided several of 15 Maffei's faults: why has he not avoided his fault of omitting to introduce, at the moment of recognition, a scene between the mother and son? Lessing thinks that he wanted the double recognition in order to enable him to fill his prescribed space, that terrible "carrière de cinq actes" of which he so grievously 20 complains. I believe, rather, that he cut the recognition in two, in order to produce for his audience two distinct shocks of surprise: for to inspire *surprise*, Voltaire considered the dramatic poet's true aim; an opinion which, as we shall hereafter see, sometimes led him astray. 25

Voltaire's *Merope* was adapted for the English stage by Aaron Hill, a singular man; by turns, poet, soldier, theatrical manager, and Lord Peterborough's private secretary; but always, and above all, an indefatigable projector. He originated a beech-oil company, a Scotch timber company, and a plan to 30 colonise Florida. He published Essays on Reducing the Price of Coals, on Repairing Dagenham Breach, and on English Grape Wines; an epic poem on Gideon, a tragedy called *The Fatal Vision, or Fall of Siam,* and a translation of Voltaire's *Zaïre*. His *Merope* was his last work. It appeared in 1749 with 35 a dedication to Lord Bolingbroke; it was brought on the stage with great success, Garrick acting in it; and Hill, who was at this time in poverty, and who died soon after, received a considerable sum from his benefit nights. I have not seen this work, which is not included in the Inchbald collection of acted plays. Warton calls Aaron Hill an affected and fustian writer, and this seems to have been his reputation among his contemporaries. His *Zara*, which I have seen, has the fault of so much of English literature of the second class—an incurable defect of *style*.

One other *Merope* remains to be noticed—the *Merope* of Alfieri. In this tragedy, which appeared in 1783, Alfieri has entirely followed Maffei and Voltaire. He seems to have followed Maffei in the first half of it; Voltaire in the second. His Polyphontes, however, does not make love to Merope: desiring to obtain her hand, in order by this marriage to make the Messenians forget their attachment to Cresphontes, he appeals to her self-interest. "You are miserable," he says; "but a throne is a great consolation. A throne is—

> la sola
> Non vile ammenda, che al fallir mio resti."

Egisto, in Alfieri's piece, falls under suspicion from the blood left on his clothes in a struggle with a stranger, whom he kills and throws into the river Pamisus. The suspicion is confirmed by the appearance of a girdle recognised by Merope as having belonged to her son; as it was confirmed in Maffei's piece by the appearance of a ring, in Voltaire's, by that of a coat of armour. The rest is, in the main, as with Voltaire, except that Alfieri makes Polyphontes perish upon the stage, under circumstances of considerable improbability.

This work of Alfieri has the characteristic merit, and the characteristic fault, of Alfieri's tragedies: it has the merit of elevation, and the fault of narrowness. *Narrow elevation;* that seems to me exactly to express the quality of Alfieri's poetry: he is a noble-minded, deeply interesting man, but a monotonous poet.

A mistake, a grave mistake it seems to me, in the treatment of their subject, is common to Maffei, Voltaire, and Alfieri. They have abandoned the tradition where they had better have followed it; they have followed it, where they had better have abandoned it. 5

The tradition is a great matter to a poet; it is an unspeakable support; it gives him the feeling that he is treading on solid ground. Aristotle tells the tragic poet that he must not destroy the received stories. A noble and accomplished living poet, M. Manzoni, has, in an admirable dissertation, developed this 10 thesis of the importance to the poet of a basis of tradition. Its importance I feel so strongly, that, where driven to invent in the false story told by Merope's son, as by Orestes in the *Electra*, of his own death, I could not satisfy myself until I discovered in Pausanias a tradition, which I took for my basis, 15 of an Arcadian hunter drowned in the lake Stymphalus, down one of those singular Katabothra, or chasms in the limestone rock, so well known in Greece, in a manner similar to that in which Æpytus is represented to have perished.

Maffei did right, I think, in altering the ancient tradition 20 where it represents Merope as actually the wife of Polyphontes. It revolts our feeling to consider her as married to her husband's murderer; and it is no great departure from the tradition to represent her as sought in marriage by him, but not yet obtained. But why did Maffei (for he, it will be re- 25 membered, gave the story its modern arrangement, which Voltaire and Alfieri have, in all its leading points, followed), why did Maffei abandon that part of the tradition which represents Æpytus, the Messenian prince, as acquainted with his own origin? Why did he and his followers prefer to attrib- 30 ute to curiosity a return which the tradition attributed to a far more tragic motive? Why did they compel themselves to invent a machinery of robbers, assassins, guards, rings, girdles, and I know not what, to effect that which the tradition effects in a far simpler manner, to place Æpytus before his mother as 35 his own murderer? Lessing imagines that Maffei, who wished to depict, above all, the maternal anxiety of Merope, conceived that this anxiety would be more naturally and powerfully awakened by the thought of her child reared in hardship and obscurity as a poor man's son, than by the thought of him reared in splendour as a prince in the palace of her own father. But what a conception of the sorrow of a queen, whose husband has been murdered, and whose son is an exile from his inheritance, to suppose that such a sorrow is enhanced by the thought that her child is rudely housed and plainly fed; to assume that it would take a less tragic complexion if she knew that he lived in luxury! No; the true tragic motive of Merope's sorrow is elsewhere: the tradition amply supplied it.

Here, then, the moderns have invented amiss, because they have invented needlessly; because, on this point, the tradition, as it stood, afforded perfect materials to the tragic poet: and, by Maffei's change, not a higher tragic complication, but merely a greater puzzle and intricacy is produced. I come now to a point on which the tradition might with advantage, as I think, have been set aside; and that is, the character of Polyphontes.

Yet, on this point, to speak of *setting aside the tradition* is to speak too strongly; for the tradition is here not complete. Neither Pausanias nor Apollodorus mention circumstances which definitely fix the character of Polyphontes; Hyginus, no doubt, represents him as a villain, and, if Hyginus follows Euripides, Euripides also thus represented him. Euripides may possibly have done so; yet a purer tragic feeling, it seems to me, is produced, if Polyphontes is represented as not wholly black and inexcusable, than if he is represented as a mere monster of cruelty and hypocrisy. Aristotle's profound remark is well known, that the tragic personage whose ruin is represented, should be a personage neither eminently good, nor yet one brought to ruin by sheer iniquity; nay, that his character should incline rather to good than to bad, but that he should have some fault which impels him to his fall. For, as he explains, the two grand tragic feelings, pity and terror, which it is the business of tragedy to excite, will not be excited by the spectacle of the ruin of a mere villain; since pity is for those who suffer undeservedly, and such a man suffers deservedly: terror is excited by the fall of one of like nature with ourselves, and we feel that the mere villain is not as ourselves. Aristotle, no doubt, is here speaking, above all, of the Protagonist, or principal personage of the drama; but the noblest tragic poets of Greece rightly extended their application of the truth on which his remark is based to all the personages of the drama: neither the Creon of Sophocles, nor the Clytemnestra of Æschylus, are wholly inexcusable; in none of the extant dramas of Æschylus or Sophocles is there a character which is entirely bad. For such a character we must go to Euripides; we must go to an art—wonderful indeed, for I entirely dissent from the unreserved disparagers of this great poet—but an art of less moral significance than the art of Sophocles and Æschylus; we must go to tragedies like the *Hecuba*, for villains like Polymestor.

What is the main dramatic difficulty of the story of Merope, as usually treated? It is, as Alfieri rightly saw, that the interest naturally declines from the moment of Merope's recognition of her son; that the destruction of the tyrant is not, after this, matter of interest enough to affect us deeply. This is true, if Polyphontes is a mere villain. It is not true, if he is one for the ruin of whom we may, in spite of his crime, feel a profound compassion. Then our interest in the story lasts to the end: for to the very end we are inspired with the powerful tragic emotions of commiseration and awe. Pausanias states circumstances which suggest the possibility of representing Polyphontes, not as a mere cruel and selfish tyrant, but as a man whose crime was a truly tragic fault, the error of a noble nature. Assume such a nature in him, and the turn of circumstances in the drama takes a new aspect: Merope and her son triumph, but the fall of their foe leaves us awestruck and compassionate: the story issues *tragically*, as Aristotle has truly said that the best tragic stories ought to issue.

Neither Maffei, nor Voltaire, nor Alfieri have drawn Polyphontes with a character to inspire any feeling but aversion, with any traits of nobleness to mitigate our satisfaction at his death. His character being such, it is difficult to render his anxiety to obtain Merope's hand intelligible, for Merope's situation is not such as to make her enmity really dangerous to

Polyphontes; he has, therefore, no sufficient motive of self-interest, and the nobler motives of reparation and pacification could have exercised, on such a character, no force. Voltaire accordingly, whose keen eye no weak place of this kind escaped, felt his difficulty. "Neither M. Maffei nor I," he confesses, "have assigned any sufficient motives for the desire of Polyphontes to marry Merope."

To criticise is easier than to create; and if I have been led, in this review of the fortunes of my story, to find fault with the works of others, I do not on that account assume that I have myself produced a work which is not a thousand times more faulty.

It remains to say something, for those who are not familiar with the Greek dramatic forms, of the form in which this tragedy is cast. Greek tragedy, as is well known, took its origin from the songs of a chorus, and the stamp of its origin remained for ever impressed upon it. A chorus, or band of dancers, moving around the altar of Bacchus, sang the adventures of the god. To this band Thespis joined an actor, who held dialogue with the chorus, and who was called ὑποκριτής, *the answerer*, because he answered the songs of the chorus. The drama thus commenced; for the dialogue of this actor with the chorus brought before the audience some action of Bacchus, or of one of the heroes; this action, narrated by the actor, was commented on in song, at certain intervals, by the chorus alone. Æschylus added a second actor, thus making the character of the representation more *dramatic*, for the chorus was never itself so much an actor as a hearer and observer of the actor: Sophocles added a third. These three actors might successively personate several characters in the same piece; but to three actors and a chorus the dramatic poet limited himself: only in a single piece of Sophocles, not brought out until after his death, was the employment of a fourth actor, it appears, necessary.

The chorus consisted, in the time of Sophocles, of fifteen persons. After their first entrance they remained before the spectators, without withdrawing, until the end of the piece. Their place was in the orchestra; that of the actors was upon the stage. The orchestra was a circular space, like the pit of our theatres: the chorus arrived in it by side-entrances, and not by the stage. In the centre of the orchestra was the altar of Bacchus, around which the chorus originally danced; but in dramatic representations their place was between this altar and the stage: here they stood, a little lower than the persons on the stage, but looking towards them, and holding, through their leaders, conversation with them: then, at pauses in the action, the united chorus sang songs expressing their feelings at what was happening upon the stage, making, as they sang, certain measured stately movements between the stage and the altar, and occasionally standing still. Steps led from the orchestra to the stage, and the chorus, or some members of it, might thus, if necessary, join the actors on the stage; but this seldom happened, the proper place for the chorus was the orchestra. The dialogue of the chorus with the actors on the stage passed generally in the ordinary form of dramatic dialogue; but, on occasions where strong feeling was excited, the dialogue took a lyrical form. Long dialogues of this kind sometimes took place between the leaders of the chorus and one of the actors upon the stage, their burden being a lamentation for the dead.

The Greek theatres were vast, and open to the sky; the actors, masked, and in a somewhat stiff tragic costume, were to be regarded from a considerable distance: a solemn, clearly marked style of gesture, a sustained tone of declamation, were thus rendered necessary. Under these conditions, intricate by-play, rapid variations in the action, requiring great mobility, ever-changing shades of tone and gesture in the actor, were impossible. Broad and simple effects were, under these conditions, above all to be aimed at; a profound and clear impression was to be effected. Unity of plan in the action, and symmetry in the treatment of it, were indispensable. The action represented, therefore, was to be a single, rigorously developed action; the masses of the composition were to be balanced, each bringing out the other into stronger and distincter relief. In the best tragedies, not only do the divisions of the full choral songs accurately correspond to one another, but the divisions of the lyrical dialogue, nay, even the divisions of the regular dramatic dialogue, form corresponding members, of which one member is the answer, the counter-stroke to the other; and an indescribable sense of distinctness and depth of impression is thus produced.

From what has been said, the reader will see that the Greek tragic forms were not chosen as being, in the nature of things, the best tragic forms; such would be a wholly false conception of them. They are an adaptation to dramatic purposes, under certain theatrical conditions, of forms previously existing for other purposes; that adaptation at which the Greeks, after several stages of improvement, finally rested. The laws of Greek tragic art, therefore, are not exclusive; they are for Greek dramatic art itself, but they do not pronounce other modes of dramatic art unlawful; they are, at most, *prophecies of the improbability of dramatic success under other conditions.* "Tragedy," says Aristotle, in a remarkable passage, "after going through many changes, got the nature which suited it, and there it stopped. Whether or no the kinds of tragedy are yet exhausted," he presently adds, "tragedy being considered either in itself, or in respect to the stage, I shall not now inquire." Travelling in a certain path, the spirit of man arrived at Greek tragedy; travelling in other paths, it may arrive at other kinds of tragedy.

But it cannot be denied that the Greek tragic forms, although not the only possible tragic forms, satisfy, in the most perfect manner, some of the most urgent demands of the human spirit. If, on the one hand, the human spirit demands variety and the widest possible range, it equally demands, on the other hand, depth and concentration in its impressions. Powerful thought and emotion, flowing in strongly marked channels, make a stronger impression: this is the main reason why a metrical form is a more effective vehicle for them than prose: in prose there is more freedom, but, in the metrical form, the very limit gives a sense [of] precision and emphasis. This sense of emphatic distinctness in our impressions rises, as the thought and emotion swell higher and higher without overflowing their boundaries, to a lofty sense of the mastery of the human spirit over its own stormiest agitations; and this, again, conducts us to a state of feeling which it is the highest aim of tragedy to produce, to *a sentiment of sublime acquiescence in the course of fate, and in the dispensations of human life.*

What has been said explains, I think, the reason of the effectiveness of the severe forms of Greek tragedy, with its strongly marked boundaries, with its recurrence, even in the most agitating situations, of mutually replying masses of metrical arrangement. Sometimes the agitation becomes overwhelming, and the correspondence is for a time lost, the torrent of feeling flows for a space without check: this disorder amid the general order produces a powerful effect; but the balance is restored before the tragedy closes: the final sentiment in the mind must be one not of trouble, but of acquiescence.

This sentiment of acquiescence is, no doubt, a sentiment of *repose;* and, therefore, I cannot agree with Mr. Lewes when he says, in his remarks on Goethe's *Iphigeneia,* that "the Greek Drama is distinguished by its absence of repose; by the currents of passion being for ever kept in agitation." I entirely agree, however, in his criticism of Goethe's tragedy; of that noble poem which Schiller so exactly characterised when he said that it was "full of soul:" I entirely agree with him when he says that "the tragic situation in the story of Iphigeneia is not touched by Goethe; that his tragedy addresses the conscience rather than the emotions." But Goethe does not err from Greek ideas when he thinks that there is repose in tragedy: he errs from Greek practice in the mode in which he strives to produce that repose. Sophocles does not produce the sentiment of repose, of acquiescence, by inculcating it, by avoiding agitating circumstances: he produces it by exhibiting to us the most agitating matter under the conditions of the severest form. Goethe has truly recognised that this sentiment is the grand final effect of Greek tragedy: but he produces it, not in the manner of Sophocles, but, as Mr. Lewes has most ably pointed out, in a manner of his own; he produces it by inculcating it; by avoiding agitating matter; by keeping himself in the domain of the soul and conscience, not in that of the passions.

I have now to speak of the chorus; for of this, as of the other forms of Greek tragedy, it is not enough, considering how Greek tragedy arose, to show that the Greeks used it; it is necessary to show that it is effective. Johnson says, that "it could only be by long prejudice and the bigotry of learning that Milton could prefer the ancient tragedies, with their encumbrance of a chorus, to the exhibitions of the French and English stages:" and his tragedy of *Irene* sufficiently proves that he himself, in his practice, adopted Greek art as arranged at Paris, by those

> "Juges plus éclairés que ceux qui dans Athène
> Firent naître et fleurir les lois de Melpomène;"

as Voltaire calls them in the prologue to his *Éryphile*. Johnson merely calls the chorus an encumbrance. Voltaire, who, in his *Œdipus*, had made use of the chorus in a singular manner, argued, at a later period, against its introduction. Voltaire is always worth listening to, because his keenness of remark is always suggestive. "In an interesting piece the intrigue generally requires," says Voltaire, "that the principal actors should have secrets to tell one another—*Eh! le moyen de dire son secret à tout un peuple*. And, if the songs of the chorus allude to what has already happened, they must," he says, "be tiresome; if they allude to what is about to happen, their effect will be to *dérober le plaisir de la surprise*." How ingenious, and how entirely in Voltaire's manner! The sense to be appealed to in tragedy is *curiosity;* the impression to be awakened in us is *surprise*. But the Greeks thought differently. For them, the aim of tragedy was *profound moral impression:* and the ideal spectator, as Schlegel and Müller have called the chorus, was designed to enable the actual spectator to feel his own impressions more distinctly and more deeply. The chorus was, at each stage in the action, to collect and weigh the impressions which the action would at that stage naturally make on a pious and thoughtful mind; and was at last, at the end of the tragedy, when the issue of the action appeared, to strike the final balance. If the feeling with which the actual spectator regarded the course of the tragedy could be deepened by reminding him of what was past, or by indicating to him what was to come, it was the province of the ideal spectator so to deepen it. To combine, to harmonise, to deepen for the spectator the feelings naturally excited in him by the sight of what was passing upon the stage—this is one grand effect produced by the chorus in Greek tragedy.

There is another. Coleridge observes that Shakspeare, after one of his grandest scenes, often plunges, as if to relax and relieve himself, into a scene of buffoonery. After tragic situations of the greatest intensity, a desire for relief and relaxation is no doubt natural, both to the poet and to the spectator; but the finer feeling of the Greeks found this relief, not in buffoonery, but in lyrical song. The noble and natural relief from the emotion produced by tragic events is in the transition to the emotion produced by lyric poetry, not in the contrast and shock of a totally opposite order of feelings. The relief afforded to excited feeling by lyrical song every one has experienced at the opera: the delight and facility of this relief renders so universal the popularity of the opera, of this "*beau monstre*," which still, as in Voltaire's time, "*étouffe Melpomène*." But in the opera, the lyrical element, the element of feeling and relaxation, is in excess: the dramatic element, the element of intellect and labour, is in defect. In the best Greek tragedy, the lyrical element occupies its true place; it is the relief and solace in the stress and conflict of the action; it is not the substantive business.

Few can have read the *Samson Agonistes* of Milton without feeling that the chorus imparts a peculiar and noble effect to that poem; but I regret that Milton determined, induced probably by his preference for Euripides, to adopt, in the songs of the chorus, "the measure," as he himself says, "called by the Greeks Monostrophic, or rather Apolelymenon, without regard had to Strophe, Antistrophe, or Epode." In this relaxed form of the later Greek tragedy, the means are sacrificed by which the chorus could produce, within the limits of a single choric song, the same effect which it was their business, as we have seen, to produce in the tragedy as a whole. The regular correspondence of part with part, the antithesis, in answering stanzas, of thought to thought, feeling to feeling, with the balance of the whole struck in one independent final stanza or epode, is lost; something of the peculiar distinctness and symmetry, which constitute the vital force of the Greek tragic forms, is thus forfeited. The story of Samson, although it has no mystery or complication, to inspire, like tragic stories of the most perfect kind, a foreboding and anxious gloom in the mind of him who hears it, is yet a truly dramatic and noble one; but the forms of Greek tragedy, which are founded on Greek manners, on the practice of chorus-dancing, and on the ancient habitual transaction of affairs in the open air in front of the dwellings of kings, are better adapted to Greek stories than to Hebrew or any other. These reserves being made, it is impossible to praise the *Samson Agonistes* too highly: it is great with all the greatness of Milton. Goethe might well say to Eckermann, after re-reading it, that hardly any work had been composed so entirely in the spirit of the ancients.

Milton's drama has the true oratorical flow of ancient tragedy, produced mainly, I think, by his making it, as the Greeks made it, the rule, not the exception, to put the pause at the end of the line, not in the middle. Shakspeare has some noble passages, particularly in his *Richard the Third*, constructed with this, the true oratorical rhythm; indeed, that wonderful poet, who has so much besides rhetoric, is also the greatest poetical rhetorician since Euripides: still, it is to the Elizabethan poets that we owe the bad habit, in dramatic poetry, of perpetually dividing the line in the middle. Italian tragedy has the same habit: in Alfieri's plays it is intolerable. The constant occurrence of such lines produces, not a sense of variety, but a sense of perpetual interruption.

Some of the measures used in the choric songs of my tragedy are ordinary measures of English verse: others are not so; but it must not be supposed that these last are the reproduction of any Greek choric measures. So to adapt Greek measures to English verse is impossible: what I have done is to try to follow rhythms which produced on my own feeling a similar impression to that produced on it by the rhythms of

Greek choric poetry. In such an endeavour, when the ear is guided solely by its own feeling, there is, I know, a continual risk of failure and of offence. I believe, however, that there are no existing English measures which produce the same effect on the ear, and therefore on the mind, as that produced by many measures indispensable to the nature of Greek lyric poetry. He, therefore, who would obtain certain effects obtained by that poetry, is driven to invent new measures, whether he will or no.

Pope and Dryden felt this. Pope composed two choruses for the Duke of Buckingham's *Brutus*, a tragedy altered from Shakspeare, and performed at Buckingham-house. A short specimen will show what these choruses were—

"Love's purer flames the Gods approve:
The Gods and Brutus bend to love:
Brutus for absent Portia sighs,
And sterner Cassius melts at Junia's eyes."

In this style he proceeds for eight lines more, and then the antistrophe duly follows. Pope felt that the peculiar effects of Greek lyric poetry were here missed; the measure in itself makes them impossible: in his ode on St. Cecilia's day, accordingly, he tries to come nearer to the Greeks. Here is a portion of his fourth stanza; of one of those stanzas in which Johnson thinks that "we have all that can be performed by sweetness of diction, or elegance of versification:"—

"Dreadful gleams,
Dismal screams,
Fires that glow,
Shrieks of woe,
Sullen moans,
Hollow groans,
And cries of tortured ghosts."

Horrible! yet how dire must have been the necessity, how strong the feeling of the inadequacy of existing metres to produce effects demanded, which could drive a man of Pope's taste to such prodigies of invention! Dryden in his *Alexander's Feast* deviates less from ordinary English measures; but to deviate from them in some degree he was compelled. My admiration for Dryden's genius is warm: my delight in this incomparable ode, the mighty son of his old age, is unbounded: but it seems to me that in only one stanza and chorus of the *Alexander's Feast*, the fourth, does the rhythm from first to last completely satisfy the ear.

I must have wearied my reader's patience: but I was desirous, in laying before him my tragedy, that it should not lose what benefit it can derive from the foregoing explanations. To his favourable reception of it there will still be obstacles enough, in its unfamiliar form, and in the incapacity of its author.

How much do I regret that the many poets of the present day who possess that capacity which I have not, should not have forestalled me in an endeavour far beyond my powers! How gladly should I have applauded their better success in the attempt to enrich with what, in the forms of the most perfectly-formed literature in the world, is most perfect, our noble English literature; to extend its boundaries in the one direction, in which, with all its force and variety, it has not yet advanced! They would have lost nothing by such an attempt, and English literature would have gained much.

Only their silence could have emboldened to undertake it one with inadequate time, inadequate knowledge, and a talent, alas! still more inadequate: one who brings to the task none of the requisite qualifications of genius or learning: nothing but a passion for the great Masters, and an effort to study them without fancifulness.

London: December, 1857.

England and the Italian Question

"Sed nondum est finis."
S. MATT. XXIV. 6

"*L'aristocratie anglaise est fort heureuse*," said a foreigner to me the other day. I replied that in the Italian question the English aristocracy had scarcely had its usual good fortune. "*Elle est fort heureuse*," he insisted; and the next day came the news of the peace of Villafranca. The condemnation by the English aristocracy of the Italian war was justified, although every reason which it had assigned for that condemnation was wrong.

To examine and dispose of these fallacious reasons is to unravel and set clear the Italian Question.

A great number of persons in England strongly desire to form for themselves a clear judgment on that question. I have had the same desire as so many others. In attempting to fulfil it, I have enjoyed peculiar opportunities for correcting myself of certain misconceptions current in England. I venture to hope that in endeavouring to record the lessons which I have learned, I may possibly be of some use to others.

Three great arguments were urged in England against the Italian war. The first was, that the Italians having never since the fall of the Empire been independent of foreign rulers, it was vain to hope that they could ever become so. The second, that the principle of nationality, in virtue of which the Italians claimed their independence, was chimerical. The third, that the result of the Emperor Napoleon's intervention in Italy could only be a French war of conquest, and the substitution, for the Italians, of French in the place of Austrian domination.

[1]

Is it true that the Italians have never, since the fall of the Roman Empire, been independent of foreign rulers?

At the fall of the Empire, Italy, like other countries of Western Europe, became the prey of conquering nations of German origin. In Italy, as in other countries, the local sovereignties established by the conquering nations became absorbed into the universal sovereignty of Charlemagne. In Italy, as in other countries, the dissolution of the Carlovingian monarchy, after the death of Charlemagne, produced that state of dismemberment and local isolation under which arose the numberless petty principalities of the feudal epoch.

The dukes and counts of these petty principalities had everywhere, as is well known, their recognised superior in a king or emperor, their feudal suzerain; but the practical authority of this recognised chief was for a long time, in all the feudal countries, difficult to enforce, and frequently resisted. In Italy it was peculiarly weak and shadowy; for while the other divisions of Charlemagne's empire fell at his death to sovereigns who at least lived in the countries which they ruled, and who spoke the language of those countries, Italy, by an exception, fell to a sovereign who lived beyond the Alps, and who did not speak her language—to the Emperor of Germany. The great feudal nobles of Italy were indeed, like their suzerain, of German origin; but they lived in Italy, they spoke the Italian language, they had become Italians. The secondary feudal nobility was for the most part Italian by race. The mass of the population was of course Italian. All classes in Italy were thus in a certain measure naturally united from the first against their foreign ruler, whom they all alike regarded, however they might resort to him for help in their quarrels among themselves, as a stranger, a barbarian, and an inferior. This was a great external impediment to the establishment in Italy of the rule of princes of Germanic race, descendants of Charlemagne.

There was a great internal impediment also. Through all the

anarchy of the barbarian invasion there had survived in the towns of Italy the remains of the ancient Roman *curia*, of the system of municipal administration founded by the Romans. As time went on, and the Italian towns, with the re-establishment of order and trade, began to grow in wealth, prosperity, and power, these vivacious remains more and more developed themselves. The habits of municipal action, of local self-government, the great legacy to modern nations of the reason of the ancient world, are essentially opposed to the habits of feudalism. Their gradual development in Europe has been the gradual emancipation of Europe from feudalism. They were developed in Italy earlier and more powerfully than in any other European nation, for they were native there, and the barbarian invasion had trodden down but not eradicated them. From the middle of the tenth century there appear traces of the revived existence in the Italian towns of a municipal administration under magistrates bearing the Roman name of consuls.

To the rule, therefore, of the German Emperor Italy early opposed two grand obstacles. To the foreign German quality of the Emperor it opposed the Italian quality of the population, the Italianised quality of the feudal nobles; to the foreign German idea of feudalism, which the German Emperor represented, it opposed the native Latin idea of municipal government.

After a long struggle, feudalism and German domination were both vanquished. The people of the Italian towns first established their independence of the great feudal lords in their neighbourhood; then carrying the war into the enemy's country, razed the castles of the nobles, reduced them to submission, became suzerains of the chiefs to whom they had been formerly vassals; and by the middle of the twelfth century had mostly established their towns, with the territory surrounding them, as self-governed republics. In the course of the struggle the feudal nobles were constantly driven to appeal for support to their disliked feudal suzerain the German Emperor. The German Emperor, though well aware of the little love entertained towards him by his Italianised German nobles beyond the Alps, could not but feel that their quarrel was in fact his own. His intervention, frequently exercised, sometimes successful, was finally baffled by the immense natural obstacles it had to encounter, and entirely ceased. Frederic Barbarossa, after maintaining a long struggle with the Italian towns, was obliged, in the Treaty of Constance, in 1183, to recognise in fact their independence. The extraordinary genius and energy of Frederic II., crowned King of the Romans in 1220, enabled him to achieve the triumph, for a time, of the imperial authority over the popular and national government of the Italian republics. But the original feudal element, on which alone the imperial authority could lean for support, had been already, before the triumph of Frederic II., almost extirpated in Italy. After the defeat of his son Manfred at Ceprano, in 1267, the Italian sovereignty of the German Emperor became more and more a shadow. The appearance in Italy of Henry of Luxemburg in 1310, so ardently hailed by the Ghibeline Dante, was the last serious effort to make that shadow a reality. This last effort terminated in loss and failure, and the government of Italy remained to the Italians.

Amid the fierce intestine commotions of the Italian republics, men of extraordinary force of character or extraordinary talent for intrigue succeeded in securing to themselves the power, and more than the power, of the old feudal dukes and marquises. Their success excluded the popular and republican elements from the governments of Italy; but it also excluded the foreign, German, and feudal elements. Their governments were Italian governments, and they were themselves Italians. By absorbing the small local republics, they prepared the way for that national unity which no one of the great European states has attained without a similar process. This went on for nearly two centuries, and these centuries are the greatest in Italian history. At the beginning of the fifteenth century there remained in Italy, instead of a multitude of petty independent republics, five powerful states—Rome, Naples, Florence, Venice, and Milan. The struggles between these were incessant, and in the nature of things one of them would probably have ended by swallowing up the rest, as each of the five had swallowed up so many smaller states; and Italy would then have been a great nation, united under one Italian government. In the fifteenth century she was still divided into five governments; but each of them was considerable, and above all each of them was Italian.

At the end of the fifteenth century Charles VIII. appeared in Italy at the head of a French army. He was followed in the sixteenth century by the armies of all the great continental States of Western Europe. The free internal development of Italy and her progress towards a national unity were thus violently interrupted. No country in the world, at such a stage of its formation, could have maintained its independent course of growth under such shocks.

But the unnatural condition of Italy, since the sixteenth century, must not make us deny the results which she had obtained before that period. From the above historical sketch, it appears how untrue is the assertion that she has never been independent of the foreigner, never been Italian. For nearly two centuries, from 1310 to 1494, she was independent of the foreigner,—she was Italian; and without resorting to commonplaces to describe what she achieved in those two centuries, it is enough to say that they were her greatest, her most fruitful. Of all the European States she had opposed to feudalism, which for her was at the same time the symbol of foreign domination, the earliest, the most enlightened, and the most successful resistance. Her success in this resistance she owed chiefly to her municipal spirit. But she had also succeeded, in the fifteenth century, in controlling the exaggerations of this spirit, which, though it achieved her liberty, yet tended to keep her forces fractionised; and she had thus not only established her independence, but had gone very far towards establishing her unity.

It is therefore not true that Italy has never, since the fall of the Roman Empire, been independent of the foreigner. The fact was asserted for the sake of an inference from it; namely, that she never would become so. With the fact falls the inference.

[II]

Is it true that the principle of nationality, in virtue of which the Italians claim their independence, is chimerical?

In some cases, to make a separate nationality the plea for a separate national existence, would be unreasonable in the highest degree. In other cases it is in the highest degree reasonable. Those who pronounce absolutely the principle of nationality chimerical, are led into error for want of attending to this distinction. The distinction is so evidently just and necessary, that they themselves, when their attention is called to it, cannot but admit its force. It would evidently be fantastical to insist on detaching Alsace from France, or the Channel Islands from England, on the plea of a separate nationality. It would as evidently be natural and reasonable, if Kent were annexed to France, or if Normandy were annexed to England, for the inhabitants of those districts to struggle to be released from a connection intolerable to their national feeling. Everything depends on the merits of the particular case in which the principle of nationality is invoked. When this principle is invoked on behalf of Italy, its invokers are to be met, not by absurdly denouncing the principle altogether, but by examining whether they invoke it reasonably. Now, what constitutes reasonableness or unreasonableness in these cases?

It is clearly unreasonable to propose, on the ground of nationality, territorial changes which no one calls for, and to redistribute, like some theorists, the map of Europe according to affinities of race and language. It is fanciful and chimerical to propose to unite Belgium and Geneva with France, Alsace and Berne with Germany, merely because the Belgians and Genevese speak French, the Alsatians and Bernese German. Here the parties alone concerned are satisfied with the existing arrangements, and if they are satisfied, it is well. To invoke with reasonableness the principle of nationality, it is necessary that the parties connected should themselves, one or other of them, be dissatisfied with their connection.

It is also necessary that the dissatisfied party, connected by constraint and against his will with an alien nation, should belong, by nature and origin, to a *great nationality*. The principle of nationality, if acted upon too early, or if pushed too far, would prevent that natural and beneficial union of conterminous or neighbouring territories into one great state, upon which the grandeur of nations and the progress of civilisation depends. It would have prevented the amalgamation of Cornwall and Wales with England, of Brittany with France. Small nationalities inevitably gravitate towards the larger nationalities in their immediate neighbourhood. Their ultimate fusion is so natural and irresistible that even the sentiment of the absorbed race ceases, with time, to struggle against it; the Cornishman and the Breton become at last, in feeling as well as in political fact, an Englishman and a Frenchman. Great nationalities refuse to be thus absorbed; their resilience from fusion is as natural and inevitable as is the gravitation of petty nationalities towards it.

There is no doubt that Lombardy and Venice were dissatisfied with their connection with Austria. Do they also belong to a great nationality, to a nationality too considerable in itself to be ever absorbed in another? In order to answer this question, we must determine in what the greatness of a nationality consists.

Let an Englishman or a Frenchman, who respectively represent the two greatest nationalities of modern Europe, sincerely ask himself what it is that makes him take pride in his nationality, what it is which would make it intolerable to his feelings to pass, or to see any part of his country pass, under foreign dominion. He will find that it is the sense of self-esteem generated by knowing the figure which his nation makes in history; by considering the achievements of his nation in war, government, arts, literature, or industry. It is the sense that his people, which has done such great things, merits to exist in freedom and dignity, and to enjoy the luxury of self-respect. It is the same feeling of self-esteem which, in the case of an individual, makes a state of dependence peculiarly galling to one who has once filled a great position, and who contrasts an eminent past with an abject present. For this feeling all the world confesses a natural sympathy, by regarding the situation of such a man as in a high degree tragic and pitiable.

Except England and France, no country can have this feeling of self-esteem in so high a degree as Italy. Except England and France, no country can suffer so much in having it wounded. No other country, not even the great powers, such as Russia, Austria, and Prussia, could cry with such just humiliation and despair in undergoing a foreign rule, "*Unde lapsus!*" What is the past of these three nations, what their elements for a national pride to feed upon, what their history, art, or literature, compared with those of Italy?—of a people, which, besides having been the most brilliant in Europe in the middle ages and at the Revival of Letters, has in addition, to swell its consciousness of its gifts and grandeur, all the glories of the Roman Empire. And it is vain to tell an Italian that he has no right to take a national pride in these, to identify his race with the Roman race, to claim an inheritance in Roman antiquity. In the first place, were his blood a thousand times more mixed than it really is, were he a thousand times less than he really is the descendant of the Romans, it would still be inevitable that, in his position, he should adopt them as his forefathers, and cherish the memory of their exploits as of those of his own race. In the second place, the modern Italian does in fact continue the old nations of Italy with far less change than is commonly supposed. The greatest of authorities on the languages of Latin origin believed that the modern dialects of Italy were the spoken dialects of Italy in the time of the Romans. The barbarian invasion changed the inhabitants of Italy far less than the Norman invasion changed the inhabitants of England. Yet we, whose language and national character were profoundly modified by that invasion, who use a language which far less resembles that of Hengist than an Italian's language resembles that of Romulus, who owe to the influence of the Latinised Normans that practical inventive and audacious genius which has made the fortune of the English nation, we take an affectionate pride in the Saxon Alfred, and esteem his glory as a national possession. Can we wonder that an Italian, with less solution of continuity, claims kinship with Scipio and Cæsar?

That the Italians, therefore, should have a national self-consciousness, strong, deep, and susceptible, is inevitable. That, having this self-consciousness, they should be perpetually restless under a foreign domination, is inevitable also. In a sentiment thus natural and necessary, and the operation of which, 5 also, is thus natural and necessary, there is nothing chimerical. A politician is not fanciful for taking such a sentiment into account. It is considerable enough to demand his notice. Because he takes it into account for Italy, he is not bound to take it into account for all countries. He has a right to ask whether, 10 for those countries, this sentiment is as legitimate, as inevitable, and as unconquerable as for Italy. If not, he may be excused if, while treating it with respect, he yet refuses to indulge it and to grant its demands; for he may fairly expect that it will in time yield to interest or convenience. He may thus weigh 15 the claims of different nationalities, and while he admits some may fairly reject others. He may fairly say to Poland, Hungary, or Ireland: "I respect your susceptibilities, but I cannot convince myself that the past history of your countries has been so great and fruitful as to give them a necessary right to 20 a place by themselves for ever; as to generate in their inhabitants an immense legitimate self-esteem which must for ever prevent their fusing themselves with another nationality." A Pole does not descend by becoming a Russian, or an Irishman by becoming an Englishman. But an Englishman, with his 25 country's history behind him, descends and deteriorates by becoming anything but an Englishman; a Frenchman, by becoming anything but a Frenchman; an Italian, by becoming anything but an Italian.

The principle of nationality, in virtue of which Italy claims 30 her independence, is not, in the case of Italy, chimerical.

[III]

A third reason assigned for looking with dislike on the late war, was that the result of the French intervention could only be a French war of conquest, and the substitution in Italy of

French for Austrian domination. This reason also was groundless.

I will not content myself with saying that the peace just concluded proves it to have been groundless, inasmuch as that
5 peace, whatever may be its faults, at any rate does not substitute French for Austrian rule in Italy. I will endeavour to show that the condition of things from the first was such as to make the groundlessness of this reason apparent to all who could judge coolly.

10 It was evident that the Emperor Napoleon, however absolute, must take some account of the dispositions of the French people. These dispositions were decidedly, at the outset, averse to the war. They were averse to it, precisely from the apprehension lest it should be a war waged to substitute French
15 for Austrian domination in Italy, lest it should be a war of conquest. What were the real feelings of the French people with regard to the wars of conquest of the first Napoleon, I know not; what are their real feelings with respect to wars of conquest at present, I have had some means of judging. Not one
20 Frenchman in a thousand wishes to enlarge the territory of France. Not one Frenchman in a thousand would thank the Emperor for annexing Savoy. Not one in a thousand would thank him for the line of the Rhine. They think, and think correctly, that their actual limits are wide enough, and that France has more
25 to gain by developing her immense natural resources within her present boundary than by extending it. That vast peasant proprietary which is the modern France, which conjointly with the army maintains Louis Napoleon's empire, and which is in entire sympathy with the army because the army issues
30 from its bosom, this powerful body has one great desire—to enjoy, in quiet and stability, its possession of the soil of France. Its supreme antipathy is for the feudal past or for any approach to a return to it; for a territorial nobility, with privileges and vast estates. The peasant feels that the death of
35 this is his life, and that the life of this would be his death. Any restoration of it endangers, he thinks, his actual state of possession which dates from its destruction. He is really averse to both branches of the Bourbons, because both are alike con-

nected in his mind with the old aristocratic order of things in France, with the times before the Revolution. He prefers Napoleonism because it represents the breach of France with the feudal past, because it represents France organised anew since the Revolution. But the peasant's second antipathy is for disorder and commotion; since this, if it does not endanger his state of possession, yet disturbs his peaceable enjoyment of what he possesses. It is needless to say that the French peasant did not make the Revolution of 1848. But perhaps it is not enough known in England how cordially the French peasant detested the state of anarchy and trouble produced by that revolution; how indignant he was with the townspeople, the *petits bourgeois,* whom he accused of producing the confusion. The burly Lorraine peasants came into the streets of Nancy on the day of the Presidential election with images of Napoleon hung round their necks; taking by the collar each bustling town-agitator whom they met, they held the image to his lips and compelled him to kiss it. But by this vigorous recourse to the sign of Napoleon the peasant was not so much betokening a romantic sentiment, as setting up a symbol of force and order amidst the anarchy which irritated him.

The French peasant, this important and positive personage, the enemy of revolution, because it disturbs his peaceable well-being, is naturally also an enemy of war, so far as it disturbs this. And war on a great scale does disturb it in a very serious manner. It increases the taxes and the conscription: it takes his money and it takes his children. It is a most grave matter for a Government to ask the French peasant for too much money or too many men. To taxes and conscription up to a certain point he has made up his mind; he regards them as institutions of his country. But the moment the pressure exceeds the usual amount, he is of all people in the world the most restive and impatient under them. And what chance of waging a European war, a war of conquest, without the infliction of this extra pressure?

The commercial classes in France, every year rising in activity and importance, are equally positive in their ideas with the peasant. They are entirely indisposed to see France plunge into adventures. They are keenly sensible of the unprofitableness and dangerousness of a war of conquest. For fear lest it should assume this character, they were at first strongly opposed to the Italian war.

5 If, in spite of the coldness of these all-important classes of the French nation, the war nevertheless obtained first their assent, then their approbation, it was that they acquired the assurance that it would not be a war of conquest.

[IV]

In order to explain this, it is necessary to insist upon a fact 10 not sufficiently appreciated in England. This fact is, the hearty confidence reposed in the Emperor Louis Napoleon by the bulk of the industrious classes in France.

The English in general regard Louis Napoleon as a skilful despot who has mastered France and who deals with it for his 15 own advantage. The vast majority of the industrious classes in France regard him as a beneficent ruler on whom they have themselves conferred power, and who wields it for the advantage of the French nation. Which of these estimates is the true one, I do not now inquire; I only note their diversity.

20 How the English impression arose, it is not hard to discover. In the first place we have a natural antipathy to absolute government, and a predisposition to believe that it cannot exist by the wish of the governed. In the second place, the English in France, if they see anything at all of French society, see 25 almost exclusively that in Paris, and, in Paris, that of members of the Orleanist or Legitimist party. These parties undoubtedly contain nearly all which in France is most distinguished by birth, manners and education. Undoubtedly they regard Louis Napoleon with aversion. Undoubtedly, for them, he is a self-30 imposed despot, not an elected chief. And the English take from them their opinion of him. But they are not the French nation. They are an almost imperceptible minority of the French nation; and their influence is every day becoming less.

The great industrious classes of France regard Louis Napoleon very differently. These classes, as has been said above, did not make the last revolution: they were irritated and humiliated by it. They called Louis Napoleon to power that he might relieve them from it. They consider that he has performed with eminent success the task entrusted to him, and they are deeply grateful. The words which one sees so often on commemorative monuments in the French provincial towns, the words which one hears so often in conversing with members of the industrious classes,—*il nous a sauvés de l'anarchie,—il nous a tirés de l'abîme,*—are not, from them, mere official flatteries, but the sincere expressions of conviction. They believe that he has restored tranquillity and prosperity at home, while by his foreign policy he has recovered for France a proud position towards the nations abroad. They attribute to him the possession, in an eminent degree, of prudence and good-fortune, both objects of high veneration to the mass of mankind. They are proud of him as regards the past, and they have confidence in him as regards the future.

The disgust which the monotonous adulation of the Imperial journals inspires, makes us reluctant to accept any of their assertions as important or true. Yet they certainly state no more than the truth, when they affirm that the Emperor has perfectly gained the confidence of the great mass of the French nation.

When the Italian war became inevitable, this confidence displayed itself in a remarkable manner. It has often been said in England that it was the natural inconstancy of the French people which made them pass in a few weeks from dislike of the war to acclamation of it. It has been said that it was their natural love of war and its excitements, which, in spite of reason, broke out and carried them away at the sight of great military operations. Neither assertion is true. They remained steady in their rooted disinclination to a war of conquest, an European war. The intoxication of the warlike spirit has less power upon the French people now than at any former period of its history. But they believed in the Emperor. When they saw that he was resolved upon the Italian war, they had confidence that he would conduct it so as to bring them advantage. They had confidence that if he really judged war necessary, it was that he did not intend the folly of a war of conquest. They accepted his manifesto, and believed that he saw the way to procure for the French nation, without exposing it to serious danger, a vast accession of prestige.

The susceptibility of French national feeling is well known, and, in spite of the positive tendencies of the French industrious classes, the prestige of France has no doubt great charms for them. They would not now plunge into adventures, they would not incur ruinous expense and danger, in order to enhance it; but to enhance it with security is extremely agreeable to them. They believed that the Emperor's skill and address would keep the war a war with Austria only: and in a war with Austria only, they believed that success was certain. Success in this war with Austria was a triumphant obliteration by France of part of the Treaties of 1815. Those treaties were undoubtedly a humiliation for her; she underwent, by virtue of them, the law of the vanquished. To tear a leaf from them with an armed hand gratified her self-esteem and raised her prestige. To this consideration the industrious classes in France were fully sensible.

They were sensible also to the gratification of playing before the world the brilliant part of generous and disinterested liberators of such a country as Italy. Neither for this gratification would they pay too high a price; but if it was to be had on reasonable terms, they accepted it gladly. "*Après tout*"—the common people were constantly saying after the Emperor's manifesto had appeared—"*après tout, c'est une belle guerre, c'est une belle guerre,*" and then followed a string of commonplaces, taken from the journals, as to the achievements of Italy in the cause of civilisation and her claims upon the gratitude of the world. It is to the honour of France, it is what distinguishes her from all other nations, that the mass of her population is so accessible to considerations of this elevated order. It is the bright feature in her civilisation that her common people can understand and appreciate language which elsewhere meets with a response only from the educated and refined classes. One is tempted to ask oneself what would the French nation be if the general knowledge equalled the general intelligence. At present the accessibility to ideas, in France, is only equalled by the ignorance of facts. To give a curious illustration: if ever a war with England is consented to by the French nation it will be from the profound conviction entertained by the mass of them (I do not speak of the Emperor or his general officers) of the inefficiency of the English army.

The assent of the French nation to the Italian war proved their conviction that it was not to be a war of conquest.

[v]

This being so, was there anything in the character of the Emperor which made it probable that he would disappoint this conviction of the French nation? This is, in fact to ask, Was there anything in his character which made it probable that he would be guilty of an outbreak of ambitious violence, that he would commit what the French call a *coup de tête?*

Nothing. From the moment that the disinclination of the French people to a war of conquest was certain, it was certain that the Emperor Napoleon would not make the Italian war a war of conquest. I am not going to insist on his moderation and magnanimity. English and American enthusiasts are to be met with who celebrate him for these virtues, and it is difficult to hear them without laughing. They are so entirely without the means of knowing whether he has them or no. On the other hand, in all that I have to say of him I shall avoid all personal condemnation and disrespect. We are too near him to judge him well: besides, he has not yet finished his career, and no man can be perfectly judged till he has finished it. Undoubtedly he broke an oath to seize power; but no usurper ever seized power without breaking some engagement of allegiance, and all usurpers history does not blacken. It is not the perjury which decides the complexion of these cases; it is the more or less of perfidy. Even if the commencements of the Emperor Napoleon are inevitably to be condemned, bad commencements have before now been retrieved by the career which followed them.

But, leaving out of sight all questions of moral disposition, it cannot be denied that the Emperor has hitherto uniformly made it his aim to comprehend and satisfy the real wishes of the French nation. He has not hitherto given any evidences of suffering himself to be guided, where the desires of the French nation were concerned, by caprice or passion. His prosecution of M. de Montalembert appeared to us in England an act of passion. But in that prosecution the feelings of the French nation were not concerned: they were, and are, profoundly indifferent to the illustrious sufferer. It has been the aim of the Emperor to consolidate his own position and that of his dynasty by firmly attaching to himself the mass of the French nation. This aim he has pursued with remarkable constancy, prudence, and success. He had long consolidated his own power: it remained for him to consolidate his dynasty. This was to be done by continuing in the course which he had hitherto pursued. If he returned from Italy able to say to France: "I have triumphantly overridden the humiliating treaties of Vienna, I have humbled the Austrian army, I have delivered a gifted and sister nation; and yet I have given no pretence for a coalition, I have not endangered France, I have not repeated the errors of the first empire," he knew that he would gratify, elate, and reassure to the highest degree the French people. He knew that this pride, pleasure, and confidence would turn to the profit of his dynasty. If, on the other hand, he returned saying: "I have renewed the triumphs of the first empire, I have established a French kingdom of Etruria, a French kingdom of Naples; but Europe is combining against me, and I must call on France for great exertions to maintain and extend our successes," then he knew that through the length and breadth of France would run a thrill of apprehension, disappointment, and dismay, menacing to the future of his dynasty, menacing even to himself. Having this knowledge, he was not the man to set it at nought.

But it was not only the negative prudence of Louis Napoleon

which rendered him unlikely to place himself in antagonism to the decided wishes of France, by plunging into a sterile war of conquest. There is a positive element in his character which makes him unapt to be out of sympathy with the masses of the people. It is an element which he has repeatedly manifested in his writings, his speeches, and his actions. It is the most interesting feature in his character. It is his great advantage over the kings and aristocracies of Europe. *It is that he possesses, largely and deeply interwoven in his constitution, the popular fibre.*

[VI]

At a time when the masses of the European populations begin more and more to make their voice heard respecting their country's affairs, at a time when sovereigns and statesmen must more and more listen to this voice, can less and less act without taking it into account, it is an extraordinary advantage for a ruler to be able to hear this voice in his own bosom, and therefore to understand it when he hears it from the people. The masses of the people are strongly susceptible to certain powerful ideas. When a ruler is himself susceptible to these ideas, he not only knows how to speak to the people a language which they will comprehend, but how to speak it with the force and effectiveness of conviction. He knows how to gain, not only the attention of the masses, but their enthusiasm.

The ideas of religious, political, and social freedom, which are commonly called the ideas of 1789, which were popularised by the French revolution, although they had long before been partly put in practice in England and in Holland, have now leavened for seventy years the populations of Europe. Politicians have used and abused them, but no politician has played a great part without taking them into account. The first Napoleon, even under the fatal spell of his personal ambition and ungovernable self-will, was profoundly influenced by them. No intelligent man can mix much and freely with the great world (a very different world from the world of the great) without becoming aware of this power. It depends on his own nature whether they are sympathetic to him. The present Emperor, in his intercourse through his varied career with all classes of men, has become aware of the influence of 5 these ideas on the world; by the constitution of his own nature he is in entire sympathy with them.

The masses who are strongly moved by these general ideas, who respond with enthusiasm, if the abolition of privilege, the right of the people to choose its own government, the claims 10 of nationalities, are involved, have little regard for considerations of policy, of respect for established facts, of compromise. They possess the graver fault of having little regard even for justice, except under a poetical and popular form. At any rate, the considerations above mentioned find them singularly deaf. 15 But it is precisely these considerations to which aristocracies in general are most sensible.

The English aristocracy is no exception. I desire to speak of it with the most unbounded respect. It is the most popular of aristocracies; it has avoided faults which have ruined other 20 aristocracies equally splendid. While the aristocracy of France was destroying its estates by its extravagance, and itself by its impertinence, the aristocracy of England was founding English agriculture, and commanding respect by a personal dignity which made even its pride forgiven. Historical and political 25 England, the England of which we are all proud, is of its making. And, although it has to reckon with powerful interests, it still governs England; he who withdraws to a little distance will best be able to observe how completely. If it ever falls before the attacks of its adversaries, if

30 "Veniet lustris labentibus ætas
Quum domus Assaraci Phthiam clarasque Mycenas
Servitio premet, ac victis dominabitur Argis,"

then the England administered by its adversaries, the England no more administered by the English aristocracy, will no 35 longer be the same England; it may be great, but it will be another. Or rather, perhaps, this is doubtful; for so astonishing has been the force and attraction of this aristocracy, that the whole English people is in a great degree formed upon its example and imbued with its spirit.

Nevertheless in regard to ideas it follows inevitably the tendencies of all aristocracies. 5

Members of an aristocracy, forming more or less a caste, and living in a society of their own, have little personal experience of the effect of ideas upon the masses of the people. They run little chance of catching the influence of these ideas by contact. On the other hand, an aristocracy has naturally a great respect 10 for the established order of things, for the *fait accompli*. It is itself a *fait accompli*, it is satisfied with things as they are, it is, above everything, prudent. Exactly the reverse of the masses, who regard themselves as in a state of transition, who are by no means satisfied with things as they are, who are, above 15 everything, adventurous.

A man naturally susceptible to popular ideas may, of course, happen to be born in the ranks of an aristocracy; Mr. Fox was such a man; but this is something exceptional. In general, an aristocracy is not sympathetic to ideas; it regards them as 20 visionary, because it has not experienced them; and as dangerous, because they are independent of existing facts. It regards them, therefore, at once with some contempt as illusory, and with some apprehension as subversive. If it can entirely convince itself that they are illusory, and deserving of uncom- 25 promising contempt and repression, it is glad. This is the secret of the immense admiration with which M. de Talleyrand was regarded by the aristocracies of Europe, even by the English aristocracy, which undoubtedly, in most respects, was immeasurably superior to him. M. de Talleyrand was, or appeared 30 to be, profoundly convinced of the illusoriness of popular ideas; while others treated them with doubtful alarm, he treated them with composed disdain. The imperturbable serenity, the majestic contempt of M. de Talleyrand's conviction, was the ideal which every aristocracy in Europe wished 35 to attain.

With this want of sympathy for ideas, aristocracies have generally been most successful in times when force and firmness and vigour of character were of more account than ideas, in the stages when society is forming. They have generally been unfortunate in times of advanced civilisation; in times when a complicated society has arisen; in times which imperiously demand the comprehension of ideas and the application of them. The Roman aristocracy fell because they could not deal with the ideas of the mature and modern period of Rome, when her struggle for existence ceased after the Punic Wars. The Venetian and French aristocracies fell because they could not deal with the ideas of modern Europe.

[VII]

The English aristocracy was misled by the success of its struggle with the French revolution. It imagined that it had conquered the ideas of the French revolution, and that these conquered ideas must be hollow. It did not conquer the ideas of the French revolution, and these ideas were, in the main, true. The defeat of France by England in the war which ended in 1815 no more proves the falsehood of the ideas of 1789, than the repulse of Mahometanism from Western Europe proves a plurality of Gods. The proclamation of the ideas of 1789 was not, as Sir Archibald Alison thinks, the revolt of Satan against God, and therefore accursed. But the French, whose moral and intellectual being was by no means grown to the stature of the ideas of 1789, organised those ideas in the crudest manner. This crude organisation they hurried, with Mahometan frenzy, to impose on the other nations of Europe. In doing so, they encountered the resistance of a people who had long since effected, with high success, the practical though partial organisation of the ideas which the French were proclaiming, and who owed to that success a power and solidity which to the French were wanting. Against such a people, as against a superior natural force, the French onset inevitably failed. Against the other nations of Europe it succeeded. In that splendid and successful resistance of the English nation the

English aristocracy bore the principal part; and here, in enduring and resisting, it was in its element.

But with the victory of Waterloo the period for endurance and resistance, for the great qualities of an aristocracy, ended: the period for intelligent reconstruction, for the application of ideas, for the exercise of faculties in which an aristocracy is weak, arrived. For the treaties of Vienna the English aristocracy is mainly answerable, so overwhelming was the preponderance, at the end of the war, of the country whose influence they wielded. The race of politicians who regard those treaties as the venerable product of wisdom is nearly extinct. So much harm has been said of them that it is almost cruel to remark on the fallacy of a commonplace often urged in their favour,—that they have maintained the peace of Europe for more than forty years. It would be more true to say that the exhaustion and weariness of war produced by a twenty-five years' struggle had maintained the peace of Europe in spite of the seeds of disturbance contained in the treaties of Vienna. This was the more possible as the most combative of the parties in the struggle, France, had suffered heaviest, and was the most exhausted. The treaties of Vienna, with their arbitrary distribution of the populations of Europe, their Mezentian copulations of the living with the dead, were eminently treaties of force—treaties which took no account of popular ideas. And they were unintelligent and capricious treaties of force. Their great object was to erect barriers against France. To accomplish this object, instead of creating a strong Germany, they created the impotent German Confederation; placing on the frontiers of France the Duchy of Baden and an outlying province of Bavaria, and splitting the action of Germany so that her two chief Powers will always be beaten by France. They created the incoherent kingdom of Holland and the insufficient kingdom of Sardinia; they strengthened Austria against France by adding to Austria provinces which have ever since been a source of weakness to her. They left to France Alsace and German Lorraine, which unity of race and language might with time have solidly re-attached to Germany.

In compensation they took from France provinces which the same unity may one day enable her to reabsorb. They denied to Switzerland her natural frontier, because the Voltairian Louis XVIII. declared he would sooner cut off his hand than sign away Ferney, the residence of his idol. They have no more claim, by intrinsic merit, to permanence as the public law of Europe, than the rotten boroughs had claim, by intrinsic merit, to permanence as public institutions of England.

[VIII]

It was necessary to enter into these considerations in order to make apparent the position of the Emperor Napoleon in regard to the English aristocracy at the beginning of the Italian war, and his advantage.

He had no intention of making that war a war of conquest. When accused of such an intention, he knew that the issue of the war would justify him and confound his accusers. He knew too that he could disavow such an intention, of which he was really innocent, with an accent of truth and sincerity which would convince France. This accusation would have been formidable if true; it would have united the public opinion of Europe and of France against him: but it was not true.

But when the English aristocracy accused him of assailing the Treaties of Vienna, of making himself the champion of nationalities, they accused him of what was true. He was conscious of this intention. But he listened to the accusation with complacency. He knew that it would do him no harm. He knew that it would not excite against him a murmur of public opinion in France. He knew that it appealed to no popular ideas, that it even wounded them, and that he might safely defy it. He knew that, so far as European sentiment was concerned, he might securely proceed to violate the Treaties of Vienna, though a hundred Cassandras in the English Upper House bewailed them with dishevelled hair. He knew that when he was accused of undertaking, in behalf of Italian nationality, "the most unjustifiable war ever commenced," he was accused of what would go far to reconcile to him popular feeling in all nations, and to make it forgive his despotism. He felt that his attitude was procuring for him the immense advantage (which I sincerely believe he had not sought) of drawing the English aristocracy on to a most dangerous ground, where, in attacking him, they would meet with no favour from Europe, with little favour even from their own country.

The position of the Emperor Napoleon was almost impregnable. I shall not touch the question, most delicate and most difficult, as to what course England should have pursued in the Italian complications. I will only say what might need development for foreign readers, but for English readers needs none,—that it was impossible she could enter into the Italian war as the ally of France. The Crimean experience was too near. That she could enter into the war as the ally of Austria could only be the frantic hope of German terror. England was thus placed on one side. Russia was a not unpleased spectator of Austrian humiliation. Prussia remained: but Prussia is a great power only in name; and neither the Emperor nor the French nation really dreaded her interference. Prussia, with neither territory nor population enough for her support as a great military power, can only have a large efficient army at the expense of having her finances in ruin. She sensibly chooses to have her finances in prosperity. But her army, therefore, is a shadow. In her regular forces she has not a man who has served three full years. The majority of her *landwehr* are respectable married citizens, fathers of families. To require such troops to repel a charge of Zouaves would be as reasonable as to make this demand of the Marylebone Vestry. French military men know this perfectly well. They speak with great respect of the Austrian army. "*C'est une belle armée*," they say of the Austrian army, "*mais elle est malheureuse*;" of the Prussian army they say, "*C'est une garde nationale*."

The French Emperor was master of the situation. It seemed inevitable that the end of the war would see him crowned with complete material and moral predominance in Europe; with material predominance as the disposer of the immense and successful forces of France; with moral predominance as the triumphant agent of popular ideas.

[IX]

Here is the place to remark two facts, which must, I think, strike a careful observer of the present state of France:

First: The development which the spirit of the French nation is assuming, under the present Empire, is not, upon the whole, a good one.

Secondly: The Emperor and his government, from a very exaggerated estimate of the influence of the clergy in France, bid for the support of the clergy a far higher price than it is worth.

On the first of these propositions I shall not now dilate, but I have a few words to add respecting the second.

There are hardly any remains of a Gallican clergy in France. The immense majority of the bishops are ultramontane. If the French clergy is still legitimist at heart, it is certainly no longer warmly legitimist. Its members are much more the men of the Pope than the men of the Comte de Chambord. The present French government spares nothing to gain them, and they have extended to it a certain conditional support. But they have done far less for it than it imagines; they will never be its sincere allies; nor, if they were, would their best services be worth the price they would exact for them. The vast majority of them regarded the Italian war with extreme disquietude. They had no wish to see Austria injured, whose Emperor, an ardent Catholic, had displayed in his Concordat with the Pope a Catholicism as indubitable as that of Louis Napoleon is enigmatical. Above all, they foresaw dangers for the Pope. As the war proceeded, and the position of the Pope as a temporal sovereign became extremely critical, the French clergy became more and more dissatisfied. The impunity with which they expressed this dissatisfaction proved the reluctance of the government to come into collision with them. Indeed, it did its best to pacify and reassure them. But it was of no avail. The language of the *Univers*, the great clerical organ, the newspaper which lies on the table of every bishop in France, became violent, menacing, outrageous. The *Univers* deserves to be more read in England. Its fanaticism is insane: 5 but it is almost the only journal in France written with entire freedom and vigour. The intelligent *Journal des Débats* is too scrupulously discreet for the intense war of politics. It appears to be written by old men, who, if they deliver themselves in the morning of the most covert sarcasm, the most remote 10 innuendo, chuckle for the remainder of the day over their juvenile audacity. The *Siècle* writes in fetters. Of the *Constitutionnel* and the *Patrie* there is only to be said, that the one adores the Divinity of the Tuileries in the morning, and the other in the evening. But the *Univers* is written with a free 15 impetuosity, which recalls to the English reader the *Times* in its most aggressive and stormy moments. If it lacks the effect which impersonality lends to the invective of the *Times*, it has a special interest from the singular individuality of its principal writer, M. Louis Veuillot. M. Louis Veuillot is a polemic 20 worthy of the golden age of polemics. He is singly devoted to ultramontanism; he lives on a small fixed salary from the proprietors of the *Univers;* he is a man of the purest and simplest domestic life; he is poor, and has a large family, but he has refused all offers of place and salary from the govern- 25 ment, and maintains his entire independence. M. Louis Veuillot began to denounce the war with more and more vehemence; he held it up to the suspicion and aversion of all good Catholics; he cordially defended the conduct of the Papal troops at Perugia. When reproached for this, with terrible plainness 30 of speech he produced chapter and verse from the records of the *coup d'état* of December 1851, to parallel all the brutal acts of violence of the Papal troops by similar acts of the Imperial soldiery. For this he received a warning. With mocking contempt, he printed this warning the next day, at the head of his 35 journal. The organ of the French clergy not only condemned the Emperor and his government: it began to defy them.

[x]

The Emperor recoiled. It may be true that the actual sight of the fields of carnage in Italy produced a profoundly painful impression upon him, for he has neither the practice nor the iron nerves of his uncle; it may be true that he was struck 5 by hearing of the emotion shown by the common people at the aspect of their kinsfolk and acquaintance returning, in the prime of life, wounded and mutilated to their homes, for in no previous war has the feeling of the French people so markedly paid this homage to civilisation. It may be true, as he 10 himself intimates, that a certain lassitude and despondency seized him at encountering the unconquerable suspicion and hostility of the governments of Europe. But there can be little doubt that what really determined him to end the war abruptly, and to make peace at a great sacrifice, was his uneasiness at the 15 daily thickening complications in the Papal States, and his dread to push matters to an extremity with the Catholicism of Europe and with the clergy of France.

I believe that he was in error. The Catholicism of Europe, out of France, need have occasioned him no apprehension 20 whatever. In Italy itself, the seat of the Papacy, its moral force is perfectly insignificant; nowhere is the party of the priests so little loved or respected as here, where it is best known. In France it is more powerful; and, from the decorous life of the majority of the clergy, deservedly so. But even in France it has 25 no real hold on the masses of the population, and the Emperor dangerously overrates its power.

His own mortification at his peace must have been immense. I have said that he is evidently, by nature, sincerely susceptible to certain great popular ideas; and there is no doubt that the 30 idea of Italian nationality powerfully stirred his spirit. He must have felt, in concluding the peace of Villafranca, that he renounced, for this occasion at least, probably for ever, the hope so attractive to the imagination of men, of initiating one of those great changes which commence new periods in history. In one of the addresses, defaced by an oriental servility, in which the great bodies of the State the other day saluted his return, the orator compared him to Scipio, who, after conquering at Zama, forebore to press Carthage. He is more like Hannibal, who, after an astonishing march, encamped within sight of Rome, hesitated, and lost it for ever.

In France the peace is severely criticised. The masses of the people, susceptible to popular ideas as their sovereign, are keenly disappointed at the lame and impotent conclusion of the exciting drama commenced so lately. The Emperor has given them, indeed, a great military triumph over the Austrian empire. But this they had often had before, and did not eagerly covet. To obtain no more than this, the war, they think, was not worth undertaking; the Emperor should have estimated difficulties beforehand, and should never have undertaken it.

And Italy! Who can sound the depth of Italy's disappointment? Austria is still entrenched in Italy. But there is the Italian Confederation! It would be too bold to augur beforehand what shape this project may ultimately assume, and what results may flow from it. But, at present, what aspect must it wear to an Italian? A confederation in which but one member is a great power, and that member not Italian,—that member Austria! A confederation which restores the Duke of Modena! A confederation in which the Pope has the post of honour, and retains his temporal dominion! The Italians see that the peace which founds this confederation drives M. de Cavour from office in despair, while it fills M. Louis Veuillot with triumph. They hear M. Louis Veuillot devoutly thanking God that this peace, in which one Emperor gives Lombardy away and another receives it, affords no consecration to the hateful doctrine that nations have any voice in their own disposal. What an ally for the man whom his admirers call "the incarnation of the modern spirit"! What a creditable, what an agreeable, adherent for *L'Uomo del Secolo!*

[XI]

Although the bitter disappointment of the Italians is to be deeply pitied, yet there is no need to regret the abortive termination of the great design of the Emperor of the French.

In the first place, to an Englishman, to a man not only proud of his country, but sincerely convinced of the utility of her moral influence for the nations abroad, it could not have been an agreeable sight to witness the chief of another country invested, as the complete realisation of his design would have invested Louis Napoleon, with entire moral and material predominance in Europe. England may not concern herself with material predominance in Europe; but a share in moral predominance may and must be dear to her. At present she has no reason for disquietude. His material predominance may remain to the Emperor Louis Napoleon, but moral predominance has escaped him.

But this consideration is for the English. On the Continent of Europe, although there are some persons whom their knowledge and admiration of English institutions may induce to sympathise in it, yet we cannot expect it to be widely or deeply entertained.

But on the Continent of Europe, in Italy herself, the true friends of freedom may well feel it a relief to be spared from witnessing an experiment which would have been without parallel in history, and which it was impossible to watch without apprehension. *Non tali auxilio*. It would have been a prodigious and sinister spectacle to behold Italian freedom given as a boon by the present French Empire. The future of a liberty so bestowed would have been at least ambiguous. Over the free institutions of Italy there would have rested a shadow from the great liberating power, impossible to be complained of, alien to their nature, unfavourable to their growth.

[XII]

At this abortive close of the Italian war, what course should be pursued by the English aristocracy?

At the commencement of the war the English aristocracy said to the Italian people: "This war will bring you no good; we dissuade you from it."

They added: "We dissuade you from it, because Italy never has been, and never can be, independent; because the claims of nationalities are a dream; because the French Emperor will inevitably make the war a war of conquest."

The reasons were unsubstantial, but the dissuasion was sage. To this day the orators of the English aristocracy keep repeating their fallacious reasons; keep urging that Italy has no more claim to independence than Ireland or Canada: and they are wrong. They have solely to insist on the indisputable and fortunate fact that they prophesied a null result of the war to Italy. They have only to receive the peace of the French Emperor with the same coldness as they received his war. They have only to extend to his confederation the same incredulity which they extended to his manifesto.

Happily there is now at the head of the English government a statesman who has never committed himself to the arguments of the majority of his order. It is the same statesman who, in 1848, with supreme felicity, or it is more just to say with supreme sagacity, took a step which at the present moment almost gives him the command of the situation. In 1848 Lord Palmerston refused to guarantee her Venetian possessions to Austria, even at the price of her surrender of Lombardy. The refusal would perhaps have been made by no other statesman in Europe. For the firmness and foresight it displayed it may take rank with the warning addressed at the occupation of Cracow by the same statesman to Austria in the fulness of her power, that the treaties which counted for nothing on the Vistula might one day come to count for nothing on the Po. It has subjected him to the most unintelligent, but the most sincere, abuse. It has never been disavowed by him, always defended. It is now of incalculable advantage to England. It enables her to say, with perfect sincerity and dignity, that her programme for Italy was, is, and will be, "Italy for the Italians, 5 and the removal of all foreign interference between the Italians and their governments."

In fact, what nation in Europe should desire the establishment of a great and free Italy with such cordiality as England? What nation in Europe can have such prospect of advantage 10 from it, such impossibility of disadvantage? Can France? Would France be on permanent good terms with a great Latin nation on her frontier? She once had such a neighbour in Spain, and she never rested till she had ruined her. Would she contemplate, with the same perfect freedom from jealousy 15 as England, the growth as a great people of those extraordinary populations, who even now, though the most misgoverned and neglected in Europe, are equal to the French in intelligence, and superior to them in refinement of nature?

[XIII]

But England is blamed for keeping her sympathies for na- 20 tions of the future, and refusing them to the actual nations of Europe. She is warned of the dangers of her isolation. She is counselled to go to the congress to avoid them. She is advised not to estrange from her at the same moment, by her fastidiousness and coldness, Germany and France.

25 But can she help herself? Is it her fault if she cannot build a firm alliance where a real basis of likeness of nature, community of interests, or equality of strength, is wanting? She must naturally desire the existence of a great Germany, as of a great Italy. At present there is a great German stock, but no 30 great German state. Is England to be blamed because she does not contract an intimate alliance with Austria? We are told that Mr. Pitt set the highest value on the Austrian alliance, and we are blamed for not following his example. But Mr. Pitt lived in very different times. Would that great and practical

minister have set the same value, in these days of the triumph of the modern spirit, on his country's alliance with a state whose government is incurably opposed to the modern spirit, and the most retrograde in Europe? The Prussian alliance is desirable; but is the alliance on equal terms between England and a state immeasurably overmatched by France, and which can subsist only by a temporising policy? We are the natural friends of Germany; but we have a right to say to the Germans, if they ask for our intimate alliance, "Constitute yourselves so as to have some real strength of your own, so as to be able to give as well as to receive support. Create a Germany which may be able to meet France upon another field of Leipsic without the help of a quarter of a million Russians, which may fight a Ligny that the English have not to redeem by their Waterloo."

As to France, the intimate alliance of the English with the French nation is no doubt ardently to be wished for, but is it possible? It is my profound conviction that at present it is not, and that the obstacles to it, the incurable want of sympathy, exist more on the side of the French nation than on ours. There remains the alliance between the two governments. And here let me render justice to the Emperor Louis Napoleon. I believe that he is unfeignedly, disinterestedly, and deeply inclined to the English alliance. I believe that he knows and values the English nation almost as well as the truest friends of England, M. Guizot or the lamented M. de Tocqueville. I believe that, in many respects, and putting out of question his strong natural leaning to ideas, which is not English, the English character is more sympathetic to him than the French. But he must not be expected to remain firm to the English alliance to the detriment of his position in France. He remains firm to it as long as he can, but the moment fatally arrives, when his perseverance brings him into collision with the sympathies and wishes of the French people; then he releases his hold on it, sorrowfully, hesitatingly, but inevitably. We saw this in the Russian war. Few will now deny that England ought either never to have entered into that war at all, or not to have ended it when she did. But the French clamoured for its conclusion. England wished to continue it. The Emperor adhered to England for a time, and resisted the clamours of his own subjects. But at last he yielded.

May the English aristocracy comprehend the gravity of the situation in which their country is placed! May they understand that the present Europe is no longer the Europe of Mr. Pitt, and cannot be dealt with on Mr. Pitt's principles! When I consider the governing skill which the English aristocracy have displayed since 1688, and the extraordinary height of grandeur to which they have conducted their country, I almost doubt whether the law of nature, which seems to have given to aristocracies the rule of the old order of things, and to have denied them that of the new, may not be destined to be reversed in their favour. May it be so! May their inimitable prudence and firmness have this signal reward! May they have the crowning good fortune, as in the ancient world of force, so in the modern world of ideas, to command the respect and even the enthusiasm of their countrymen!

On Translating Homer

. . . . Nunquamne reponam?

[1]

It has more than once been suggested to me that I should translate Homer. That is a task for which I have neither the time nor the courage; but the suggestion led me to regard yet more closely a poet whom I had already long studied, and for one or two years the works of Homer were seldom out of my hands. The study of classical literature is probably on the decline; but, whatever may be the fate of this study in general, it is certain that, as instruction spreads and the number of readers increases, attention will be more and more directed to the poetry of Homer, not indeed as part of a classical course, but as the most important poetical monument existing. Even within the last ten years two fresh translations of the *Iliad* have appeared in England: one by a man of great ability and genuine learning, Professor Newman; the other by Mr. Wright, the conscientious and painstaking translator of Dante. It may safely be asserted that neither of these works will take rank as the standard translation of Homer; that the task of rendering him will still be attempted by other translators. It may perhaps be possible to render to these some service, to save them some loss of labour, by pointing out rocks on which their predecessors have split, and the right objects on which a translator of Homer should fix his attention.

It is disputed what aim a translator should propose to himself in dealing with his original. Even this preliminary is not yet settled. On one side it is said that the translation ought to be such 'that the reader should, if possible, forget that it is a translation at all, and be lulled into the illusion that he is reading an original work,—something original' (if the translation be in English), 'from an English hand.' The real original is in this case, it is said, 'taken as a basis on which to rear a poem that shall affect our countrymen as the original may be conceived to have affected its natural hearers.' On the other hand, Mr. Newman, who states the foregoing doctrine only to condemn it, declares that he 'aims at precisely the opposite: to retain every peculiarity of the original, so far as he is able, *with the greater care the more foreign it may happen to be;*' so that it may 'never be forgotten that he is imitating, and imitating in a different material.' The translator's 'first duty,' says Mr. Newman, 'is a historical one: to be *faithful*.' Probably both sides would agree that the translator's 'first duty is to be faithful;' but the question at issue between them is, in what faithfulness consists.

My one object is to give practical advice to a translator; and I shall not the least concern myself with theories of translation as such. But I advise the translator not to try 'to rear on the basis of the *Iliad*, a poem that shall affect our countrymen as the original may be conceived to have affected its natural hearers;' and for this simple reason, that we cannot possibly tell *how* the *Iliad* 'affected its natural hearers.' It is probably meant merely that he should try to affect Englishmen powerfully, as Homer affected Greeks powerfully; but this direction is not enough, and can give no real guidance. For all great poets affect their hearers powerfully, but the effect of one poet is one thing, that of another poet another thing: it is our translator's business to reproduce the effect of Homer, and the most powerful emotion of the unlearned English reader can never assure him whether he has *re*produced this, or whether he has produced something else. So, again, he may follow Mr. Newman's directions, he may try to be 'faithful,' he may 'retain every peculiarity of his original;' but who is to assure him, who is to assure Mr. Newman himself, that, when he has done this, he has done that for which Mr. Newman enjoins this to be done, 'adhered closely to Homer's manner and habit of thought'? Evidently the translator needs some more practical directions than these. No one can tell him how Homer affected the Greeks; but there are those who can tell him how Homer affects *them.* These are scholars; who possess, at the same time with knowledge of Greek, adequate poetical taste and feeling. No translation will seem to them of much worth compared with the original; but they alone can say whether the translation produces more or less the same effect upon them as the original. They are the only competent tribunal in this matter: the Greeks are dead; the unlearned Englishman has not the data for judging; and no man can safely confide in his own single judgment of his own work. Let not the translator, then, trust to his notions of what the ancient Greeks would have thought of him; he will lose himself in the vague. Let him not trust to what the ordinary English reader thinks of him; he will be taking the blind for his guide. Let him not trust to his own judgment of his own work; he may be misled by individual caprices. Let him ask how his work affects those who both know Greek and can appreciate poetry; whether to read it gives the Provost of Eton, or Professor Thompson at Cambridge, or Professor Jowett here in Oxford, at all the same feeling which to read the original gives them. I consider that when Bentley said of Pope's translation, 'It was a pretty poem, but must not be called Homer,' the work, in spite of all its power and attractiveness, was judged.

Ὡς ἂν ὁ φρόνιμος ὁρίσειεν,—'as the judicious would determine,' —that is a test to which every one professes himself willing to submit his works. Unhappily, in most cases, no two persons agree as to who 'the judicious' are. In the present case, the ambiguity is removed: I suppose the translator at one with me as to the tribunal to which alone he should look for judgment; and he has thus obtained a practical test by which to estimate the real success of his work. How is he to proceed, in order that his work, tried by this test, may be found most successful?

First of all, there are certain negative counsels which I will give him. Homer has occupied men's minds so much, such a literature has arisen about him, that every one who approaches him should resolve strictly to limit himself to that which may directly serve the object for which he approaches him. I advise the translator to have nothing to do with the questions, whether Homer ever existed; whether the poet of the *Iliad* be one or many; whether the *Iliad* be one poem or an *Achilleis* and an *Iliad* stuck together; whether the Christian doctrine of the Atonement is shadowed forth in the Homeric mythology; 5 whether the Goddess Latona in any way prefigures the Virgin Mary, and so on. These are questions which have been discussed with learning, with ingenuity, nay, with genius; but they have two inconveniences,—one general for all who approach them, one particular for the translator. The general incon- 10 venience is that there really exist no data for determining them. The particular inconvenience is that their solution by the translator, even were it possible, could be of no benefit to his translation.

I advise him, again, not to trouble himself with constructing 15 a special vocabulary for his use in translation; with excluding a certain class of English words, and with confining himself to another class, in obedience to any theory about the peculiar qualities of Homer's style. Mr. Newman says that 'the entire dialect of Homer being essentially archaic, that of a translator 20 ought to be as much Saxo-Norman as possible, and owe as little as possible to the elements thrown into our language by classical learning.' Mr. Newman is unfortunate in the observance of his own theory; for I continually find in his translation words of Latin origin, which seem to me quite alien to the 25 simplicity of Homer,—'responsive,' for instance, which is a favourite word of Mr. Newman, to represent the Homeric ἀμειβόμενος:

> Great Hector of the motley helm thus spake to her *responsive.*
>
> But thus *responsively* to him spake god-like Alexander.

30 And the word 'celestial,' again, in the grand address of Zeus to the horses of Achilles,

> You, who are born *celestial*, from Eld and Death exempted!

seems to me in that place exactly to jar upon the feeling as too bookish. But, apart from the question of Mr. Newman's 35 fidelity to his own theory, such a theory seems to me both dangerous for a translator and false in itself. Dangerous for a translator; because, wherever one finds such a theory announced (and one finds it pretty often), it is generally followed by an explosion of pedantry; and pedantry is of all things in the world the most un-Homeric. False in itself; because, in fact, we owe to the Latin element in our language most of that very rapidity and clear decisiveness by which it is contradistinguished from the German, and in sympathy with the languages of Greece and Rome: so that to limit an English translator of Homer to words of Saxon origin is to deprive him of one of his special advantages for translating Homer. In Voss's well-known translation of Homer, it is precisely the qualities of his German language itself, something heavy and trailing both in the structure of its sentences and in the words of which it is composed, which prevent his translation, in spite of the hexameters, in spite of the fidelity, from creating in us the impression created by the Greek. Mr. Newman's prescription, if followed, would just strip the English translator of the advantage which he has over Voss.

The frame of mind in which we approach an author influences our correctness of appreciation of him; and Homer should be approached by a translator in the simplest frame of mind possible. Modern sentiment tries to make the ancient not less than the modern world its own; but against modern sentiment in its applications to Homer the translator, if he would feel Homer truly—and unless he feels him truly, how can he render him truly?—cannot be too much on his guard. For example: the writer of an interesting article on English translations of Homer, in the last number of the *National Review*, quotes, I see, with admiration, a criticism of Mr. Ruskin on the use of the epithet φυσίζοος, 'life-giving,' in that beautiful passage in the third book of the *Iliad*, which follows Helen's mention of her brothers Castor and Pollux as alive, though they were in truth dead:

> ὣς φάτο · τοὺς δ' ἤδη κάτεχεν φυσίζοος αἶα
> ἐν Λακεδαίμονι αὖθι, φίλῃ ἐν πατρίδι γαίῃ.[1]

[1] *Iliad*, iii. 243.

'The poet,' says Mr. Ruskin, 'has to speak of the earth in sadness; but he will not let that sadness affect or change his thought of it. No; though Castor and Pollux be dead, yet the earth is our mother still,—fruitful, life-giving.' This is a just specimen of that sort of application of modern sentiment to the ancients, against which a student, who wishes to feel the ancients truly, cannot too resolutely defend himself. It reminds one, as, alas! so much of Mr. Ruskin's writing reminds one, of those words of the most delicate of living critics: 'Comme tout genre de composition a son écueil particulier, *celui du genre romanesque, c'est le faux*.' The reader may feel moved as he reads it; but it is not the less an example of 'le faux' in criticism; it is false. It is not true, as to that particular passage, that Homer called the earth φυσίζοος because, 'though he had to speak of the earth in sadness, he would not let that sadness change or affect his thought of it,' but consoled himself by considering that 'the earth is our mother still,—fruitful, life-giving.' It is not true, as a matter of general criticism, that this kind of sentimentality, eminently modern, inspires Homer at all. 'From Homer and Polygnotus I every day learn more clearly,' says Goethe, 'that in our life here above ground we have, properly speaking, to enact Hell:' [1]—if the student must absolutely have a keynote to the *Iliad*, let him take this of Goethe, and see what he can do with it; it will not, at any rate, like the tender pantheism of Mr. Ruskin, falsify for him the whole strain of Homer.

These are negative counsels; I come to the positive. When I say, the translator of Homer should above all be penetrated by a sense of four qualities of his author:—that he is eminently rapid; that he is eminently plain and direct, both in the evolution of his thought and in the expression of it, that is, both in his syntax and in his words; that he is eminently plain and direct in the substance of his thought, that is, in his matter and ideas; and, finally that he is eminently noble;—I probably seem to be saying what is too general to be of much service to anybody. Yet it is strictly true that, for want of duly pene-

[1] *Briefwechsel zwischen Schiller und Goethe*, vi. 230.

trating themselves with the first-named quality of Homer, his rapidity, Cowper and Mr. Wright have failed in rendering him; that, for want of duly appreciating the second-named quality, his plainness and directness of style and diction, Pope and Mr. Sotheby have failed in rendering him; that for want of appreciating the third, his plainness and directness of ideas, Chapman has failed in rendering him; while for want of appreciating the fourth, his nobleness, Mr. Newman, who has clearly seen some of the faults of his predecessors, has yet failed more conspicuously than any of them.

Coleridge says, in his strange language, speaking of the union of the human soul with the divine essence, that this takes place

> Whene'er the mist, which stands 'twixt God and thee,
> Defecates to a pure transparency;

and so, too, it may be said of that union of the translator with his original, which alone can produce a good translation, that it takes place when the mist which stands between them—the mist of alien modes of thinking, speaking, and feeling on the translator's part—'defecates to a pure transparency,' and disappears. But between Cowper and Homer—(Mr. Wright repeats in the main Cowper's manner, as Mr. Sotheby repeats Pope's manner, and neither Mr. Wright's translation nor Mr. Sotheby's has, I must be forgiven for saying, any proper reason for existing)—between Cowper and Homer there is interposed the mist of Cowper's elaborate Miltonic manner, entirely alien to the flowing rapidity of Homer; between Pope and Homer there is interposed the mist of Pope's literary artificial manner, entirely alien to the plain naturalness of Homer's manner; between Chapman and Homer there is interposed the mist of the fancifulness of the Elizabethan age, entirely alien to the plain directness of Homer's thought and feeling; while between Mr. Newman and Homer is interposed a cloud of more than Egyptian thickness,—namely, a manner, in Mr. Newman's version, eminently ignoble, while Homer's manner is eminently noble.

I do not despair of making all these propositions clear to a student who approaches Homer with a free mind. First, Homer is eminently rapid, and to this rapidity the elaborate movement of Miltonic blank verse is alien. The reputation of Cowper,
5 that most interesting man and excellent poet, does not depend on his translation of Homer; and in his preface to the second edition, he himself tells us that he felt,—he had too much poetical taste not to feel,—on returning to his own version after six or seven years, 'more dissatisfied with it himself than the
10 most difficult to be pleased of all his judges.' And he was dissatisfied with it for the right reason,—that 'it seemed to him deficient *in the grace of ease*.' Yet he seems to have originally misconceived the manner of Homer so much, that it is no wonder he rendered him amiss. 'The similitude of Milton's
15 manner to that of Homer is such,' he says, 'that no person familiar with both can read either without being reminded of the other; and it is in those breaks and pauses to which the numbers of the English poet are so much indebted, both for their dignity and variety, that he chiefly copies the Grecian.'
20 It would be more true to say: 'The unlikeness of Milton's manner to that of Homer is such, that no person familiar with both can read either without being struck with his difference from the other; and it is in his breaks and pauses that the English poet is most unlike the Grecian.'
25 The inversion and pregnant conciseness of Milton or Dante are, doubtless, most impressive qualities of style; but they are the very opposites of the directness and flowingness of Homer, which he keeps alike in passages of the simplest narrative, and in those of the deepest emotion. Not only, for example, are
30 these lines of Cowper un-Homeric:—

> So numerous seemed those fires the banks between
> Of Xanthus, blazing, and the fleet of Greece
> In prospect all of Troy;

where the position of the word 'blazing' gives an entirely un-
35 Homeric movement to this simple passage, describing the fires of the Trojan camp outside of Troy; but the following lines, in that very highly-wrought passage where the horse of

Achilles answers his master's reproaches for having left Patroclus on the field of battle, are equally un-Homeric:—

> For not through sloth or tardiness on us
> Aught chargeable, have Ilium's sons thine arms
> Stript from Patroclus' shoulders; but a God 5
> Matchless in battle, offspring of bright-haired
> Latona, him contending in the van
> Slew, for the glory of the chief of Troy.

Here even the first inversion, 'have Ilium's sons thine arms Stript from Patroclus' shoulders,' gives the reader a sense of 10 a movement not Homeric; and the second inversion, 'a God him contending in the van Slew,' gives this sense ten times stronger. Instead of moving on without check, as in reading the original, the reader twice finds himself, in reading the translation, brought up and checked. Homer moves with the 15 same simplicity and rapidity in the highly-wrought as in the simple passage.

It is in vain that Cowper insists on his fidelity: 'my chief boast is that I have adhered closely to my original:'—'the matter found in me, whether the reader like it or not, is found 20 also in Homer; and the matter not found in me, how much soever the reader may admire it, is found only in Mr. Pope.' To suppose that it is *fidelity* to an original to give its matter, unless you at the same time give its manner; or, rather, to suppose that you can really give its matter at all, unless you can 25 give its manner, is just the mistake of our pre-Raphaelite school of painters, who do not understand that the peculiar effect of nature resides in the whole and not in the parts. So the peculiar effect of a poet resides in his manner and movement, not in his words taken separately. It is well known how conscien- 30 tiously literal is Cowper in his translation of Homer. It is well known how extravagantly free is Pope.

> So let it be!
> Portents and prodigies are lost on me:

that is Pope's rendering of the words, 35

Ξάνθε, τί μοι θάνατον μαντεύεαι; οὐδέ τί σε χρή·[1]

Xanthus, why prophesiest thou my death to me? thou needest not at all:—

yet, on the whole, Pope's translation of the *Iliad* is more Homeric than Cowper's, for it is more rapid.

Pope's movement, however, though rapid, is not of the same kind as Homer's; and here I come to the real objection to rhyme in a translation of Homer. It is commonly said that rhyme is to be abandoned in a translation of Homer, because 'the exigences of rhyme,' to quote Mr. Newman, 'positively forbid faithfulness;' because 'a just translation of any ancient poet in rhyme,' to quote Cowper, 'is impossible.' This, however, is merely an accidental objection to rhyme. If this were all, it might be supposed that if rhymes were more abundant, Homer could be adequately translated in rhyme. But this is not so; there is a deeper, a substantial objection to rhyme in a translation of Homer. It is, that rhyme inevitably tends to pair lines which in the original are independent, and thus the movement of the poem is changed. In these lines of Chapman, for instance, from Sarpedon's speech to Glaucus, in the twelfth book of the *Iliad*:—

O friend, if keeping back
Would keep back age from us, and death, and that we might not wrack
In this life's human sea at all, but that deferring now
We shunned death ever,—nor would I half this vain valor show,
Nor glorify a folly so, to wish thee to advance;
But since we *must* go, though not here, and that besides the chance
Proposed now, there are infinite fates, etc.

Here the necessity of making the line,

Nor glorify a folly so, to wish thee to advance,

rhyme with the line which follows it, entirely changes and spoils the movement of the passage.

[1] *Iliad*, xix. 420.

οὔτε κεν αὐτὸς ἐνὶ πρώτοισι μαχοίμην,
οὔτε κε σὲ στέλλοιμι μάχην ἐς κυδιάνειραν·[1]

Neither would I myself go forth to fight with the foremost,
Nor would I urge thee on to enter the glorious battle,

says Homer; there he stops, and begins an opposed movement: 5

νῦν δ'—ἔμπης γὰρ Κῆρες ἐφεστᾶσιν θανάτοιο—

But—for a thousand fates of death stand close to us always—

This line, in which Homer wishes to go away with the most marked rapidity from the line before, Chapman is forced, by the necessity of rhyming, intimately to connect with the line 10 before.

But since we *must* go, though not here, and that besides the chance—

The moment the word *chance* strikes our ear, we are irresistibly carried back to *advance* and to the whole previous line, 15 which, according to Homer's own feeling, we ought to have left behind us entirely, and to be moving farther and farther away from.

Rhyme certainly, by intensifying antithesis, can intensify separation, and this is precisely what Pope does; but this bal- 20 anced rhetorical antithesis, though very effective, is entirely un-Homeric. And this is what I mean by saying that Pope fails to render Homer, because he does not render his plainness and directness of style and diction. Where Homer marks separation by moving away, Pope marks it by antithesis. No pas- 25 sage could show this better than the passage I have just quoted, on which I will pause for a moment.

Robert Wood, whose *Essay on the Genius of Homer* is mentioned by Goethe as one of the books which fell into his hands when his powers were first developing themselves, and 30 strongly interested him, relates of this passage a striking story. He says that in 1762, at the end of the Seven Years' War, being

[1] *Iliad*, xii. 324.

then Under-Secretary of State, he was directed to wait upon the President of the Council, Lord Granville, a few days before he died, with the preliminary articles of the Treaty of Paris. 'I found him,' he continues, 'so languid, that I proposed postponing my business for another time; but he insisted that I should stay, saying, it could not prolong his life to neglect his duty; and repeating the following passage out of Sarpedon's speech, he dwelled with particular emphasis on the third line, which recalled to his mind the distinguishing part he had taken in public affairs:—

> ὦ πέπον, εἰ μὲν γὰρ, πόλεμον περὶ τόνδε φυγόντε,
> αἰεὶ δὴ μέλλοιμεν ἀγήρω τ' ἀθανάτω τε
> ἔσσεσθ', ο ὔ τ ε κ ε ν α ὐ τ ὸ ς ἐ ν ὶ π ρ ώ τ ο ι σ ι μ α χ ο ί μ η ν,[1]
> οὔτε κε σὲ οτέλλοιμι μάχην ἐς κυδιάνειραν·
> νῦν δ'—ἔμπης γὰρ Κῆρες ἐφεστᾶσιν θανάτοιο
> μυρίαι, ἃς οὐκ ἔστι φυγεῖν βροτὸν, οὐδ' ὑπαλύξαι—
> ἴομεν.

His Lordship repeated the last word several times with a calm and determinate resignation; and, after a serious pause of some minutes, he desired to hear the Treaty read, to which he listened with great attention, and recovered spirits enough to declare the approbation of a dying statesman (I use his own words) "on the most glorious war, and most honourable peace, this nation ever saw." '[2]

I quote this story, first, because it is interesting as exhibiting the English aristocracy at its very height of culture, lofty spirit, and greatness, towards the middle of the last century. I quote it, secondly, because it seems to me to illustrate Goethe's saying which I mentioned, that our life, in Homer's view of it, represents a conflict and a hell; and it brings out, too, what there is tonic and fortifying in this doctrine. I quote it, lastly, because it shows that the passage is just one of those in translat-

[1] These are the words on which Lord Granville 'dwelled with particular emphasis.'

[2] Robert Wood, *Essay on the Original Genius and Writings of Homer*, London, 1775, p. vii.

ing which Pope will be at his best, a passage of strong emotion and oratorical movement, not of simple narrative or description.

Pope translates the passage thus:—

> Could all our care elude the gloomy grave 5
> Which claims no less the fearful than the brave,
> For lust of fame I should not vainly dare
> In fighting fields, nor urge thy soul to war:
> But since, alas! ignoble age must come,
> Disease, and death's inexorable doom; 10
> The life which others pay, let us bestow,
> And give to fame what we to nature owe.

Nothing could better exhibit Pope's prodigious talent; and nothing, too, could be better in its own way. But, as Bentley said, 'You must not call it Homer.' One feels that Homer's 15 thought has passed through a literary and rhetorical crucible, and come out highly intellectualised; come out in a form which strongly impresses us, indeed, but which no longer impresses us in the same way as when it was uttered by Homer. The antithesis of the last two lines— 20

> The life which others pay, let us bestow,
> And give to fame what we to nature owe—

is excellent, and is just suited to Pope's heroic couplet; but neither the antithesis itself, nor the couplet which conveys it, is suited to the feeling or to the movement of the Homeric 25 *ἴομεν*.

A literary and intellectualised language is, however, in its own way well suited to grand matters; and Pope, with a language of this kind and his own admirable talent, comes off well enough as long as he has passion, or oratory, or a great 30 crisis to deal with. Even here, as I have been pointing out, he does not render Homer; but he and his style are in themselves strong. It is when he comes to level passages, passages of narrative or description, that he and his style are sorely tried, and prove themselves weak. A perfectly plain direct style can of 35 course convey the simplest matter as naturally as the grandest; indeed, it must be harder for it, one would say, to convey a grand matter worthily and nobly, than to convey a common matter, as alone such a matter should be conveyed, plainly and simply. But the style of *Rasselas* is incomparably better fitted to describe a sage philosophising than a soldier lighting his camp-fire. The style of Pope is not the style of *Rasselas;* but it is equally a literary style, equally unfitted to describe a simple matter with the plain naturalness of Homer.

Every one knows the passage at the end of the eighth book of the *Iliad*, where the fires of the Trojan encampment are likened to the stars. It is very far from my wish to hold Pope up to ridicule, so I shall not quote the commencement of the passage, which in the original is of great and celebrated beauty, and in translating which Pope has been singularly and notoriously unfortunate. But the latter part of the passage, where Homer leaves the stars, and comes to the Trojan fires, treats of the plainest, most matter-of-fact subject possible, and deals with this, as Homer always deals with every subject, in the plainest and most straightforward style. 'So many in number, between the ships and the streams of Xanthus, shone forth in front of Troy the fires kindled by the Trojans. There were kindled a thousand fires in the plain; and by each one there sat fifty men in the light of the blazing fire. And the horses, munching white barley and rye, and standing by the chariots, waited for the bright-throned Morning.' [1]

In Pope's translation, this plain story becomes the following:—

> So many flames before proud Ilion blaze,
> And brighten glimmering Xanthus with their rays;
> The long reflections of the distant fires
> Gleam on the walls, and tremble on the spires.
> A thousand piles the dusky horrors gild,
> And shoot a shady lustre o'er the field.
> Full fifty guards each flaming pile attend,
> Whose umbered arms, by fits, thick flashes send;
> Loud neigh the coursers o'er their heaps of corn,
> And ardent warriors wait the rising morn.

[1] *Iliad*, viii. 560.

It is for passages of this sort, which, after all, form the bulk of a narrative poem, that Pope's style is so bad. In elevated passages he is powerful, as Homer is powerful, though not in the same way; but in plain narrative, where Homer is still powerful and delightful, Pope, by the inherent fault of his style, is ineffective and out of taste. Wordsworth says somewhere, that wherever Virgil seems to have composed 'with his eye on the object,' Dryden fails to render him. Homer invariably composes 'with his eye on the object,' whether the object be a moral or a material one: Pope composes with his eye on his style, into which he translates his object, whatever it is. That, therefore, which Homer conveys to us immediately, Pope conveys to us through a medium. He aims at turning Homer's sentiments pointedly and rhetorically; at investing Homer's description with ornament and dignity. A sentiment may be changed by being put into a pointed and oratorical form, yet may still be very effective in that form; but a description, the moment it takes its eyes off that which it is to describe, and begins to think of ornamenting itself, is worthless.

Therefore, I say, the translator of Homer should penetrate himself with a sense of the plainness and directness of Homer's style; of the simplicity with which Homer's thought is evolved and expressed. He has Pope's fate before his eyes, to show him what a divorce may be created even between the most gifted translator and Homer by an artificial evolution of thought and a literary cast of style.

Chapman's style is not artificial and literary like Pope's nor his movement elaborate and self-retarding like the Miltonic movement of Cowper. He is plain-spoken, fresh, vigorous, and, to a certain degree, rapid; and all these are Homeric qualities. I cannot say that I think the movement of his fourteen-syllable line, which has been so much commended, Homeric; but on this point I shall have more to say by and by, when I come to speak of Mr. Newman's metrical exploits. But it is not distinctly anti-Homeric, like the movement of Milton's blank verse; and it has a rapidity of its own. Chapman's diction, too, is generally good, that is, appropriate to Homer; above all, the syntactical character of his style is appropriate. With these merits, what prevents his translation from being a satisfactory version of Homer? Is it merely the want of literal faithfulness to his original, imposed upon him, it is said, by the exigences of rhyme? Has this celebrated version, which has so many advantages, no other and deeper defect than that? Its author is a poet, and a poet, too, of the Elizabethan age; the golden age of English literature as it is called, and on the whole truly called; for, whatever be the defects of Elizabethan literature (and they are great), we have no development of our literature to compare with it for vigour and richness. This age, too, showed what it could do in translating, by producing a master-piece, its version of the Bible.

Chapman's translation has often been praised as eminently Homeric. Keats's fine sonnet in its honour every one knows; but Keats could not read the original, and therefore could not really judge the translation. Coleridge, in praising Chapman's version, says at the same time, 'It will give you small idea of Homer.' But the grave authority of Mr. Hallam pronounces this translation to be 'often exceedingly Homeric;' and its latest editor boldly declares that by what, with a deplorable style, he calls 'his own innative Homeric genius,' Chapman 'has thoroughly identified himself with Homer;' and that 'we pardon him even for his digressions, for they are such as we feel Homer himself would have written.'

I confess that I can never read twenty lines of Chapman's version without recurring to Bentley's cry, 'This is not Homer!' and that from a deeper cause than any unfaithfulness occasioned by the fetters of rhyme.

I said that there were four things which eminently distinguished Homer, and with a sense of which Homer's translator should penetrate himself as fully as possible. One of these four things was, the plainness and directness of Homer's ideas. I have just been speaking of the plainness and directness of his style; but the plainness and directness of the contents of his style, of his ideas themselves, is not less remarkable. But as eminently as Homer is plain, so eminently is the Elizabethan literature in general, and Chapman in particular, fanciful. Steeped in humours and fantasticality up to its very lips, the Elizabethan age, newly arrived at the free use of the human faculties after their long term of bondage, and delighting to exercise them freely, suffers from its own extravagance in this first exercise of them, can hardly bring itself to see an object quietly or to describe it temperately. Happily, in the translation of the Bible, the sacred character of their original inspired the translators with such respect that they did not dare to give the rein to their own fancies in dealing with it. But, in dealing with works of profane literature, in dealing with poetical works above all, which highly stimulated them, one may say that the minds of the Elizabethan translators were *too* active; that they could not forbear importing so much of their own, and this of a most peculiar and Elizabethan character, into their original, that they effaced the character of the original itself.

Take merely the opening pages to Chapman's translation, the introductory verses, and the dedications. You will find:—

> An Anagram of the name of our Dread Prince,
> My most gracious and sacred Mæcenas,
> Henry, Prince of Wales,
> Our Sunn, Heyr, Peace, Life,—

Henry, son of James the First, to whom the work is dedicated. Then comes an address,

> To the sacred Fountain of Princes,
> Sole Empress of Beauty and Virtue, Anne, Queen
> Of England, etc.

All the Middle Age, with its grotesqueness, its conceits, its irrationality, is still in these opening pages; they by themselves are sufficient to indicate to us what a gulf divides Chapman from the 'clearest-souled' of poets, from Homer; almost as great a gulf as that which divides him from Voltaire. Pope has been sneered at for saying that Chapman writes 'somewhat as one might imagine Homer himself to have written before he arrived at years of discretion.' But the remark is excellent: Homer expresses himself like a man of adult reason, Chapman like a man whose reason has not yet cleared itself. For instance, if Homer had had to say of a poet, that he hoped his merit was now about to be fully established in the opinion of good judges, he was as incapable of saying this as Chapman says it,—'Though truth in her very nakedness sits in so deep a pit, that from Gades to Aurora, and Ganges, few eyes can sound her, I hope yet those few here will so discover and confirm her that, the date being out of her darkness in this morning of our poet, he shall now gird his temples with the sun,'—I say, Homer was as incapable of saying this in that manner, as Voltaire himself would have been. Homer, indeed, has actually an affinity with Voltaire in the unrivalled clearness and straightforwardness of his thinking; in the way in which he keeps to one thought at a time, and puts that thought forth in its complete natural plainness, instead of being led away from it by some fancy striking him in connection with it, and being beguiled to wander off with this fancy till his original thought, in its natural reality, knows him no more. What could better show us how gifted a race was this Greek race? The same member of it has not only the power of profoundly touching that natural heart of humanity which it is Voltaire's weakness that he cannot reach, but can also address the understanding with all Voltaire's admirable simplicity and rationality.

My limits will not allow me to do more than shortly illustrate, from Chapman's version of the *Iliad*, what I mean when I speak of this vital difference between Homer and an Elizabethan poet in the quality of their thought; between the plain simplicity of the thought of the one, and the curious complexity of the thought of the other. As in Pope's case, I carefully abstain from choosing passages for the express purpose of making Chapman appear ridiculous; Chapman, like Pope, merits in himself all respect, though he too, like Pope, fails to render Homer.

In that tonic speech of Sarpedon, of which I have said so much, Homer, you may remember, has:—

εἰ μὲν γὰρ, πόλεμον περὶ τόνδε φυγόντε,
αἰεὶ δὴ μέλλοιμεν ἀγήρω τ' ἀθανάτω τε
ἔσσεσθ',—

if indeed, but once *this* battle avoided,
We were for ever to live without growing old and immortal.

Chapman cannot be satisfied with this, but must add a fancy to it:—

if keeping back
Would keep back age from us, and death, and *that we might not wrack*
In this life's human sea at all;

and so on. Again; in another passage which I have before quoted, where Zeus says to the horses of Peleus,

τί σφῶϊ δόμεν Πηλῆϊ ἄνακτι
θνητῷ; ὑμεῖς δ' ἐστὸν ἀγήρω τ' ἀθανάτω τε·[1]

Why gave we you to royal Peleus, to a mortal? but ye are without old age, and immortal.

Chapman sophisticates this into:—

Why gave we you t' a mortal king, when immortality
And *incapacity of age so dignifies your states?*

Again; in the speech of Achilles to his horses, where Achilles, according to Homer, says simply, 'Take heed that ye bring your master safe back to the host of the Danaans, in some other sort than the last time, when the battle is ended,' Chapman sophisticates this into:—

When with blood, for this day's fast observed, revenge shall yield
Our heart satiety, bring us off.

In Hector's famous speech, again, at his parting from Andromache, Homer makes him say: 'Nor does my own heart so bid me' (to keep safe behind the walls), 'since I have learned to be staunch always, and to fight among the foremost of the

[1] *Iliad*, xvii. 443.

Trojans, busy on behalf of my father's great glory, and my own.'[1] In Chapman's hands this becomes:—

The spirit I first did breathe
Did never teach me that; much less, since the contempt of death
5 Was settled in me, *and my mind knew what a worthy was,*
Whose office is to lead in fight, and give no danger pass
Without improvement. In this fire must Hector's trial shine:
Here must his country, father, friends, be in him made divine.

You see how ingeniously Homer's plain thought is *tormented,*
10 as the French would say, here. Homer goes on: 'For well I know this in my mind and in my heart, the day will be, when sacred Troy shall perish:'—

ἔσσεται ἦμαρ, ὅτ' ἄν ποτ' ὀλώλῃ Ἴλιος ἱρή.

Chapman makes this:—

15 And such a *stormy* day shall come, in mind and soul I know,
When sacred Troy *shall shed her towers, for tears of overthrow.*

I might go on for ever, but I could not give you a better illustration than this last, of what I mean by saying that the Elizabethan poet fails to render Homer because he cannot forbear
20 to interpose a play of thought between his object and its expression. Chapman translates his object into Elizabethan, as Pope translates it into the Augustan of Queen Anne; both convey it to us through a medium. Homer, on the other hand, sees his object and conveys it to us immediately.

25 And yet, in spite of this perfect plainness and directness of Homer's style, in spite of this perfect plainness and directness of his ideas, he is eminently *noble;* he works as entirely in the grand style, he is as grandiose, as Phidias, or Dante, or Michael Angelo. This is what makes his translators despair.
30 'To give relief,' says Cowper, 'to prosaic subjects' (such as dressing, eating, drinking, harnessing, travelling, going to bed), that is to treat such subjects nobly, in the grand style, 'with-

[1] *Iliad,* vi. 444.

out seeming unseasonably tumid, is extremely difficult.' It *is* difficult, but Homer has done it. Homer is precisely the incomparable poet he is, because he has done it. His translator must not be tumid, must not be artificial, must not be literary; true: but then also he must not be commonplace, must not be ignoble. I have shown you how translators of Homer fail by wanting rapidity, by wanting simplicity of style, by wanting plainness of thought: in a second lecture I will show you how a translator fails by wanting nobility.

[II]

I must repeat what I said in beginning, that the translator of Homer ought steadily to keep in mind where lies the real test of the success of his translation, what judges he is to try to satisfy. He is to try to satisfy *scholars*, because scholars alone have the means of really judging him. A scholar may be a pedant, it is true, and then his judgment will be worthless; but a scholar may also have poetical feeling, and then he can judge him truly; whereas all the poetical feeling in the world will not enable a man who is not a scholar to judge him truly. For the translator is to reproduce Homer, and the scholar alone has the means of knowing that Homer who is to be reproduced. He knows him but imperfectly, for he is separated from him by time, race, and language; but he alone knows him at all. Yet people speak as if there were two real tribunals in this matter,—the scholar's tribunal, and that of the general public. They speak as if the scholar's judgment was one thing, and the general public's judgment another; both with their shortcomings, both with their liability to error; but both to be regarded by the translator. The translator who makes verbal literalness his chief care 'will,' says a writer in the *National Review* whom I have already quoted, 'be appreciated by the scholar accustomed to test a translation rigidly by comparison with the original, to look perhaps with excessive care to finish in detail rather than boldness and general effect, and find pardon even for a version that seems bare and bald, so it be scholastic and faithful.' But, if the scholar in judging a translation looks to detail rather than to general effect, he judges it pedantically and ill. The appeal, however, lies not from the pedantic scholar 5 to the general public, which can only like or dislike Chapman's version, or Pope's, or Mr. Newman's, but cannot *judge* them; it lies from the pedantic scholar to the scholar who is not pedantic, who knows that Homer is Homer by his general effect, and not by his single words, and who demands but one 10 thing in a translation,—that it shall, as nearly as possible, reproduce for him the *general effect* of Homer. This, then, remains the one proper aim of the translator: to reproduce on the intelligent scholar, as nearly as possible, the general effect of Homer. Except so far as he reproduces this, he loses 15 his labour, even though he may make a spirited *Iliad* of his own, like Pope, or translate Homer's *Iliad* word for word, like Mr. Newman. If his proper aim were to stimulate in any manner possible the general public, he might be right in following Pope's example; if his proper aim were to help schoolboys to 20 construe Homer, he might be right in following Mr. Newman's. But it is not: his proper aim is, I repeat it yet once more, to reproduce on the intelligent scholar, as nearly as he can, the general effect of Homer.

When, therefore, Cowper says, 'My chief boast is that I have 25 adhered closely to my original;' when Mr. Newman says, 'My aim is to retain every peculiarity of the original, to be *faithful*, exactly as is the case with the draughtsman of the Elgin marbles;' their real judge only replies: 'It may be so: reproduce then upon us, reproduce the effect of Homer, as 30 a good copy reproduces the effect of the Elgin marbles.'

When, again, Mr. Newman tells us that 'by an exhaustive process of argument and experiment' he has found a metre which is at once the metre of 'the modern Greek epic,' and a metre 'like in moral genius' to Homer's metre, his judge has 35 still but the same answer for him: 'It may be so: reproduce then on our ear something of the effect produced by the movement of Homer.'

But what is the general effect which Homer produces on

Mr. Newman himself? because, when we know this, we shall know whether he and his judges are agreed at the outset, whether we may expect him, if he can reproduce the effect he feels, if his hand does not betray him in the execution, to satisfy his judges and to succeed. If, however, Mr. Newman's impression from Homer is something quite different from that of his judges, then it can hardly be expected that any amount of labour or talent will enable him to reproduce for them *their* Homer.

Mr. Newman does not leave us in doubt as to the general effect which Homer makes upon him. As I have told you what is the general effect which Homer makes upon me,—that of a most rapidly moving poet, that of a poet most plain and direct in his style, that of a poet most plain and direct in his ideas, that of a poet eminently noble,—so Mr. Newman tells us his general impression of Homer. 'Homer's style,' he says, 'is direct, popular, forcible, quaint, flowing, garrulous.' Again: 'Homer rises and sinks with his subject, is prosaic when it is tame, is low when it is mean.'

I lay my finger on four words in these two sentences of Mr. Newman, and I say that the man who could apply those words to Homer can never render Homer truly. The four words are these: *quaint*, *garrulous*, *prosaic*, *low*. Search the English language for a word which does not apply to Homer, and you could not fix on a better than *quaint*, unless perhaps you fixed on one of the other three.

Again; 'to translate Homer suitably,' says Mr. Newman, 'we need a diction sufficiently antiquated to obtain pardon of the reader for its frequent homeliness.' 'I am concerned,' he says again, 'with the artistic problem of attaining a plausible aspect of moderate antiquity, while remaining easily intelligible.' And again, he speaks of 'the more antiquated style suited to this subject.' Quaint! antiquated!—but to whom? Sir Thomas Browne is quaint, and the diction of Chaucer is antiquated: does Mr. Newman suppose that Homer seemed quaint to Sophocles, when he read him, as Sir Thomas Browne seems quaint to us, when we read him? or that Homer's diction seemed antiquated to Sophocles, as Chaucer's diction seems antiquated to us? But we cannot really know, I confess, how Homer seemed to Sophocles: well then, to those who can tell us how he seems to them, to the living scholar, to our only present witness on this matter,—does Homer make on the Provost of Eton, when he reads him, the impression of a poet quaint and antiquated? does he make this impression on Professor Thompson or Professor Jowett? When Shakspeare says, 'The princes *orgulous*,' meaning 'the proud princes,' we say, 'This is antiquated;' when he says of the Trojan gates, that they

> With massy staples
> And corresponsive and fulfilling bolts
> *Sperr* up the sons of Troy,

we say, 'This is both quaint and antiquated.' But does Homer ever compose in a language which produces on the scholar at all the same impression as this language which I have quoted from Shakspeare? Never once. Shakspeare is quaint and antiquated in the lines which I have just quoted; but Shakspeare—need I say it?—can compose, when he likes, when he is at his best, in a language perfectly simple, perfectly intelligible; in a language which, in spite of the two centuries and a half which part its author from us, stops us or surprises us as little as the language of a contemporary. And Homer has not Shakspeare's variations: Homer always composes as Shakspeare composes at his best; Homer is always simple and intelligible, as Shakspeare is often; Homer is never quaint and antiquated, as Shakspeare is sometimes.

When Mr. Newman says that Homer is garrulous, he seems, perhaps, to depart less widely from the common opinion than when he calls him quaint; for is there not Horace's authority for asserting that 'the good Homer sometimes nods,' *bonus dormitat Homerus?* and a great many people have come, from the currency of this well-known criticism, to represent Homer to themselves as a diffuse old man, with the full-stocked mind, but also with the occasional slips and weaknesses, of old age. Horace has said better things than his 'bonus dormitat Homerus;' but he never meant by this, as I need not remind any one who knows the passage, that Homer was garrulous, or anything of the kind. Instead, however, of either discussing what Horace meant, or discussing Homer's garrulity as a general question, I prefer to bring to my mind some style which *is* garrulous, and to ask myself, to ask you, whether anything at all of the impression made by that style is ever made by the style of Homer. The mediæval romancers, for instance, are garrulous; the following, to take out of a thousand instances the first which comes to hand, is in a garrulous manner. It is from the romance of Richard Cœur de Lion.

> Of my tale be not a-wondered!
> The French says he slew an hundred
> (Whereof is made this English saw)
> Or he rested him any thraw.
> Him followed many an English knight
> That eagerly holp him for to fight,—

and so on. Now the manner of that composition I call garrulous; every one will feel it to be garrulous; every one will understand what is meant when it is called garrulous. Then I ask the scholar,—does Homer's manner ever make upon you, I do not say, the same impression of its garrulity as that passage, but does it make, ever for one moment, an impression in the slightest way resembling, in the remotest degree akin to, the impression made by that passage of the mediæval poet? I have no fear of the answer.

I follow the same method with Mr. Newman's two other epithets, *prosaic* and *low*. 'Homer rises and sinks with his subject,' says Mr. Newman; 'is prosaic when it is tame, is low when it is mean.' First I say, Homer is never, in any sense, to be with truth called prosaic; he is never to be called low. He does not rise and sink with his subject; on the contrary, his manner invests his subject, whatever his subject be, with nobleness. Then I look for an author of whom it may with truth be said, that he 'rises and sinks with his subject, is prosaic when it is tame, is low when it is mean.' Defoe is eminently such an author; of Defoe's manner it may with perfect precision be said, that it follows his matter; his lifelike composition takes its character from the facts which it conveys, not from the nobleness of the composer. In *Moll Flanders* and *Colonel Jack,* Defoe is undoubtedly prosaic when his subject is tame, low when his subject is mean. Does Homer's manner in the *Iliad,* I ask the scholar, ever make upon him an impression at all like the impression made by Defoe's manner in *Moll Flanders* and *Colonel Jack?* Does it not, on the contrary, leave him with an impression of nobleness, even when it deals with Thersites or with Irus?

Well then, Homer is neither quaint, nor garrulous, nor prosaic, nor mean: and Mr. Newman, in seeing him so, sees him differently from those who are to judge Mr. Newman's rendering of him. By pointing out how a wrong conception of Homer affects Mr. Newman's translation, I hope to place in still clearer light those four cardinal truths which I pronounce essential for him who would have a right conception of Homer: that Homer is rapid, that he is plain and direct in word and style, that he is plain and direct in his ideas, and that he is noble.

Mr. Newman says that in fixing on a style for suitably rendering Homer, as he conceives him, he 'alights on the delicate line which separates the *quaint* from the *grotesque*.' 'I ought to be quaint,' he says, 'I ought not to be grotesque.' This is a most unfortunate sentence. Mr. Newman is grotesque, which he himself says he ought not to be; and he ought not to be quaint, which he himself says he ought to be.

'No two persons will agree,' says Mr. Newman, 'as to where the quaint ends and the grotesque begins;' and perhaps this is true. But, in order to avoid all ambiguity in the use of the two words, it is enough to say, that most persons would call an expression which produced on them a very strong sense of its incongruity, and which violently surprised them, *grotesque;* and an expression, which produced on them a slighter sense of its incongruity, and which more gently surprised them, *quaint*. Using the two words in this manner, I say, that when Mr. Newman translates Helen's words to Hector in the sixth book,

> Δᾶερ ἐμεῖο, κυνὸς κακομηχάνου, ὀκρυοέσσης,[1]—
>
> O, brother thou of me, who am a mischief-working vixen,
> A numbing horror,—

he is grotesque; that is, he expresses himself in a manner which produces on us a very strong sense of its incongruity, and which violently surprises us. I say, again, that when Mr. Newman translates the common line,

> Τὴν δ' ἠμείβετ' ἔπειτα μέγας κορυθαίολος Ἕκτωρ,—
>
> Great Hector of the motley helm then spake to her responsive,—

or the common expression ἐϋκνήμιδες Ἀχαιοί, 'dapper-greaved Achaians,' he is quaint; that is, he expresses himself in a manner which produces on us a slighter sense of incongruity, and which more gently surprises us. But violent and gentle surprise are alike far from the scholar's spirit when he reads in Homer κυνὸς κακομηχάνου, or κορυθαίολος Ἕκτωρ, or, ἐϋκνήμιδες Ἀχαιοί. These expressions no more seem odd to him than the simplest expressions in English. He is not more checked by any feeling of strangeness, strong or weak, when he reads them, than when he reads in an English book 'the painted savage,' or, 'the phlegmatic Dutchman.' Mr. Newman's renderings of them must, therefore, be wrong expressions in a translation of Homer, because they excite in the scholar, their only competent judge, a feeling quite alien to that excited in him by what they profess to render.

Mr. Newman, by expressions of this kind, is false to his original in two ways. He is false to him inasmuch as he is ignoble; for a noble air, and a grotesque air, the air of the address,

> Δᾶερ ἐμεῖο, κυνὸς κακομηχάνου, ὀκρυοέσσης,—

and the air of the address,

> O, brother thou of me, who am a mischief-working vixen,
> A numbing horror,—

---

[1] *Iliad*, vi. 344.

are just contrary the one to the other: and he is false to him inasmuch as he is odd; for an odd diction like Mr. Newman's, and a perfectly plain natural diction like Homer's,—'dapper-greaved Achaians' and ἐϋκνήμιδες Ἀχαιοί,—are also just contrary the one to the other. Where, indeed, Mr. Newman got his diction, with whom he can have lived, what can be his test of antiquity and rarity for words, are questions which I ask myself with bewilderment. He has prefixed to his translation a list of what he calls 'the more antiquated or rarer words' which he has used. In this list appear, on the one hand, such words as *doughty*, *grisly*, *lusty*, *noisome*, *ravin*, which are familiar, one would think, to all the world; on the other hand such words as *bragly*, meaning, Mr. Newman tells us, 'proudly fine;' *bulkin*, 'a calf;' *plump*, 'a mass;' and so on. 'I am concerned,' says Mr. Newman, 'with the artistic problem of attaining a plausible aspect of moderate antiquity, while remaining easily intelligible.' But it seems to me that *lusty* is not antiquated: and that *bragly* is not a word readily understood. That this word, indeed, and *bulkin*, may have 'a plausible aspect of moderate antiquity,' I admit; but that they are 'easily intelligible,' I deny.

Mr. Newman's syntax has, I say it with pleasure, a much more Homeric cast than his vocabulary; his syntax, the mode in which his thought is evolved, although not the actual words in which it is expressed, seems to me right in its general character, and the best feature of his version. It is not artificial or rhetorical like Cowper's syntax or Pope's: it is simple, direct, and natural, and so far it is like Homer's. It fails, however, just where, from the inherent fault of Mr. Newman's conception of Homer, one might expect it to fail,—it fails in nobleness. It presents the thought in a way which is something more than unconstrained,—over-familiar; something more than easy,—free and easy. In this respect it is like the movement of Mr. Newman's version, like his rhythm, for this, too, fails, in spite of some good qualities, by not being noble enough; this, while it avoids the faults of being slow and elaborate, falls into a fault in the opposite direction, and is slip-shod. Homer presents his thought naturally; but when Mr. Newman has,

A thousand fires along the plain, *I say*, that night were burning,—

he presents his thought familiarly; in a style which may be the genuine style of ballad-poetry, but which is not the style of Homer. Homer moves freely; but when Mr. Newman has,

Infatuate! O that thou wert lord to some other army,—[1] 5

he gives himself too much freedom; he leaves us too much to do for his rhythm ourselves, instead of giving to us a rhythm like Homer's, easy indeed, but mastering our ear with a fulness of power which is irresistible.

I said that a certain style might be the genuine style of ballad- 10 poetry, but yet not the style of Homer. The analogy of the ballad is ever present to Mr. Newman's thoughts in considering Homer; and perhaps nothing has more caused his faults than this analogy,—this popular, but, it is time to say, this erroneous analogy. 'The moral qualities of Homer's style,' says Mr. New- 15 man, 'being like to those of the English ballad, we need a metre of the same genius. Only those metres, which by the very possession of these qualities are liable to degenerate into *doggerel,* are suitable to reproduce the ancient epic.' 'The style of Homer,' he says, in a passage which I have before quoted, 20 'is direct, popular, forcible, quaint, flowing, garrulous: in all these respects it is similar to the old English ballad.' Mr. Newman, I need not say, is by no means alone in this opinion. 'The most really and truly Homeric of all the creations of the English muse is,' says Mr. Newman's critic in the *National Review,* 25 'the ballad-poetry of ancient times; and the association between metre and subject is one that it would be true wisdom to preserve.' 'It is confessed,' says Chapman's last editor, Mr.

[1] From the reproachful answer of Ulysses to Agamemnon, who had proposed an abandonment of their expedition. This is one of the 'tonic' 30 passages of the *Iliad,* so I quote it:—

Ah, unworthy king, some other inglorious army
Should'st thou command, not rule over *us,* whose portion for ever
Zeus hath made it, from youth right up to age, to be winding
Skeins of grievous wars, till every soul of us perish. 35

Iliad, xiv. 84.

Hooper, 'that the fourteen-syllable verse' (that is, a ballad-verse) 'is peculiarly fitting for Homeric translation.' And the editor of Dr. Maginn's clever and popular *Homeric Ballads* assumes it as one of his author's greatest and most undisputable merits, that he was 'the first who consciously realised to himself the truth that Greek ballads can be really represented in English only by a similar measure.'

This proposition that Homer's poetry is *ballad-poetry*, analogous to the well-known ballad-poetry of the English and other nations, has a certain small portion of truth in it, and at one time probably served a useful purpose, when it was employed to discredit the artificial and literary manner in which Pope and his school rendered Homer. But it has been so extravagantly over-used, the mistake which it was useful in combating has so entirely lost the public favour, that it is now much more important to insist on the large part of error contained in it, than to extol its small part of truth. It is time to say plainly that, whatever the admirers of our old ballads may think, the supreme form of epic poetry, the genuine Homeric mould, is not the form of the Ballad of Lord Bateman. I have myself shown the broad difference between Milton's manner and Homer's; but, after a course of Mr. Newman and Dr. Maginn, I turn round in desperation upon them and upon the balladists who have misled them, and I exclaim: 'Compared with you, Milton is Homer's double; there is, whatever you may think, ten thousand times more of the real strain of Homer in,

> Blind Thamyris, and blind Mæonides,
> And Tiresias, and Phineus, prophets old,—

than in,

> Now Christ thee save, thou proud portèr,
> Now Christ thee save and see,[1]—

or in,

[1] From the ballad of *King Estmere*, in Percy's *Reliques of Ancient English Poetry*, i. 69 (edit. of 1767).

While the tinker did dine, he had plenty of wine.[1]

For Homer is not only rapid in movement, simple in style, plain in language, natural in thought; he is also, and above all, *noble*. I have advised the translator not to go into the vexed question of Homer's identity. Yet I will just remind him that the grand argument—or rather, not argument, for the matter affords no data for arguing, but the grand source from which conviction, as we read the *Iliad*, keeps pressing in upon us, that there is one poet of the *Iliad*, one Homer—is precisely this nobleness of the poet, this grand manner; we feel that the analogy drawn from other joint compositions does not hold good here, because those works do not bear, like the *Iliad*, the magic stamp of a master; and the moment you have *anything* less than a masterwork, the co-operation or consolidation of several poets becomes possible, for talent is not uncommon; the moment you have *much* less than a masterwork, they become easy, for mediocrity is everywhere. I can imagine fifty Bradies joined with as many Tates to make the New Version of the Psalms. I can imagine several poets having contributed to any one of the old English ballads in Percy's collection. I can imagine several poets, possessing, like Chapman, the Elizabethan vigour and the Elizabethan mannerism, united with Chapman to produce his version of the *Iliad*. I can imagine several poets, with the literary knack of the twelfth century, united to produce the *Nibelungen Lay* in the form in which we have it,—a work which the Germans, in their joy at discovering a national epic of their own, have rated vastly higher than it deserves. And lastly, though Mr. Newman's translation of Homer bears the strong mark of his own idiosyncrasy, yet I can imagine Mr. Newman and a school of adepts trained by him in his art of poetry, jointly producing that work, so that Aristarchus himself should have difficulty in pronouncing which line was the master's, and which a pupil's. But I cannot imagine several poets, or one poet, joined with Dante in the composition of his *Inferno*, though many poets have taken for their subject a descent into Hell. Many artists, again, have

[1] *Reliques*, i. 241.

represented Moses; but there is only one Moses of Michael Angelo. So the insurmountable obstacle to believing the *Iliad* a consolidated work of several poets is this: that the work of great masters is unique; and the *Iliad* has a great master's genuine stamp, and that stamp is *the grand style*.

Poets who cannot work in the grand style instinctively seek a style in which their comparative inferiority may feel itself at ease, a manner which may be, so to speak, indulgent to their inequalities. The ballad-style offers to an epic poet, quite unable to fill the canvas of Homer, or Dante, or Milton, a canvas which he is capable of filling. The ballad-measure is quite able to give due effect to the vigour and spirit which its employer, when at his very best, may be able to exhibit; and, when he is not at his best, when he is a little trivial, or a little dull, it will not betray him, it will not bring out his weaknesses into broad relief. This is a convenience; but it is a convenience which the ballad-style purchases by resigning all pretensions to the highest, to the grand manner. It is true of its movement, as it is *not* true of Homer's, that it is 'liable to degenerate into doggerel.' It is true of its 'moral qualities,' as it is *not* true of Homer's, that 'quaintness' and 'garrulity' are among them. It is true of its employers, as it is *not* true of Homer, that they 'rise and sink with their subject, are prosaic when it is tame, are low when it is mean.' For this reason the ballad-style and the ballad-measure are eminently *in*appropriate to render Homer. Homer's manner and movement are always both noble and powerful: the ballad-manner and movement are often either jaunty and smart, so not noble; or jog-trot and humdrum, so not powerful.

The *Nibelungen Lay* affords a good illustration of the qualities of the ballad-manner. Based on grand traditions, which had found expression in a grand lyric poetry, the German epic poem of the *Nibelungen Lay*, though it is interesting, and though it has good passages, is itself anything rather than a grand poem. It is a poem of which the composer is, to speak the truth, a very ordinary mortal, and often, therefore, like other ordinary mortals, very prosy. It is in a measure which eminently adapts itself to this commonplace personality of its composer, which has much the movement of the well-known measures of Tate and Brady, and can jog on, for hundreds of lines at a time, with a level ease which reminds one of Sheridan's saying that easy writing may be often such hard reading. But, instead of occupying myself with the *Nibelungen Lay*, I prefer to look at the ballad-style as directly applied to Homer, in Chapman's version and Mr. Newman's, and in the *Homeric Ballads* of Dr. Maginn.

First I take Chapman. I have already shown that Chapman's conceits are un-Homeric, and that his rhyme is un-Homeric; I will now show how his manner and movement are un-Homeric. Chapman's diction, I have said, is generally good; but it must be called good with this reserve, that, though it has Homer's plainness and directness, it often offends him who knows Homer, by wanting Homer's nobleness. In a passage which I have already quoted, the address of Zeus to the horses of Achilles, where Homer has—

> ἆ δειλώ, τί σφῶϊ δόμεν Πηλῆϊ ἄνακτι
> θνητῷ; ὑμεῖς δ' ἐστὸν ἀγήρω τ' ἀθανάτω τε!
> ἦ ἵνα δυστήνοισι μετ' ἀνδράσιν ἄλγε' ἔχητον;[1]

Chapman has—

> *'Poor wretched beasts*,' said he,
> 'Why gave we you to a mortal king, when immortality
> And incapacity of age so dignifies your states?
> Was it to haste[2] the miseries poured out on human fates?'

There are many faults in this rendering of Chapman's, but what I particularly wish to notice in it is the expression 'Poor wretched beasts' for ἆ δειλώ. This expression just illustrates the difference between the ballad-manner and Homer's. The ballad-manner—Chapman's manner—is, I say, pitched sensibly lower than Homer's. The ballad-manner requires that an expression shall be plain and natural, and then it asks no more. Homer's

[1] *Iliad*, xvii. 443.

[2] All the editions which I have seen have 'haste,' but the right reading must certainly be 'taste.'

manner requires that an expression shall be plain and natural, but it also requires that it shall be noble. Ἆ δειλώ is as plain, as simple as 'Poor wretched beasts;' but it is also noble, which 'Poor wretched beasts' is not. 'Poor wretched beasts' is, in truth, a little over-familiar, but this is no objection to it for the ballad-manner; it is good enough for the old English ballad, good enough for the *Nibelungen Lay*, good enough for Chapman's *Iliad*, good enough for Mr. Newman's *Iliad*, good enough for Dr. Maginn's *Homeric Ballads;* but it is not good enough for Homer.

To feel that Chapman's measure, though natural, is not Homeric; that, though tolerably rapid, it has not Homer's rapidity; that it has a jogging rapidity rather than a flowing rapidity; and a movement familiar rather than nobly easy, one has only, I think, to read half a dozen lines in any part of his version. I prefer to keep as much as possible to passages which I have already noticed, so I will quote the conclusion of the nineteenth book, where Achilles answers his horse Xanthus, who has prophesied his death to him.[1]

> Achilles, far in rage,
> Thus answered him:—It fits not thee thus proudly to presage
> My overthrow. I know myself it is my fate to fall
> Thus far from Phthia; yet that fate shall fail to vent her gall
> Till mine vent thousands.—These words said, he fell to horrid deeds,
> Gave dreadful signal, and forthright made fly his one-hoofed steeds.

For what regards the manner of this passage, the words 'Achilles Thus answered him,' and 'I know myself it is my fate to fall Thus far from Phthia,' are in Homer's manner, and all the rest is out of it. But for what regards its movement, who, after being jolted by Chapman through such verse as this,—

> These words said, he fell to horrid deeds,
> Gave dreadful signal, and forthright made fly his one-hoofed steeds,—

[1] *Iliad*, xix. 419.

who does not feel the vital difference of the movement of Homer,—

ἦ ῥα, καὶ ἐν πρώτοις ἰάχων ἔχε μώνυχας ἵππους?

To pass from Chapman to Dr. Maginn. His *Homeric Ballads* are vigorous and genuine poems in their own way; they are not one continual falsetto, like the pinchbeck *Roman Ballads* of Lord Macaulay; but just because they are ballads in their manner and movement, just because, to use the words of his applauding editor, Dr. Maginn has 'consciously realised to himself the truth that Greek ballads can be really represented in English only by a similar manner,'—just for this very reason they are not at all Homeric, they have not the least in the world the manner of Homer. There is a celebrated incident in the nineteenth book of the *Odyssey*, the recognition by the old nurse Eurycleia of a scar on the leg of her master Ulysses, who has entered his own hall as an unknown wanderer, and whose feet she has been set to wash. 'Then she came near,' says Homer, 'and began to wash her master; and straightway she recognised a scar which he had got in former days from the white tusk of a wild boar, when he went to Parnassus unto Autolycus and the sons of Autolycus, his mother's father and brethren.' [1] This, 'really represented' by Dr. Maginn, in 'a measure similar' to Homer's, becomes:—

> And scarcely had she begun to wash
> Ere she was aware of the grisly gash
>   Above his knee that lay.
> It was a wound from a wild boar's tooth,
>   All on Parnassus' slope,
> Where he went to hunt in the days of his youth
> With his mother's sire,—

and so on. That is the true ballad-manner, no one can deny; 'all on Parnassus' slope' is, I was going to say, the true ballad-slang; but never again shall I be able to read,

[1] *Odyssey*, xix. 392.

νίζε δ' ἄρ' ἆσσον ἰοῦσα ἄναχθ' ἑόν · αὐτίκα δ' ἔγνω
οὐλήν,

without having the detestable dance of Dr. Maginn's,—

And scarcely had she begun to wash
5 Ere she was aware of the grisly gash,—

jigging in my ears, to spoil the effect of Homer, and to torture me. To apply that manner and that rhythm to Homer's incidents, is not to imitate Homer, but to travesty him.

Lastly I come to Mr. Newman. His rhythm, like Chapman's
10 and Dr. Maginn's, is a ballad-rhythm, but with a modification of his own. 'Holding it,' he tells us, 'as an axiom, that rhyme must be abandoned,' he found, on abandoning it, 'an unpleasant void until he gave a double ending to the verse.' In short, instead of saying,

15 Good people all with one accord
Give ear unto my *tale*,—

Mr. Newman would say,

Good people all with one accord
Give ear unto my *story*.

20 A recent American writer[1] gravely observes that for his countrymen this rhythm has a disadvantage in being like the rhythm of the American national air *Yankee Doodle*, and thus provoking ludicrous associations. *Yankee Doodle* is not our national air: for us Mr. Newman's rhythm has not this disad-
25 vantage. He himself gives us several plausible reasons why this rhythm of his really ought to be successful: let us examine how far it *is* successful.

Mr. Newman joins to a bad rhythm so bad a diction that it is difficult to distinguish exactly whether in any given passage
30 it is his words or his measure which produces a total impression

[1] Mr. Marsh, in his *Lectures on the English Language*, New York, 1860, p. 520.

of such an unpleasant kind. But with a little attention we may analyse our total impression, and find the share which each element has in producing it. To take the passage which I have so often mentioned, Sarpedon's speech to Glaucus. Mr. Newman translates this as follows:— 5

O gentle friend! if thou and I, from this encounter 'scaping,
Hereafter might forever be from Eld and Death exempted
As heavenly gods, not I in sooth would fight among the foremost,
Nor liefly thee would I advance to man-ennobling battle.
Now,—sith ten thousand shapes of Death do any-gait pursue us 10
Which never mortal may evade, though sly of foot and nimble;—
Onward! and glory let us earn, or glory yield to some one.—

Could all our care elude the gloomy grave
Which claims no less the fearful than the brave—

I am not going to quote Pope's version over again, but I must 15 remark in passing, how much more, with all Pope's radical difference of manner from Homer, it gives us of the real effect of

εἰ μὲν γὰρ, πόλεμον περὶ τόνδε φυγόντε—

than Mr. Newman's lines. And now, why are Mr. Newman's 20 lines faulty? They are faulty, first, because, as a matter of diction, the expressions 'O gentle friend,' 'eld,' 'in sooth,' 'liefly,' 'advance,' 'man-ennobling,' 'sith,' 'any-gait,' and 'sly of foot,' are all bad; some of them worse than others, but all bad: that is, they all of them as here used excite in the scholar, 25 their sole judge,—excite, I will boldly affirm, in Professor Thompson or Professor Jowett,—a feeling totally different from that excited in them by the words of Homer which these expressions profess to render. The lines are faulty, secondly, because, as a matter of rhythm, any and every line among them 30 has to the ear of the same judges (I affirm it with equal boldness) a movement as unlike Homer's movement in the corresponding line as the single words are unlike Homer's words. Οὔτε κε σὲ στέλλοιμι μάχην ἐς κυδιάνειραν,—'Nor liefly thee would

I advance to man-ennobling battle;'—for whose ears do those two rhythms produce impressions of, to use Mr. Newman's own words, 'similar moral genius'?

I will by no means make search in Mr. Newman's version for passages likely to raise a laugh; that search, alas! would be far too easy. I will quote but one other passage from him, and that a passage where the diction is comparatively inoffensive, in order that disapproval of the words may not unfairly heighten disapproval of the rhythm. The end of the nineteenth book, the answer of Achilles to his horse Xanthus, Mr. Newman gives thus:—

> 'Chestnut! why bodest death to me? from thee this was not needed.
> Myself right surely know alsó, that 't is my doom to perish,
> From mother and from father dear apart, in Troy; but never
> Pause will I make of war, until the Trojans be glutted.'
>   He spake, and yelling, held afront the single-hoofed horses.

Here Mr. Newman calls Xanthus *Chestnut*, indeed, as he calls Balius *Spotted*, and Podarga *Spry-foot;* which is as if a Frenchman were to call Miss Nightingale *Mdlle. Rossignol*, or Mr. Bright *M. Clair*. And several other expressions, too,—'yelling,' 'held afront,' 'single-hoofed,'—leave, to say the very least, much to be desired. Still, for Mr. Newman, the diction of this passage is pure. All the more clearly appears the profound vice of a rhythm, which, with comparatively few faults of words, can leave a sense of such incurable alienation from Homer's manner as, 'Myself right surely know alsó that 't is my doom to perish,' compared with the εὖ νυ τὸ οἶδα καὶ αὐτὸς, ὅ μοι μόρος ἐνθάδ' ὀλέσθαι of Homer.

But so deeply seated is the difference between the ballad-manner and Homer's, that even a man of the highest powers, even a man of the greatest vigour of spirit and of true genius,—the Coryphæus of balladists, Sir Walter Scott,—fails with a manner of this kind to produce an effect at all like the effect of Homer. 'I am not so rash,' declares Mr. Newman, 'as to say that if *freedom* be given to rhyme as in Walter Scott's poetry,'—Walter Scott, 'by far the most Homeric of our poets,' as in another place he calls him,—'a genius may not arise who will translate Homer into the melodies of *Marmion*.' 'The *truly* classical and the *truly* romantic,' says Dr. Maginn, 'are one; the moss-trooping Nestor reappears in the moss-trooping heroes of Percy's *Reliques*;' and a description by Scott, which he quotes, 5 he calls 'graphic, and therefore Homeric.' He forgets our fourth axiom,—that Homer is not *only* graphic; he is also noble, and has the grand style. Human nature under like circumstances is probably in all ages much the same; and so far it may be said that 'the truly classical and the truly romantic are one;' 10 but it is of little use to tell us this, because we know the human nature of other ages only through the representations of them which have come down to us, and the classical and the romantic modes of representation are so far from being 'one,' that they remain eternally distinct, and have created for us a separa- 15 tion between the two worlds which they respectively represent. Therefore to call Nestor the 'moss-trooping Nestor' is absurd, because, though Nestor may possibly have been much the same sort of man as many a moss-trooper, he has yet come to us through a mode of representation so unlike that of Percy's 20 *Reliques*, that instead of 'reappearing in the moss-trooping heroes' of these poems, he exists in our imagination as something utterly unlike them, and as belonging to another world. So the Greeks in Shakspeare's *Troilus and Cressida* are no longer the Greeks whom we have known in Homer, because 25 they come to us through a mode of representation of the romantic world. But I must not forget Scott.

I suppose that when Scott is in what may be called full ballad swing, no one will hesitate to pronounce his manner neither Homeric nor the grand manner. When he says, for instance, 30

> I do not rhyme to that dull elf
> Who cannot image to himself,[1]

and so on, any scholar will feel that *this* is not Homer's manner. But let us take Scott's poetry at its best; and when it is at its best, it is undoubtedly very good indeed:— 35

[1] *Marmion*, canto vi. 38.

Tunstall lies dead upon the field,
His life-blood stains the spotless shield;
Edmund is down,—my life is reft,—
The Admiral alone is left.
5 Let Stanley charge with spur of fire,—
With Chester charge, and Lancashire,
Full upon Scotland's central host,
Or victory and England's lost.[1]

That is, no doubt, as vigorous as possible, as spirited as possible;
10 it is exceedingly fine poetry. And still I say, it is not in the grand manner, and therefore it is not like Homer's poetry. Now, how shall I make him who doubts this feel that I say true; that these lines of Scott are essentially neither in Homer's style nor in the grand style? I may point out to him that the
15 movement of Scott's lines, while it is rapid, is also at the same time what the French call *saccadé*, its rapidity is 'jerky;' whereas Homer's rapidity is a flowing rapidity. But this is something external and material; it is but the outward and visible sign of an inward and spiritual diversity. I may discuss
20 what, in the abstract, constitutes the grand style; but that sort of general discussion never much helps our judgment of particular instances. I may say that the presence or absence of the grand style can only be spiritually discerned; and this is true, but to plead this looks like evading the difficulty. My best way
25 is to take eminent specimens of the grand style, and to put them side by side with this of Scott. For example, when Homer says:—

ἀλλά, φίλος, θάνε καὶ σύ · τίη ὀλοφύρεαι οὕτως;
κάτθανε καὶ Πάτροκλος, ὅπερ σέο πολλὸν ἀμείνων,[2]

30 that is in the grand style. When Virgil says:—

[1] *Marmion*, canto vi. 29.

[2] 'Be content, good friend, die also thou! why lamentest thou thyself on this wise? Patroclus, too, died, who was a far better than thou.'—*Iliad*, xxi. 106.

> Disce, puer, virtutem ex me verumque laborem,
> Fortunam ex aliis,[1]

that is in the grand style. When Dante says:—

> Lascio lo fele, e vo per dolci pomi
> Promessi a me per lo verace Duca;
> Ma fino al centro pria convien ch' io tomi,[2]

that is in the grand style. When Milton says:—

> His form had yet not lost
> All her original brightness, nor appeared
> Less than archangel ruined, and the excess
> Of glory obscured,[3]

that, finally, is in the grand style. Now let any one, after repeating to himself these four passages, repeat again the passage of Scott, and he will perceive that there is something in style which the four first have in common, and which the last is without; and this something is precisely the grand manner. It is no disrespect to Scott to say that he does not attain to this manner in his poetry; to say so, is merely to say that he is not among the five or six supreme poets of the world. Among these he is not; but, being a man of far greater powers than the ballad-poets, he has tried to give to their instrument a compass and an elevation which it does not naturally possess, in order to enable him to come nearer to the effect of the instrument used by the great epic poets,—an instrument which he felt he could not truly use,—and in this attempt he has but imperfectly succeeded. The poetic style of Scott is—(it becomes necessary to say so when it is proposed to 'translate Homer into the melodies

[1] 'From me, young man, learn nobleness of soul and true effort: learn success from others.'—*Æneid*, xii. 435.

[2] 'I leave the gall of bitterness, and I go for the apples of sweetness promised unto me by my faithful Guide; but far as the centre it behoves me first to fall.'—*Hell*, xvi. 61.

[3] *Paradise Lost*, i. 591.

of *Marmion*')—it is, tried by the highest standards, a bastard epic style; and that is why, out of his own powerful hands, it has had so little success. It is a less natural, and therefore a less good style, than the original ballad-style; while it shares with the ballad-style the inherent incapacity of rising into the grand style, of adequately rendering Homer. Scott is certainly at his best in his battles. Of Homer you could not say this; he is not better in his battles than elsewhere; but even between the battle-pieces of the two there exists all the difference which there is between an able work and a masterpiece.

> Tunstall lies dead upon the field,
> His life-blood stains the spotless shield:
> Edmund is down,—my life is reft,—
> The Admiral alone is left.

—'For not in the hands of Diomede the son of Tydeus rages the spear, to ward off destruction from the Danaans; neither as yet have I heard the voice of the son of Atreus, shouting out of his hated mouth; but the voice of Hector the slayer of men bursts round me, as he cheers on the Trojans; and they with their yellings fill all the plain, overcoming the Achaians in the battle.'—I protest that, to my feeling, Homer's performance, even through that pale and far-off shadow of a prose translation, still has a hundred times more of the grand manner about it, than the original poetry of Scott.

Well, then, the ballad-manner and the ballad-measure, whether in the hands of the old ballad poets, or arranged by Chapman, or arranged by Mr. Newman, or, even, arranged by Sir Walter Scott, cannot worthily render Homer. And for one reason: Homer is plain, so are they; Homer is natural, so are they; Homer is spirited, so are they; but Homer is sustainedly noble, and they are not. Homer and they are both of them natural, and therefore touching and stirring; but the grand style, which is Homer's, is something more than touching and stirring; it can form the character, it is edifying. The old English balladist may stir Sir Philip Sidney's heart like a trumpet, and this is much: but Homer, but the few artists in the grand style, can do more; they can refine the raw natural man, they can transmute him. So it is not without cause that I say, and say again, to the translator of Homer: 'Never for a moment suffer yourself to forget our fourth fundamental proposition, *Homer is noble*.' For it is seen how large a share this nobleness has in producing that general effect of his, which it is the main business of a translator to *re*produce.

I shall have to try your patience yet once more upon this subject, and then my task will be completed. I have shown what the four axioms respecting Homer which I have laid down, exclude, what they bid a translator not to do; I have still to show what they supply, what positive help they can give to the translator in his work. I will even, with their aid, myself try my fortune with some of those passages of Homer which I have already noticed; not indeed with any confidence that I more than others can succeed in adequately rendering Homer, but in the hope of satisfying competent judges, in the hope of making it clear to the future translator, that I at any rate follow a right method, and that, in coming short, I come short from weakness of execution, not from original vice of design. This is why I have so long occupied myself with Mr. Newman's version; that, apart from all faults of execution, his original design was wrong, and that he has done us the good service of declaring that design in its naked wrongness. To bad practice he has prefixed the bad theory which made the practice bad; he has given us a false theory in his preface, and he has exemplified the bad effects of that false theory in his translation. It is because his starting-point is so bad that he runs so badly; and to save others from taking so false a starting-point, may be to save them from running so futile a course.

Mr. Newman, indeed, says in his preface, that if any one dislikes his translation, 'he has his easy remedy; to keep aloof from it.' But Mr. Newman is a writer of considerable and deserved reputation; he is also a Professor of the University of London, an institution which by its position and by its merits acquires every year greater importance. It would be a very grave thing if the authority of so eminent a Professor led his students to misconceive entirely the chief work of the Greek world; that work which, whatever the other works of classical antiquity have to give us, gives it more abundantly than they all. The eccentricity too, the arbitrariness, of which Mr. Newman's conception of Homer offers so signal an example, are not a peculiar failing of Mr. Newman's own; in varying degrees they are the great defect of English intellect, the great blemish of English literature. Our literature of the eighteenth century, the literature of the school of Dryden, Addison, Pope, Johnson, is a long reaction against this eccentricity, this arbitrariness; that reaction perished by its own faults, and its enemies are left once more masters of the field. It is much more likely that any new English version of Homer will have Mr. Newman's faults than Pope's. Our present literature, which is very far, certainly, from having the spirit and power of Elizabethan genius, yet has in its own way these faults, eccentricity and arbitrariness, quite as much as the Elizabethan literature ever had. They are the cause that, while upon none, perhaps, of the modern literatures has so great a sum of force been expended as upon the English literature, at the present hour this literature, regarded not as an object of mere literary interest but as a living intellectual instrument, ranks only third in European effect and importance among the literatures of Europe; it ranks after the literatures of France and Germany. Of these two literatures, as of the intellect of Europe in general, the main effort, for now many years, has been a *critical* effort; the endeavour, in all branches of knowledge,—theology, philosophy, history, art, science,—to see the object as in itself it really is. But, owing to the presence in English literature of this eccentric and arbitrary spirit, owing to the strong tendency of English writers to bring to the consideration of their object some individual fancy, almost the last thing for which one would come to English literature is just that very thing which now Europe most desires—*criticism*. It is useful to notice any signal manifestation of those faults, which thus limit and impair the action of our literature. And therefore I have pointed out how widely, in translating Homer, a man even of real ability and learning may go astray, unless he brings to the study of this clearest of poets one quality in which our English authors, with all their great gifts, are apt to be somewhat wanting—simple lucidity of mind.

[III]

Homer is rapid in his movement, Homer is plain in his words and style, Homer is simple in his ideas, Homer is noble in his manner. Cowper renders him ill because he is slow in his movement, and elaborate in his style; Pope renders him ill because he is artificial both in his style and in his words; Chapman renders him ill because he is fantastic in his ideas; Mr. Newman renders him ill because he is odd in his words and ignoble in his manner. All four translators diverge from their original at other points besides those named; but it is at the points thus named that their divergence is greatest. For instance, Cowper's diction is not as Homer's diction, nor his nobleness as Homer's nobleness; but it is in movement and grammatical style that he is most unlike Homer. Pope's rapidity is not of the same sort as Homer's rapidity, nor are his plainness of ideas and his nobleness as Homer's plainness of ideas and nobleness: but it is in the artificial character of his style and diction that he is most unlike Homer. Chapman's movement, words, style, and manner, are often far enough from resembling Homer's movement, words, style, and manner; but it is the fantasticality of his ideas which puts him farthest from resembling Homer. Mr. Newman's movement, grammatical style, and ideas, are a thousand times in strong contrast with Homer's; still it is by the oddness of his diction and the ignobleness of his manner that he contrasts with Homer the most violently.

Therefore the translator must not say to himself: 'Cowper is noble, Pope is rapid, Chapman has a good diction, Mr. Newman has a good cast of sentence; I will avoid Cowper's slowness, Pope's artificiality, Chapman's conceits, Mr. Newman's oddity; I will take Cowper's dignified manner, Pope's impetuous movement, Chapman's vocabulary, Mr. Newman's syntax, and so make a perfect translation of Homer.' Undoubtedly in certain points the versions of Chapman, Cowper, Pope, and Mr. Newman, all of them have merit; some of them very high merit, others a lower merit; but even in these points they have none of them precisely the same kind of merit as Homer, and therefore the new translator, even if he can imitate them in their good points, will still not satisfy his judge, the scholar, who asks him for Homer and Homer's kind of merit, or, at least, for as much of them as it is possible to give.

So the translator really has no good model before him for any part of his work, and has to invent everything for himself. He is to be rapid in movement, plain in speech, simple in thought, and noble; and *how* he is to be either rapid, or plain, or simple, or noble, no one yet has shown him. I shall try to-day to establish some practical suggestions which may help the translator of Homer's poetry to comply with the four grand requirements which we make of him.

His version is to be rapid; and of course, to make a man's poetry rapid, as to make it noble, nothing can serve him so much as to have, in his own nature, rapidity and nobleness. *It is the spirit that quickeneth;* and no one will so well render Homer's swift-flowing movement as he who has himself something of the swift-moving spirit of Homer. Yet even this is not quite enough. Pope certainly had a quick and darting spirit, as he had, also, real nobleness; yet Pope does not render the movement of Homer. To render this the translator must have, besides his natural qualifications, an appropriate metre.

I have sufficiently shown why I think all forms of our ballad-metre unsuited to Homer. It seems to me to be beyond question that, for epic poetry, only three metres can seriously claim to be accounted capable of the grand style. Two of these will at once occur to every one,—the ten-syllable, or so-called *heroic*, couplet, and blank verse. I do not add to these the Spenserian stanza, although Dr. Maginn, whose metrical eccentricities I have already criticised, pronounces this stanza the one right measure for a translation of Homer. It is enough to observe that if Pope's couplet, with the simple system of correspondences that its rhymes introduce, changes the movement of Homer, in which no such correspondences are found, and is therefore a bad measure for a translator of Homer to employ, Spenser's stanza, with its far more intricate system of correspondences, must change Homer's movement far more profoundly, and must therefore be for the translator a far worse measure than the couplet of Pope. Yet I will say, at the same time, that the verse of Spenser is more fluid, slips more easily and quickly along, than the verse of almost any other English poet.

> By this the northern wagoner had set
> His seven-fold team behind the steadfast star
> That was in ocean waves yet never wet,
> But firm is fixt, and sendeth light from far
> To all that in the wide deep wandering are.[1]

One cannot but feel that English verse has not often moved with the fluidity and sweet ease of these lines. It is possible that it may have been this quality of Spenser's poetry which made Dr. Maginn think that the stanza of *The Faery Queen* must be a good measure for rendering Homer. This it is not: Spenser's verse is fluid and rapid, no doubt, but there are more ways than one of being fluid and rapid, and Homer is fluid and rapid in quite another way than Spenser. Spenser's manner is no more Homeric than is the manner of the one modern inheritor of Spenser's beautiful gift,—the poet, who evidently caught from Spenser his sweet and easy-slipping movement, and who has exquisitely employed it; a Spenserian genius, nay, a genius by natural endowment richer probably than even Spenser; that light which shines so unexpected and without fellow in our century, an Elizabethan born too late, the early lost and admirably gifted Keats.

I say then that there are really but three metres,—the ten-syllable couplet, blank verse, and a third metre which I will not yet name, but which is neither the Spenserian stanza nor any form of ballad-verse,—between which, as vehicles for Homer's poetry, the translator has to make his choice. Every one will at once remember a thousand passages in which both the ten-syllable couplet and blank verse prove themselves to

[1] *The Faery Queen,* Canto ii. stanza 1.

have nobleness. Undoubtedly the movement and manner of this,—

> Still raise for good the supplicating voice,
> But leave to Heaven the measure and the choice,—

are noble. Undoubtedly, the movement and manner of this:—

> High on a throne of royal state, which far
> Outshone the wealth of Ormus and of Ind,—

are noble also. But the first is in a rhymed metre; and the unfitness of a rhymed metre for rendering Homer I have already shown. I will observe, too, that the fine couplet which I have quoted comes out of a satire, a didactic poem; and that it is in didactic poetry that the ten-syllable couplet has most successfully essayed the grand style. In narrative poetry this metre has succeeded best when it essayed a sensibly lower style, the style of Chaucer, for instance; whose narrative manner, though a very good and sound manner, is certainly neither the grand manner nor the manner of Homer.

The rhymed ten-syllable couplet being thus excluded, blank verse offers itself for the translator's use. The first kind of blank verse which naturally occurs to us is the blank verse of Milton, which has been employed, with more or less modification, by Mr. Cary in translating Dante, by Cowper and by Mr. Wright in translating Homer. How noble this metre is in Milton's hands, how completely it shows itself capable of the grand, nay, of the grandest, style, I need not say. To this metre, as used in the *Paradise Lost,* our country owes the glory of having produced one of the only two poetical works in the grand style which are to be found in the modern languages; the *Divine Comedy* of Dante is the other. England and Italy here stand alone; Spain, France, and Germany have produced great poets, but neither Calderon, nor Corneille, nor Schiller, nor even Goethe, has produced a body of poetry in the true grand style, in the sense in which the style of the body of Homer's poetry, or Pindar's, or Sophocles's, is grand. But Dante has, and so has Milton; and in this respect Milton possesses a distinction which even Shakspeare, undoubtedly the supreme poetical power in our literature, does not share with him. Not a tragedy of Shakspeare but contains passages in the worst of all styles, the affected style; and the grand style, although it may be harsh, or obscure, or cumbrous, or over-laboured, is never affected. In spite, therefore, of objections which may justly be urged against the plan and treatment of the *Paradise Lost*, in spite of its possessing, certainly, a far less enthralling force of interest to attract and to carry forward the reader than the *Iliad* or the *Divine Comedy*, it fully deserves, it can never lose, its immense reputation; for, like the *Iliad* and the *Divine Comedy*, nay, in some respects to a higher degree than either of them, it is in the grand style.

But the grandeur of Milton is one thing, and the grandeur of Homer is another. Homer's movement, I have said again and again, is a flowing, a rapid movement; Milton's, on the other hand, is a laboured, a self-retarding movement. In each case, the movement, the metrical cast, corresponds with the mode of evolution of the thought, with the syntactical cast, and is indeed determined by it. Milton charges himself so full with thought, imagination, knowledge, that his style will hardly contain them. He is too full-stored to show us in much detail one conception, one piece of knowledge; he just shows it to us in a pregnant allusive way, and then he presses on to another; and all this fulness, this pressure, this condensation, this self-constraint, enters into his movement, and makes it what it is,—noble, but difficult and austere. Homer is quite different; he says a thing, and says it to the end, and then begins another, while Milton is trying to press a thousand things into one. So that whereas, in reading Milton, you never lose the sense of laborious and condensed fulness, in reading Homer you never lose the sense of flowing and abounding ease. With Milton line runs into line, and all is straitly bound together: with Homer line runs off from line, and all hurries away onward. Homer begins, Μῆνιν ἄειδε, Θεά,—at the second word announcing the proposed action: Milton begins:

> Of man's first disobedience, and the fruit
> Of that forbidden tree, whose mortal taste
> Brought death into the world, and all our woe,
> With loss of Eden, till one greater Man
> Restore us, and regain the blissful seat,
> Sing, heavenly muse.

So chary of a sentence is he, so resolute not to let it escape him till he has crowded into it all he can, that it is not till the thirty-ninth word in the sentence that he will give us the key to it, the word of action, the verb. Milton says:

> O for that warning voice, which he, who saw
> The Apocalypse, heard cry in heaven aloud.

He is not satisfied, unless he can tell us, all in one sentence, and without permitting himself to actually mention the name, that the man who had the warning voice was the same man who saw the Apocalypse. Homer would have said, 'O for that warning voice, which *John* heard'—and if it had suited him to say that John also saw the Apocalypse, he would have given us that in another sentence. The effect of this allusive and compressed manner of Milton is, I need not say, often very powerful; and it is an effect which other great poets have often sought to obtain much in the same way: Dante is full of it, Horace is full of it; but wherever it exists, it is always an un-Homeric effect. 'The losses of the heavens,' says Horace, 'fresh moons speedily repair; we, when we have gone down where the pious Æneas, where the rich Tullus and Ancus are, —*pulvis et umbra sumus*.'[1] He never actually says *where* we go to; he only indicates it by saying that it is that place where Æneas, Tullus, and Ancus are. But Homer, when he has to speak of going down to the grave, says, definitely, ἐς Ἠλύσιον πεδίον—ἀθάνατοι πέμψουσιν,[2]—'The immortals shall send thee *to the Elysian plain*;' and it is not till after he has definitely said this, that he adds, that it is there that the abode of departed worthies is placed: ὅθι ξανθὸς Ῥαδάμανθυς—'Where the yellow-

[1] *Odes*, IV. vii. 13.

[2] *Odyssey* iv. 563.

haired Rhadamanthus is.' Again; Horace, having to say that punishment sooner or later overtakes crime, says it thus:

> Raro antecedentem scelestum
> Deseruit pede Pœna claudo.[1]

The thought itself of these lines is familiar enough to Homer and Hesiod; but neither Homer nor Hesiod, in expressing it, could possibly have so complicated its expression as Horace complicates it, and purposely complicates it, by his use of the word *deseruit*. I say that this complicated evolution of the thought necessarily complicates the movement and rhythm of a poet; and that the Miltonic blank verse, of course the first model of blank verse which suggests itself to an English translator of Homer, bears the strongest marks of such complication, and is therefore entirely unfit to render Homer.

If blank verse is used in translating Homer, it must be a blank verse of which English poetry, naturally swayed much by Milton's treatment of this metre, offers at present hardly any examples. It must not be Cowper's blank verse, who has studied Milton's pregnant manner with such effect, that, having to say of Mr. Throckmorton that he spares his avenue, although it is the fashion with other people to cut down theirs, he says that Benevolus 'reprieves The obsolete prolixity of shade.' It must not be Mr. Tennyson's blank verse.

> For all experience is an arch, wherethrough
> Gleams that untravelled world, whose distance fades
> For ever and for ever, as we gaze.

It is no blame to the thought of those lines, which belongs to another order of ideas than Homer's, but it is true, that Homer would certainly have said of them, 'It is to consider too curiously to consider so.' It is no blame to their rhythm, which belongs to another order of movement than Homer's, but it is true that these three lines by themselves take up nearly as much time as a whole book of the *Iliad*. No; the blank verse used in rendering Homer must be a blank verse of which per-

[1] *Odes*, III. ii. 31.

haps the best specimens are to be found in some of the most rapid passages of Shakspeare's plays,—a blank verse which does not dovetail its lines into one another, and which habitually ends its lines with monosyllables. Such a blank verse might no doubt be very rapid in its movement, and might perfectly adapt itself to a thought plainly and directly evolved; and it would be interesting to see it well applied to Homer. But the translator who determines to use it, must not conceal from himself that in order to pour Homer into the mould of this metre, he will have entirely to break him up and melt him down, with the hope of then successfully composing him afresh; and this is a process which is full of risks. It may, no doubt, be the real Homer that issues new from it; it is not certain beforehand that it cannot be the real Homer, as it is certain that from the mould of Pope's couplet or Cowper's Miltonic verse it cannot be the real Homer that will issue; still, the chances of disappointment are great. The result of such an attempt to renovate the old poet may be an Æson; but it may also, and more probably will, be a Pelias.

When I say this, I point to the metre which seems to me to give the translator the best chance of preserving the general effect of Homer,—that third metre which I have not yet expressly named, the hexameter. I know all that is said against the use of hexameters in English poetry; but it comes only to this, that, among us, they have not yet been used on any considerable scale with success. *Solvitur ambulando:* this is an objection which can best be met by *producing* good English hexameters. And there is no reason in the nature of the English language why it should not adapt itself to hexameters as well as the German language does; nay, the English language, from its greater rapidity, is in itself better suited than the German for them. The hexameter, whether alone or with the pentameter, possesses a movement, an expression, which no metre hitherto in common use amongst us possesses, and which I am convinced English poetry, as our mental wants multiply, will not always be content to forego. Applied to Homer, this metre affords to the translator the immense support of keeping him more nearly than any other metre to Homer's movement; and, since a poet's movement makes so large a part of his general effect, and to reproduce this general effect is at once the translator's indispensable business and so difficult for him, it is a great thing to have this part of your model's general effect already given you in your metre, instead of having to get it entirely for yourself. 5

These are general considerations; but there are also one or two particular considerations which confirm me in the opinion that for translating Homer into English verse the hexameter should be used. The most successful attempt hitherto made at 10 rendering Homer into English, the attempt in which Homer's general effect has been best retained, is an attempt made in the hexameter measure. It is a version of the famous lines in the third book of the *Iliad*, which end with that mention of Castor and Pollux from which Mr. Ruskin extracts the sentimental 15 consolation already noticed by me. The author is the accomplished Provost of Eton, Dr. Hawtrey; and this performance of his must be my excuse for having taken the liberty to single him out for mention, as one of the natural judges of a translation of Homer, along with Professor Thompson and Professor 20 Jowett, whose connection with Greek literature is official. The passage is short; [1] and Dr. Hawtrey's version of it is suf-

[1] So short, that I quote it entire:—

Clearly the rest I behold of the dark-eyed sons of Achaia;
Known to me well are the faces of all; their names I remember; 25
Two, two only remain, whom I see not among the commanders,
Castor fleet in the car,—Polydeukes brave with the cestus,—
Own dear brethren of mine,—one parent loved us as infants.
Are they not here in the host, from the shores of loved Lacedæmon,
Or, though they came with the rest in ships that bound through the waters, 30
Dare they not enter the fight or stand in the council of Heroes,
All for fear of the shame and the taunts my crime has awakened?
So said she;—they long since in Earth's soft arms were reposing,
There, in their own dear land, their Fatherland, Lacedæmon.

English Hexameter Translations; London, 1847; p. 242. 35

I have changed Dr. Hawtrey's 'Kastor,' 'Lakedaimon,' back to the familiar 'Castor,' 'Lacedæmon,' in obedience to my own rule that everything *odd* is to be avoided in rendering Homer, the most natural and least odd of poets. I see Mr. Newman's critic in the *National Review* urges our generation to bear with the unnatural effect of these rewritten Greek 40

fused with a pensive grace which is, perhaps, rather more Virgilian than Homeric; still it is the one version of any part of the *Iliad* which in some degree reproduces for me the original effect of Homer: it is the best, and it is in hexameters.

5 This is one of the particular considerations that incline me to prefer the hexameter, for translating Homer, to our established metres. There is another. Most of you, probably, have some knowledge of a poem by Mr. Clough, *The Bothie of Toper-na-fuosich*, a long-vacation pastoral, in hexameters. 10 The general merits of that poem I am not going to discuss: it is a serio-comic poem, and, therefore, of essentially different nature from the *Iliad*. Still in two things it is, more than any other English poem which I can call to mind, like the *Iliad:* in the rapidity of its movement, and the plainness and direct- 15 ness of its style. The thought in this poem is often curious and subtle, and that is not Homeric; the diction is often grotesque, and that is not Homeric. Still, by its rapidity of movement, and plain and direct manner of presenting the thought however curious in itself, this poem, which, being as I say a serio- 20 comic poem, has a right to be grotesque, is grotesque *truly*, not, like Mr. Newman's version of the *Iliad*, *falsely*. Mr. Clough's odd epithets, 'The grave man nicknamed Adam,' 'The hairy Aldrich,' and so on, grow vitally and appear naturally in their place; while Mr. Newman's 'dapper-greaved Achaians,' and

---

25 names, in the hope that by this means the effect of them may have to the next generation become natural. For my part, I feel no disposition to pass all my own life in the wilderness of pedantry, in order that a posterity which I shall never see may one day enter an orthographical Canaan; and, after all, the real question is this: whether our living apprehension of the 30 Greek world is more checked by meeting in an English book about the Greeks, names not spelt letter for letter as in the original Greek, or by meeting names which make us rub our eyes and call out, 'How exceedingly odd!'

The Latin names of the Greek deities raise in most cases the idea of 35 quite distinct personages from the personages whose idea is raised by the Greek names. Hera and Juno are actually, to every scholar's imagination, two different people. So in all these cases the Latin names must, at any inconvenience, be abandoned when we are dealing with the Greek world. But I think it can be in the sensitive imagination of Mr. Grote only, that 40 'Thucydides' raises the idea of a different man from Θουκυδίδης.

'motley-helmed Hector,' have all the air of being mechanically elaborated and artificially stuck in. Mr. Clough's hexameters are excessively, needlessly rough; still, owing to the native rapidity of this measure, and to the directness of style which so well allies itself with it, his composition produces a sense in the reader which Homer's composition also produces, and which Homer's translator ought to *re*produce,—the sense of having, within short limits of time, a large portion of human life presented to him, instead of a small portion.

Mr. Clough's hexameters are, as I have just said, too rough and irregular; and indeed a good model, on any considerable scale, of this metre, the English translator will nowhere find. He must not follow the model offered by Mr. Longfellow in his pleasing and popular poem of *Evangeline;* for the merit of the manner and movement of *Evangeline*, when they are at their best, is to be tenderly elegant; and their fault, when they are at their worst, is to be lumbering; but Homer's defect is not lumberingness, neither is tender elegance his excellence. The lumbering effect of most English hexameters is caused by their being much too dactylic; [1] the translator must learn to use spondees freely. Mr. Clough has done this, but he has not sufficiently observed another rule which the translator cannot follow too strictly; and that is, to have no lines which will not, as it is familiarly said, *read themselves*. This is of the last importance for rhythms with which the ear of the English public is not thoroughly acquainted. Lord Redesdale, in two papers on the subject of Greek and Roman metres, has some good remarks on the outrageous disregard of quantity in which English verse, trusting to its force of accent, is apt to indulge itself. The predominance of accent in our language is so great, that it would be pedantic not to avail one's self of it; and Lord Redesdale suggests rules which might easily be pushed too far. Still, it is undeniable that in English hexameters

[1] For instance; in a version (I believe, by the late Mr. Lockhart) of Homer's description of the parting of Hector and Andromache, there occurs, in the first five lines, but one spondee besides the necessary spondees in the sixth place; in the corresponding five lines of Homer there occur ten. See *English Hexameter Translations*, 244.

we generally force the quantity far too much; we rely on justification by accent with a security which is excessive. But not only do we abuse accent by shortening long syllables and lengthening short ones; we perpetually commit a far worse fault, by requiring the removal of the accent from its natural place to an unnatural one, in order to make our line scan. This is a fault, even when our metre is one which every English reader knows, and when he can see what we want and can correct the rhythm according to our wish; although it is a fault which a great master may sometimes commit knowingly to produce a desired effect, as Milton changes the natural accent on the word *Tirésias* in the line:—

> And Tíresias and Phineus, prophets old;

and then it ceases to be a fault, and becomes a beauty. But it is a real fault, when Chapman has:—

> By him the golden-throned Queen slept, the Queen of Deities;

for in this line, to make it scan, you have to take away the accent from the word *Queen*, on which it naturally falls, and to place it on *throned*, which would naturally be unaccented; and yet, after all, you get no peculiar effect or beauty of cadence to reward you. It is a real fault, when Mr. Newman has:—

> Infatuate! O that thou wert lord to some other army—

for here again the reader is required, not for any special advantage to himself, but simply to save Mr. Newman trouble, to place the accent on the insignificant word *wert*, where it has no business whatever. But it is still a greater fault, when Spenser has (to take a striking instance):—

> Wot ye why his mother with a veil hath covered his face?

for a hexameter; because here not only is the reader causelessly required to make havoc with the natural accentuation of the line in order to get it to run as a hexameter; but also he, in nine cases out of ten, will be utterly at a loss how to perform the process required, and the line will remain a mere monster for him. I repeat, it is advisable to construct *all* verses so that by reading them naturally—that is, according to the sense and legitimate accent,—the reader gets the right rhythm; but, for English hexameters, that they be so constructed is indispensable.

If the hexameter best helps the translator to the Homeric rapidity, what style may best help him to the Homeric plainness and directness? It is the merit of a metre appropriate to your subject, that it in some degree suggests and carries with itself a style appropriate to the subject; the elaborate and self-retarding style, which comes so naturally when your metre is the Miltonic blank verse, does not come naturally with the hexameter; is, indeed, alien to it. On the other hand, the hexameter has a natural dignity which repels both the jaunty style and the jog-trot style, to both of which the ballad-measure so easily lends itself. These are great advantages; and, perhaps, it is nearly enough to say to the translator who uses the hexameter that he cannot too religiously follow, in style, the inspiration of his metre. He will find that a loose and idiomatic grammar—a grammar which follows the essential rather than the formal logic of the thought—allies itself excellently with the hexameter; and that, while this sort of grammar ensures plainness and naturalness, it by no means comes short in nobleness. It is difficult to pronounce, certainly, what is idiomatic in the ancient literature of a language which, though still spoken, has long since entirely adopted, as modern Greek has adopted, modern idioms. Still one may, I think, clearly perceive that Homer's grammatical style is idiomatic,—that it may even be called, not improperly, a loose grammatical style.[1] Examples, however, of what I mean by a loose grammatical style, will be

[1] See, for instance, in the *Iliad*, the loose construction of ὥστε, xvii. 658; that of ἴδοιτο, xvii. 681; that of οἵτε, xviii. 209; and the elliptical construction at xix. 42, 43; also the idiomatic construction of ἐγὼν ὅδε παρασχεῖν, xix. 140. These instances are all taken within a range of a thousand lines; any one may easily multiply them for himself.

of more use to the translator if taken from English poetry than if taken from Homer. I call it, then, a loose and idiomatic grammar which Shakspeare uses in the last line of the following three:—

5 He's here in double trust:
First, as I am his kinsman and his subject,
Strong both against the deed;—

or in this:—

Wit, *whither wilt?*

10 What Shakspeare means is perfectly clear, clearer, probably, than if he had said it in a more formal and regular manner; but his grammar is loose and idiomatic, because he leaves out the subject of the verb 'wilt' in the second passage quoted, and because, in the first, a prodigious addition to the sentence has 15 to be, as we used to say in our old Latin grammar days, *understood*, before the word 'both' can be properly parsed. So, again, Chapman's grammar is loose and idiomatic where he says,

Even share hath he that keeps his tent, and *he to field* doth go,—

20 because he leaves out, in the second clause, the relative which in formal writing would be required. But Chapman here does not lose dignity by this idiomatic way of expressing himself, any more than Shakspeare loses it by neglecting to confer on 'both' the blessings of a regular government: neither loses 25 dignity, but each gives that impression of a plain, direct, and natural mode of speaking, which Homer, too, gives, and which it is so important, as I say, that Homer's translator should succeed in giving. Cowper calls blank verse 'a style farther removed than rhyme from the vernacular idiom, both in the 30 language itself and in the arrangement of it;' and just in proportion as blank verse is removed from the vernacular idiom, from that idiomatic style which is of all styles the plainest and most natural. blank verse is unsuited to render Homer.

Shakspeare is not only idiomatic in his grammar or style, he is also idiomatic in his words or diction; and here too, his example is valuable for the translator of Homer. The translator must not, indeed, allow himself all the liberty that Shakspeare allows himself; for Shakspeare sometimes uses expressions which pass perfectly well as he uses them, because Shakspeare thinks so fast and so powerfully, that in reading him we are borne over single words as by a mighty current; but, if our mind were less excited,—and who may rely on exciting our mind like Shakspeare?—they would check us. 'To grunt and sweat under a weary load;'—that does perfectly well where it comes in Shakspeare; but if the translator of Homer, who will hardly have wound our minds up to the pitch at which these words of Hamlet find them, were to employ, when he has to speak of one of Homer's heroes under the load of calamity, this figure of 'grunting' and 'sweating,' we should say, *He Newmanises*, and his diction would offend us. For he is to be noble; and no plea of wishing to be plain and natural can get him excused from being this: only, as he is to be also, like Homer, perfectly simple and free from artificiality, and as the use of idiomatic expressions undoubtedly gives this effect,[1] he should be as idiomatic as he can be without ceasing to be noble. Therefore the idiomatic language of Shakspeare—such language as, 'prate of his *whereabout*;' '*jump* the life to come;' 'the damnation of his *taking-off*;' 'his *quietus make* with a bare *bodkin*'—should be carefully observed by the translator of Homer, although in every case he will have to decide for himself whether the use, by him, of Shakspeare's liberty, will or will not clash with his indispensable duty of nobleness. He will find one English book and one only, where, as in the *Iliad*

[1] Our knowledge of Homer's Greek is hardly such as to enable us to pronounce quite confidently what is idiomatic in his diction, and what is not, any more than in his grammar; but I seem to myself clearly to recognise an idiomatic stamp in such expressions as τολυπεύειν πολέμους, xiv. 86; *φάος ἐν νήεσσιν θήῃς*, xvi. 94; *τιν' οἴω ἀσπασίως αὐτῶν γόνυ κάμψειν*, xix. 71; κλοτοπεύειν, xix. 149; and many others. The first-quoted expression, τολυπεύειν ἀργαλέους πολέμους, seems to me to have just about the same degree of freedom as the '*jump* the life to come,' or the '*shuffle off* this mortal coil,' of Shakspeare.

itself, perfect plainness of speech is allied with perfect nobleness; and that book is the Bible. No one could see this more clearly than Pope saw it: 'This pure and noble simplicity,' he says, 'is nowhere in such perfection as in the Scripture and Homer:' yet even with Pope a woman is a 'fair,' a father is a 'sire,' and an old man a 'reverend sage,' and so on through all the phrases of that pseudo-Augustan, and most unbiblical, vocabulary. The Bible, however, is undoubtedly the grand mine of diction for the translator of Homer; and, if he knows how to discriminate truly between what will suit him and what will not, the Bible may afford him also invaluable lessons of style.

I said that Homer, besides being plain in style and diction, was plain in the quality of his thought. It is possible that a thought may be expressed with idiomatic plainness, and yet not be in itself a plain thought. For example, in Mr. Clough's poem, already mentioned, the style and diction is almost always idiomatic and plain, but the thought itself is often of a quality which is not plain; it is *curious*. But the grand instance of the union of idiomatic expression with curious or difficult thought is in Shakspeare's poetry. Such, indeed, is the force and power of Shakspeare's idiomatic expression, that it gives an effect of clearness and vividness even to a thought which is imperfect and incoherent; for instance, when Hamlet says,—

> To take arms against a sea of troubles,—

the figure there is undoubtedly most faulty, it by no means runs on four legs; but the thing is said so freely and idiomatically, that it passes. This, however, is not a point to which I now want to call your attention; I want you to remark, in Shakspeare and others, only that which we may directly apply to Homer. I say, then, that in Shakspeare the thought is often, while most idiomatically uttered, nay, while good and sound in itself, yet of a quality which is curious and difficult; and that this quality of thought is something entirely un-Homeric. For example, when Lady Macbeth says,—

natural effect. The double epithets so constantly occurring in Homer must be dealt with according to this rule; these epithets come quite naturally in Homer's poetry; in English poetry they, in nine cases out of ten, come, when literally rendered, quite unnaturally. I will not now discuss why this is so, I assume it as an indisputable fact that it is so; that Homer's μερόπων ἀνθρώπων comes to the reader as something perfectly natural, while Mr. Newman's 'voice-dividing mortals' comes to him as something perfectly unnatural. Well then, as it is Homer's general effect which we are to reproduce, it is to be false to Homer to be so verbally faithful to him as that we lose this effect: and by the English translator Homer's double epithets must be, in many places, renounced altogether; in all places where they are rendered, rendered by equivalents which come naturally. Instead of rendering Θέτι τανύπεπλε by Mr. Newman's 'Thetis trailing-robed,' which brings to one's mind long petticoats sweeping a dirty pavement, the translator must render the Greek by English words which come as naturally to us as Milton's words when he says, 'Let gorgeous Tragedy With sceptred pall come sweeping by.' Instead of rendering μώνυχας ἵππους by Chapman's 'one-hoofed steeds,' or Mr. Newman's 'single-hoofed horses,' he must speak of horses in a way which surprises us as little as Shakspeare surprises us when he says, 'Gallop apace, you fiery-footed steeds.' Instead of rendering μελιηδέα θυμόν by 'life as honey pleasant,' he must characterise life with the simple pathos of Gray's 'warm precincts of the cheerful day.' Instead of converting ποῖόν σε ἔπος φύγεν ἕρκος ὀδόντων; into the portentous remonstrance, 'Betwixt the outwork of thy teeth what word hath slipt?' he must remonstrate in English as straightforward as this of St. Peter, 'Be it far from thee, Lord: this shall not be unto thee;' or as this of the disciples, 'What is this that he saith, a little while? we cannot tell what he saith.' Homer's Greek, in each of the places quoted, reads as naturally as any of those English passages: the expression no more calls away the attention from the sense in the Greek than in the English. But when, in order to render literally in English one of Homer's double epithets, a strange unfamiliar adjective is invented,—such as 'voice-dividing' for μέροψ,—an improper share of the reader's attention is necessarily diverted to this ancillary word, to this word which Homer never intended should receive so much notice; and a total effect quite different from Homer's is thus produced. Therefore Mr. Newman, though he does not purposely import, like Chapman, conceits of his own into the *Iliad*, does actually import them; for the result of his singular diction is to raise ideas, and odd ideas, not raised by the corresponding diction in Homer; and Chapman himself does no more. Cowper says: 'I have cautiously avoided all terms of new invention, with an abundance of which persons of more ingenuity than judgment have not enriched our language but encumbered it;' and this criticism so exactly hits the diction of Mr. Newman that one is irresistibly led to imagine his present appearance in the flesh to be at least his second.

A translator cannot well have a Homeric rapidity, style, diction, and quality of thought, without at the same time having what is the result of these in Homer,—nobleness. Therefore I do not attempt to lay down any rules for obtaining this effect of nobleness,—the effect, too, of all others the most impalpable, the most irreducible to rule, and which most depends on the individual personality of the artist. So I proceed at once to give you, in conclusion, one or two passages in which I have tried to follow those principles of Homeric translation which I have laid down. I give them, it must be remembered, not as specimens of perfect translation, but as specimens of an attempt to translate Homer on certain principles; specimens which may very aptly illustrate those principles by falling short as well as by succeeding.

I take first a passage of which I have already spoken, the comparison of the Trojan fires to the stars. The first part of that passage is, I have said, of splendid beauty; and to begin with a lame version of that would be the height of imprudence in me. It is the last and more level part with which I shall concern myself. I have already quoted Cowper's version of this part in order to show you how unlike his stiff and Miltonic manner of telling a plain story is to Homer's easy and rapid manner:—

> So numerous seemed those fires the bank between
> Of Xanthus, blazing, and the fleet of Greece,
> In prospect all of Troy—

I need not continue to the end. I have also quoted Pope's version of it, to show you how unlike his ornate and artificial manner is to Homer's plain and natural manner:

> So many flames before proud Ilion blaze,
> And brighten glimmering Xanthus with their rays;
> The long reflections of the distant fires
> Gleam on the walls, and tremble on the spires,—

and much more of the same kind. I want to show you that it is possible, in a plain passage of this sort, to keep Homer's simplicity without being heavy and dull; and to keep his dignity without bringing in pomp and ornament. 'As numerous as are the stars on a clear night,' says Homer,

> So shone forth, in front of Troy, by the bed of Xanthus,
> Between that and the ships, the Trojans' numerous fires.
> In the plain there were kindled a thousand fires: by each one
> There sat fifty men, in the ruddy light of the fire:
> By their chariots stood the steeds, and champed the white barley
> While their masters sat by the fire, and waited for Morning.

Here, in order to keep Homer's effect of perfect plainness and directness, I repeat the word 'fires' as he repeats πυρά, without scruple; although in a more elaborate and literary style of poetry this recurrence of the same word would be a fault to be avoided. I omit the epithet of Morning, and whereas Homer says that the steeds 'waited for Morning,' I prefer to attribute this expectation of Morning to the master and not to the horse. Very likely in this particular, as in any other single particular, I may be wrong: what I wish you to remark is my endeavour after absolute plainness of speech, my care to avoid anything which may the least check or surprise the reader, whom Homer does not check or surprise. Homer's lively personal familiarity with war, and with the war-horse as his master's companion, is such that, as it seems to me, his attributing to the one the other's feelings comes to us quite naturally; but, from a poet without this familiarity, the attribution strikes as a little unnatural; and therefore, as everything the least unnatural is un-Homeric, I avoid it.

Again, in the address of Zeus to the horses of Achilles, Cowper has:

> Jove saw their grief with pity, and his brows
> Shaking, within himself thus, pensive, said.
> 'Ah hapless pair! wherefore by gift divine
> Were ye to Peleus given, a mortal king,
> Yourselves immortal and from age exempt?'

There is no want of dignity here, as in the versions of Chapman and Mr. Newman, which I have already quoted: but the whole effect is much too slow. Take Pope:—

> Nor Jove disdained to cast a pitying look
> While thus relenting to the steeds he spoke.
> 'Unhappy coursers of immortal strain!
> Exempt from age and deathless now in vain;
> Did we your race on mortal man bestow
> Only, alas! to share in mortal woe?'

Here there is no want either of dignity or rapidity, but all is too artificial. 'Nor Jove disdained,' for instance, is a very artificial and literary way of rendering Homer's words, and so is, 'coursers of immortal strain.'

Μυρομένω δ' ἄρα τώ γε ἰδὼν, ἐλέησε Κρονίων.—

And with pity the son of Saturn saw them bewailing,
And he shook his head, and thus addressed his own bosom:—
'Ah, unhappy pair, to Peleus why did we give you,
To a mortal? but ye are without old age and immortal.
Was it that ye, with man, might have your thousands of sorrows?
For than man, indeed, there breathes no wretcheder creature,
Of all living things, that on earth are breathing and moving.'

Here I will observe that the use of 'own,' in the second line, for the last syllable of a dactyl, and the use of 'To a,' in the fourth, for a complete spondee, though they do not, I think, actually spoil the run of the hexameter, are yet undoubtedly instances of that over-reliance on accent, and too free disregard of quantity, which Lord Redesdale visits with just reprehension.[1]

I now take two longer passages in order to try my method more fully; but I still keep to passages which have already come under our notice. I quoted Chapman's version of some passages in the speech of Hector at his parting with Andromache. One astounding conceit will probably still be in your remembrance,—

When sacred Troy shall *shed her tow'rs for tears of overthrow*,—

as a translation of ὅτ' ἄν ποτ' ὀλώλῃ Ἴλιος ἱρή. I will quote a few lines which may give you, also, the key-note to the Anglo-Augustan manner of rendering this passage and to the Miltonic manner of rendering it. What Mr. Newman's manner of rendering it would be, you can by this time sufficiently imagine

[1] It must be remembered, however, that, if we disregard quantity too much in constructing English hexameters, we also disregard accent too much in reading Greek hexameters. We read every Greek dactyl so as to make a pure dactyl of it; but, to a Greek, the accent must have hindered many dactyls from sounding as pure dactyls. When we read α ἰ ό λ ο ς ἵππος, for instance, or α ἰ γ ι ό χ ο ι ο, the dactyl in each of these cases is made by us as pure a dactyl as 'Tityre,' or 'dignity;' but to a Greek it was not so. To him αἰόλος must have been nearly as impure a dactyl as 'death-destined' is to us; and αἰγιόχ nearly as impure as the 'dressed his own' of my text. Nor, I think, does this right mode of pronouncing the two words at all spoil the run of the line as a hexameter. The effect of α ἰ ό λ λ ο ς ἵππος (or something like that), though not *our* effect, is not a disagreeable one. On the other hand, κορυθαιόλος as a paroxytonon, although it has the respectable authority of Liddell and Scott's *Lexicon* (following Heyne), is certainly wrong; for then the word cannot be pronounced without throwing an accent on the first syllable as well as the third, and μέγας κ ο ῤ ῥ υ θ α ι ό λ λ ο ς Ἕκτωρ would have been to a Greek as intolerable an ending for a hexameter line as 'accurst *orphanhood-destined* houses' would be to us. The best authorities, accordingly, accent κορυθαίολος as a proparoxytonon.

for yourselves. Mr. Wright,—to quote for once from his meritorious version instead of Cowper's, whose strong and weak points are those of Mr. Wright also,—Mr. Wright begins his version of this passage thus:

> All these thy anxious cares are also mine, 5
> Partner beloved; but how could I endure
> The scorn of Trojans and their long-robed wives,
> Should they behold their Hector shrink from war,
> And act the coward's part? Nor doth my soul
> Prompt the base thought. 10

Ex pede Herculem: you see just what the manner is. Mr. Sotheby, on the other hand (to take a disciple of Pope instead of Pope himself), begins thus:

> 'What moves thee, moves my mind,' brave Hector said,
> 'Yet Troy's upbraiding scorn I deeply dread, 15
> If, like a slave, where chiefs with chiefs engage,
> The warrior Hector fears the war to wage.
> Not thus my heart inclines.'

From that specimen, too, you can easily divine what, with such a manner, will become of the whole passage. But Homer 20 has neither

> What moves thee, moves my mind,—

nor has he

> All these thy anxious cares are also mine.
>
> Ἦ καὶ ἐμοὶ τάδε πάντα μέλει, γύναι· ἀλλὰ μάλ' αἰνῶς,— 25

that is what Homer has, that is his style and movement, if one could but catch it. Andromache, as you know, has been entreating Hector to defend Troy from within the walls, instead of exposing his life, and, with his own life, the safety of all those dearest to him, by fighting in the open plain. Hector 30 replies:—

Woman, I too take thought for this; but then I bethink me
What the Trojan men and Trojan women might murmur,
If like a coward I skulked behind, apart from the battle.
Nor would my own heart let me; my heart, which has bid me be
valiant
5 Always, and always fighting among the first of the Trojans,
Busy for Priam's fame and my own, in spite of the future.
For that day will come, my soul is assured of its coming,
It will come, when sacred Troy shall go to destruction,
Troy, and warlike Priam too, and the people of Priam.
10 And yet not that grief, which then will be, of the Trojans,
Moves me so much—not Hecuba's grief, nor Priam my father's,
Nor my brethren's, many and brave, who then will be lying
In the bloody dust, beneath the feet of their foemen—
As thy grief, when, in tears, some brazen-coated Achaian
15 Shall transport thee away, and the day of thy freedom be ended.
Then, perhaps, thou shalt work at the loom of another, in Argos,
Or bear pails to the well of Messeïs, or Hypereia,
Sorely against thy will, by strong Necessity's order.
And some man may say, as he looks and sees thy tears falling:
20 *See, the wife of Hector, that great pre-eminent captain*
Of the horsemen of Troy, in the day they fought for their city.
So some man will say; and then thy grief will redouble
At thy want of a man like me, to save thee from bondage.
But let me be dead, and the earth be mounded above me,
25 Ere I hear thy cries, and thy captivity told of.

The main question, whether or no this version reproduces for him the movement and general effect of Homer better than other versions[1] of the same passage, I leave for the judgment of the scholar. But the particular points, in which the opera-
30 tion of my own rules is manifested, are as follows. In the second line I leave out the epithet of the Trojan women, ἑλκεσιπέπλους, altogether. In the sixth line I put in five words, 'in spite of the future,' which are in the original by implication only, and are not there actually expressed. This I do, because
35 Homer, as I have before said, is so remote from one who reads him in English, that the English translator must be even plainer,

[1] Dr. Hawtrey also has translated this passage; but here, he has not, I think, been so successful as in his 'Helen on the walls of Troy.'

if possible, and more unambiguous than Homer himself; the connection of meaning must be even more distinctly marked in the translation than in the original. For in the Greek language itself there is something which brings one nearer to Homer, which gives one a clue to his thought, which makes a hint enough; but in the English language this sense of nearness, this clue, is gone; hints are insufficient, everything must be stated with full distinctness. In the ninth line Homer's epithet for Priam is ἐϋμμελίω,—'armed with good ashen spear,' say the dictionaries; 'ashen-speared,' translates Mr. Newman, following his own rule to 'retain every peculiarity of his original,'—I say, on the other hand, that ἐϋμμελίω has not the effect of a 'peculiarity' in the original, while 'ashen-speared' has the effect of a 'peculiarity' in English; and 'warlike' is as marking an equivalent as I dare give for ἐϋμμελίω, for fear of disturbing the balance of expression in Homer's sentence. In the fourteenth line, again, I translate χαλκοχιτώνων by 'brazen-coated.' Mr. Newman, meaning to be perfectly literal, translates it by 'brazen-cloaked,' an expression which comes to the reader oddly and unnaturally, while Homer's word comes to him quite naturally; but I venture to go as near to a literal rendering as 'brazen-coated,' because a 'coat of brass' is familiar to us all from the Bible, and familiar, too, as distinctly specified in connection with the wearer. Finally, let me further illustrate from the twentieth line the value which I attach, in a question of diction, to the authority of the Bible. The word 'pre-eminent' occurs in that line; I was a little in doubt whether that was not too bookish an expression to be used in rendering Homer, as I can imagine Mr. Newman to have been a little in doubt whether his 'responsively accosted,' for ἀμειβόμενος προσέφη, was not too bookish an expression. Let us both, I say, consult our Bibles: Mr. Newman will nowhere find it in his Bible that David, for instance, '*responsively accosted* Goliath;' but I do find in mine that 'the right hand of the Lord hath the *pre-eminence*;' and forthwith I use 'pre-eminent,' without scruple. My Bibliolatry is perhaps excessive; and no doubt a true poetic feeling is the Homeric translator's best guide in the use of words; but where this feeling does not exist, or is at fault, I think he cannot do better than take for a mechanical guide Cruden's *Concordance.* To be sure, here as elsewhere, the consulter must know how to consult,—must know how very slight a variation of word or circumstance makes the difference between an authority in his favour, and an authority which gives him no countenance at all; for instance, the 'Great simpleton!' (for μέγα νήπιος) of Mr. Newman, and the 'Thou fool!' of the Bible, are something alike; but 'Thou fool!' is very grand, and 'Great simpleton!' is an atrocity. So, too, Chapman's 'Poor wretched beasts' is pitched many degrees too low; but Shakspeare's 'Poor venomous fool, Be angry and despatch!' is in the grand style.

One more piece of translation and I have done. I will take the passage in which both Chapman and Mr. Newman have already so much excited our astonishment, the passage at the end of the nineteenth book of the *Iliad,* the dialogue between Achilles and his horse Xanthus, after the death of Patroclus. Achilles begins:—

'Xanthus and Balius both, ye far-famed seed of Podarga!
See that ye bring your master home to the host of the Argives
In some other sort than your last, when the battle is ended;
And not leave him behind, a corpse on the plain, like Patroclus.'
Then, from beneath the yoke, the fleet horse Xanthus addressed him:
Sudden he bowed his head, and all his mane, as he bowed it,
Streamed to the ground by the yoke, escaping from under the collar:
And he was given a voice by the white-armed Goddess Hera.
'Truly, yet this time will we save thee, mighty Achilles!
But thy day of death is at hand; nor shall *we* be the reason—
No, but the will of heaven, and Fate's invincible power.
For by no slow pace or want of swiftness of ours
Did the Trojans obtain to strip the arms from Patroclus;
But that prince among Gods, the son of the lovely-haired Leto,
Slew him fighting in front of the fray, and glorified Hector.
But, for us, we vie in speed with the breath of the West-Wind,
Which, men say, is the fleetest of winds; 't is thou who art fated
To lie low in death, by the hand of a God and a Mortal.'
Thus far he; and here his voice was stopped by the Furies.

Then, with a troubled heart, the swift Achilles addressed him:
'Why dost thou prophesy so my death to me, Xanthus? It needs not.
I of myself know well, that here I am destined to perish,
Far from my father and mother dear: for all that, I will not
Stay this hand from fight, till the Trojans are utterly routed.' 5

So he spake, and drove with a cry his steeds into battle.

Here the only particular remark which I will make is, that in the fourth and eighth line the grammar is what I call a loose and idiomatic grammar. In writing a regular and literary style, one would in the fourth line have to repeat before 'leave' 10 the words 'that ye' from the second line, and to insert the word 'do;' and in the eighth line one would not use such an expression as 'he was given a voice.' But I will make one general remark on the character of my own translations, as I have made so many on that of the translations of others. It is, that 15 over the graver passages there is shed an air somewhat too strenuous and severe, by comparison with that lovely ease and sweetness which Homer, for all his noble and masculine way of thinking, never loses.

Here I stop. I have said so much, because I think that the task 20 of translating Homer into English verse both will be re-attempted, and may be re-attempted successfully. There are great works composed of parts so disparate that one translator is not likely to have the requisite gifts for poetically rendering all of them. Such are the works of Shakspeare, and Goethe's 25 *Faust;* and these it is best to attempt to render in prose only. People praise Tieck and Schlegel's version of Shakspeare: I, for my part, would sooner read Shakspeare in the French prose translation, and that is saying a great deal; but in the German poets' hands Shakspeare so often gets, especially where he is 30 humorous, an air of what the French call *niaiserie!* and can anything be more un-Shakspearian than that? Again; Mr. Hayward's prose translation of the first part of *Faust*—so good that it makes one regret Mr. Hayward should have abandoned the line of translation for a kind of literature which is, 35 to say the least, somewhat slight—is not likely to be surpassed by any translation in verse. But poems like the *Iliad,* which, in the main, are in one manner, may hope to find a poetical translator so gifted and so trained as to be able to learn that one manner, and to reproduce it. Only, the poet who would 5 reproduce this must cultivate in himself a Greek virtue by no means common among the moderns in general, and the English in particular,—*moderation.* For Homer has not only the English vigour, he has the Greek grace; and when one observes the boisterous, rollicking way in which his English admirers— 10 even men of genius, like the late Professor Wilson—love to talk of Homer and his poetry, one cannot help feeling that there is no very deep community of nature between them and the object of their enthusiasm. 'It is very well, my good friends,' I always imagine Homer saying to them, if he could 15 hear them: 'you do me a great deal of honour, but somehow or other you praise me too like barbarians.' For Homer's grandeur is not the mixed and turbid grandeur of the great poets of the north, of the authors of *Othello* and *Faust;* it is a perfect, a lovely grandeur. Certainly his poetry has all the 20 energy and power of the poetry of our ruder climates; but it has, besides, the pure lines of an Ionian horizon, the liquid clearness of an Ionian sky.

LAST WORDS

'Multi, qui persequuntur me, et tribulant me: a testimoniis non declinavi.'

25 Buffon, the great French naturalist, imposed on himself the rule of steadily abstaining from all answer to attacks made upon him. 'Je n'ai jamais répondu à aucune critique,' he said to one of his friends who, on the occasion of a certain criticism, was eager to take up arms in his behalf; 'je n'ai jamais répondu 30 à aucune critique, et je garderai le même silence sur celle-ci.' On another occasion, when accused of plagiarism, and pressed by his friends to answer, 'Il vaut mieux,' he said, 'laisser ces mauvaises gens dans l'incertitude.' Even when reply to an

attack was made successfully, he disapproved of it, he regretted that those he esteemed should make it. Montesquieu, more sensitive to criticism than Buffon, had answered, and successfully answered, an attack made upon his great work, the *Esprit des Lois*, by the *Gazetier Janséniste*. This Jansenist Gazetteer was a periodical of those times,—a periodical such as other times, also, have occasionally seen,—very pretentious, very aggressive, and, when the point to be seized was at all a delicate one, very apt to miss it. 'Notwithstanding this example,' said Buffon,—who, as well as Montesquieu, had been attacked by the Jansenist Gazetteer,—'notwithstanding this example, I think I may promise my course will be different. I shall not answer a single word.'

And to any one who has noticed the baneful effects of controversy, with all its train of personal rivalries and hatreds, on men of letters or men of science; to any one who has observed how it tends to impair, not only their dignity and repose, but their productive force, their genuine activity; how it always checks the free play of the spirit, and often ends by stopping it altogether; it can hardly seem doubtful, that the rule thus imposed on himself by Buffon was a wise one. His own career, indeed, admirably shows the wisdom of it. That career was as glorious as it was serene; but it owed to its serenity no small part of its glory. The regularity and completeness with which he gradually built up the great work which he had designed, the air of equable majesty which he shed over it, struck powerfully the imagination of his contemporaries, and surrounded Buffon's fame with a peculiar respect and dignity. 'He is,' said Frederick the Great of him, 'the man who has best deserved the great celebrity which he has acquired.' And this regularity of production, this equableness of temper, he maintained by his resolute disdain of personal controversy.

Buffon's example seems to me worthy of all imitation, and in my humble way I mean always to follow it. I never have replied, I never will reply, to any literary assailant; in such encounters tempers are lost, the world laughs, and truth is not served. Least of all should I think of using this Chair as a place from which to carry on such a conflict. But when a learned and estimable man thinks he has reason to complain of language used by me in this Chair,—when he attributes to me intentions and feelings towards him which are far from my 5 heart, I owe him some explanation,—and I am bound, too, to make the explanation as public as the words which gave offence. This is the reason why I revert once more to the subject of translating Homer. But being thus brought back to that subject, and not wishing to occupy you solely with an 10 explanation which, after all, is Mr. Newman's affair and mine, not the public's, I shall take the opportunity,—not certainly to enter into any conflict with any one,—but to try to establish our old friend, the coming translator of Homer, yet a little firmer in the positions which I hope we have now secured for 15 him; to protect him against the danger of relaxing, in the confusion of dispute, his attention to those matters which alone I consider important for him; to save him from losing sight, in the dust of the attacks delivered over it, of the real body of Patroclus. He will, probably, when he arrives, requite 20 my solicitude very ill, and be in haste to disown his benefactor: but my interest in him is so sincere that I can disregard his probable ingratitude.

First, however, for the explanation. Mr. Newman has published a reply to the remarks which I made on his translation of 25 the *Iliad*. He seems to think that the respect which at the outset of those remarks I professed for him must have been professed ironically; he says that I use 'forms of attack against him which he does not know how to characterise;' that I 'speak scornfully' of him, treat him with 'gratuitous insult, gratuitous 30 rancour;' that I 'propagate slanders' against him, that I wish to 'damage him with my readers,' to 'stimulate my readers to despise' him. He is entirely mistaken. I respect Mr. Newman sincerely; I respect him as one of the few learned men we have, one of the few who love learning for its own sake; this 35 respect for him I had before I read his translation of the *Iliad*, I retained it while I was commenting on that translation, I have not lost it after reading his reply. Any vivacities of expression which may have given him pain I sincerely regret, and can only assure him that I used them without a thought of insult or rancour. When I took the liberty of creating the verb *to Newmanise*, my intentions were no more rancorous than if I had said to *Miltonise;* when I exclaimed, in my astonishment at his vocabulary, 'With whom can Mr. Newman have lived?' I meant merely to convey, in a familiar form of speech, the sense of bewilderment one has at finding a person to whom words one thought all the world knew seem strange, and words one thought entirely strange, intelligible. Yet this simple expression of my bewilderment Mr. Newman construes into an accusation that he is 'often guilty of keeping low company,' and says that I shall 'never want a stone to throw at him.' And what is stranger still, one of his friends gravely tells me that Mr. Newman 'lived with the fellows of Balliol.' As if that made Mr. Newman's glossary less inexplicable to me! As if he could have got his glossary from the fellows of Balliol! As if I could believe that the members of that distinguished society—of whose discourse, not so many years afterwards, I myself was an unworthy hearer—were in Mr. Newman's time so far removed from the Attic purity of speech which we all of us admired, that when one of them called a calf a *bulkin*, the rest 'easily understood' him; or, when he wanted to say that a newspaper-article was 'proudly fine,' it mattered little whether he said it was that or *bragly!* No; his having lived with the fellows of Balliol does not explain Mr. Newman's glossary to me. I will no longer ask 'with whom he can have lived,' since that gives him offence; but I must still declare that where he got his test of rarity or intelligibility for words is a mystery to me.

That, however, does not prevent me from entertaining a very sincere respect for Mr. Newman, and since he doubts it, I am glad to reiterate my expression of it. But the truth of the matter is this: I unfeignedly admire Mr. Newman's ability and learning; but I think in his translation of Homer he has employed that ability and learning quite amiss. I think he has chosen quite the wrong field for turning his ability and learning to account. I think that in England, partly from the want of an Academy, partly from a national habit of intellect to which that want of an Academy is itself due, there exists too little of what I may call a public force of correct literary opinion, possessing within certain limits a clear sense of what is right and wrong, sound and unsound, and sharply recalling men of ability and learning from any flagrant misdirection of these their advantages. I think, even, that in our country a powerful misdirection of this kind is often more likely to subjugate and pervert opinion than to be checked and corrected by it.[1] Hence a chaos of false tendencies, wasted efforts, impotent conclusions, works which ought never to have been undertaken. Any one who can introduce a little order into this chaos by establishing in any quarter a single sound rule of criticism, a single rule which clearly marks what is right as right, and what is wrong as wrong, does a good deed; and his deed is so much the better the greater force he counteracts of learning and ability applied to thicken the chaos. Of course no one can be sure that he has fixed any such rules; he can only do his best to fix them; but somewhere or other, in the literary opinion of Europe, if not in the literary opinion of one nation, in fifty years, if not in five, there is a final judgment on these matters, and the critic's work will at last stand or fall by its true merits.

Meanwhile, the charge of having in one instance misapplied his powers, of having once followed a false tendency, is no such grievous charge to bring against a man; it does not exclude a great respect for himself personally, or for his powers in the happier manifestation of them. False tendency is, I have said, an evil to which the artist or the man of letters in England is peculiarly prone; but everywhere in our time he is liable to it,—the greatest as well as the humblest. 'The first beginnings of my *Wilhelm Meister*,' says Goethe, 'arose out

[1] 'It is the fact, that scholars of fastidious refinement, but of a judgment which I think far more masculine than Mr. Arnold's, have passed a most encouraging sentence on large specimens of my translation. I at present count eight such names.'—'Before venturing to print, I sought to ascertain how unlearned women and children would accept my verses. I could boast how children and half-educated women have extolled them, how greedily a working man has inquired for them, without knowing who was the translator.'—Mr. Newman's Reply, pp. 2, 12, 13.

of an obscure sense of the great truth that man will often attempt something for which nature has denied him the proper powers, will undertake and practise something in which he cannot become skilled. An inward feeling warns him to desist' (yes, but there are, unhappily, cases of absolute judicial blindness!), 'nevertheless he cannot get clear in himself about it, and is driven along a false road to a false goal, without knowing how it is with him. To this we may refer everything which goes by the name of false tendency, dilettantism, and so on. A great many men waste in this way the fairest portion of their lives, and fall at last into wonderful delusion.' Yet after all,—Goethe adds,—it sometimes happens that even on this false road a man finds, not indeed that which he sought, but something which is good and useful for him; 'like Saul, the son of Kish, who went forth to look for his father's asses, and found a kingdom.' And thus false tendency as well as true, vain effort as well as fruitful, go together to produce that great movement of life, to present that immense and magic spectacle of human affairs, which from boyhood to old age fascinates the gaze of every man of imagination, and which would be his terror, if it were not at the same time his delight.

So Mr. Newman may see how wide-spread a danger it is, to which he has, as I think, in setting himself to translate Homer, fallen a prey. He may be well satisfied if he can escape from it by paying it the tribute of a single work only. He may judge how unlikely it is that I should 'despise' him for once falling a prey to it. I know far too well how exposed to it we all are; how exposed to it I myself am. At this very moment, for example, I am fresh from reading Mr. Newman's Reply to my Lectures, a reply full of that erudition in which (as I am so often and so good-naturedly reminded, but indeed I know it without being reminded) Mr. Newman is immeasurably my superior. Well, the demon that pushes us all to our ruin is even now prompting me to follow Mr. Newman into a discussion about the digamma, and I know not what providence holds me back. And some day, I have no doubt, I shall lecture on the language of the Berbers, and give him his entire revenge.

But Mr. Newman does not confine himself to complaints on

his own behalf, he complains on Homer's behalf too. He says that my 'statements about Greek literature are against the most notorious and elementary fact;' that I 'do a public wrong to literature by publishing them;' and that the Professors to whom I appealed in my three Lectures, 'would only lose credit if they sanctioned the use I make of their names.' He does these eminent men the kindness of adding, however, that 'whether they are pleased with this parading of their names in behalf of paradoxical error, he may well doubt,' and that 'until they endorse it themselves, he shall treat my process as a piece of forgery.' He proceeds to discuss my statements at great length, and with an erudition and ingenuity which nobody can admire more than I do. And he ends by saying that my ignorance is great.

Alas! that is very true. Much as Mr. Newman was mistaken when he talked of my rancour, he is entirely right when he talks of my ignorance. And yet, perverse as it seems to say so, I sometimes find myself wishing, when dealing with these matters of poetical criticism, that my ignorance were even greater than it is. To handle these matters properly there is needed a poise so perfect that the least overweight in any direction tends to destroy the balance. Temper destroys it, a crotchet destroys it, even erudition may destroy it. To press to the sense of the thing itself with which one is dealing, not to go off on some collateral issue about the thing, is the hardest matter in the world. The 'thing itself' with which one is here dealing,—the critical perception of poetic truth,—is of all things the most volatile, elusive, and evanescent; by even pressing too impetuously after it, one runs the risk of losing it. The critic of poetry should have the finest tact, the nicest moderation, the most free, flexible, and elastic spirit imaginable; he should be indeed the 'ondoyant et divers,' the *undulating and diverse* being of Montaigne. The less he can deal with his object simply and freely, the more things he has to take into account in dealing with it,—the more, in short, he has to encumber himself,—so much the greater force of spirit he needs to retain his elasticity. But one cannot exactly have this greater force by wishing for it; so, for the force of spirit one has, the load put upon it is often heavier than it will well bear. The late Duke of Wellington said of a certain peer that 'it was a great pity his education had been so far too much for his abilities.' In like manner, one often sees erudition out of all proportion to its owner's critical faculty. Little as I know, therefore, I am always apprehensive, in dealing with poetry, lest even that little should prove 'too much for my abilities.'

With this consciousness of my own lack of learning,—nay, with this sort of acquiescence in it, with this belief that for the labourer in the field of poetical criticism learning has its disadvantages,—I am not likely to dispute with Mr. Newman about matters of erudition. All that he says on these matters in his Reply I read with great interest; in general I agree with him; but only, I am sorry to say, up to a certain point. Like all learned men, accustomed to desire definite rules, he draws his conclusions too absolutely; he wants to include too much under his rules; he does not quite perceive that in poetical criticism the shade, the fine distinction, is everything; and that, when he has once missed this, in all he says he is in truth but beating the air. For instance: because I think Homer noble, he imagines I must think him elegant; and in fact he says in plain words that I do think him so,—that to me Homer seems 'pervadingly elegant.' But he does not. Virgil is elegant,—'pervadingly elegant,'—even in passages of the highest emotion:

> O, ubi campi,
> Spercheosque, et virginibus bacchata Lacænis
> Taygeta! [1]

Even there Virgil, though of a divine elegance, is still elegant: but Homer is not elegant; the word is quite a wrong one to apply to him, and Mr. Newman is quite right in blaming any one he finds so applying it. Again; arguing against my assertion that Homer is not quaint, he says: 'It is quaint to call waves *wet*, milk *white*, blood *dusky*, horses *single-hoofed*, words *winged*, Vulcan *Lobfoot* (Κυλλοποδίων), a spear *longshadowy*,'

[1] 'O for the fields of Thessaly and the streams of Spercheios! O for the hills alive with the dances of the Laconian maidens, the hills of Taygetus!'—*Georgics*, ii. 486.

and so on. I find I know not how many distinctions to draw here. I do not think it quaint to call waves *wet*, or milk *white*, or words *winged;* but I do think it quaint to call horses *single-hoofed*, or Vulcan *Lobfoot*, or a spear *longshadowy*. As to
5 calling blood *dusky*, I do not feel quite sure; I will tell Mr. Newman my opinion when I see the passage in which he calls it so. But then, again, because it is quaint to call Vulcan *Lobfoot*, I cannot admit that it was quaint to call him Κυλλοποδίων; nor that, because it is quaint to call a spear *longshadowy*, it
10 was quaint to call it δολιχόσκιον. Here Mr. Newman's erudition misleads him: he knows the literal value of the Greek so well, that he thinks his literal rendering identical with the Greek, and that the Greek must stand or fall along with his rendering. But the real question is, not whether he has given us, so to
15 speak, full change for the Greek, but *how* he gives us our change: we want it in gold, and he gives it us in copper. Again: 'It is quaint,' says Mr. Newman, 'to address a young friend as "O Pippin!"—it is quaint to compare Ajax to an ass whom boys are belabouring.' Here, too, Mr. Newman goes much too
20 fast, and his category of quaintness is too comprehensive. To address a young friend as 'O Pippin!' is, I cordially agree with him, very quaint; although I do not think it was quaint in Sarpedon to address Glaucus as ὦ πέπον: but in comparing, whether in Greek or in English, Ajax to an ass whom boys are
25 belabouring, I do not see that there is of necessity anything quaint at all. Again; because I said that *eld*, *lief*, *in sooth*, and other words, are, as Mr. Newman uses them in certain places, bad words, he imagines that I must mean to stamp these words with an absolute reprobation; and because I said that 'my
30 Bibliolatry is excessive,' he imagines that I brand all words as ignoble which are not in the Bible. Nothing of the kind: there are no such absolute rules to be laid down in these matters. The Bible vocabulary is to be used as an assistance, not as an authority. Of the words which, placed where Mr.
35 Newman places them, I have called bad words, every one may be excellent in some other place. Take *eld*, for instance: when Shakspeare, reproaching man with the dependence in which his youth is passed, says:

> all thy blessed youth
> Becomes as aged, and doth beg the alms
> Of palsied *eld*, . . .

it seems to me that *eld* comes in excellently there, in a passage of curious meditation; but when Mr. Newman renders ἀγήρω τ' ἀθανάτω τε by 'from *Eld* and Death exempted,' it seems to me he infuses a tinge of quaintness into the transparent simplicity of Homer's expression, and so I call *eld* a bad word in that place.

Once more. Mr. Newman lays it down as a general rule that 'many of Homer's energetic descriptions are expressed in coarse physical words.' He goes on: 'I give one illustration,—Τρῶες προὔτυψαν ἀολλέες. Cowper, misled by the *ignis fatuus* of "stateliness," renders it absurdly:

> The powers of Ilium gave the first assault
> Embattled close;

but it is, strictly, "The Trojans *knocked forward* (or, thumped, butted forward) *in close pack*." The verb is too coarse for later polished prose, and even the adjective is very strong (*packed together*). I believe, that "forward in pack the Trojans pitched," would not be really unfaithful to the Homeric colour; and I maintain, that "forward in mass the Trojans pitched," would be an irreprovable rendering.' He actually gives us all that as if it were a piece of scientific deduction; and as if, at the end, he had arrived at an incontrovertible conclusion. But, in truth, one cannot settle these matters quite in this way. Mr. Newman's general rule may be true or false (I dislike to meddle with general rules), but every part in what follows must stand or fall by itself, and its soundness or unsoundness has nothing at all to do with the truth or falsehood of Mr. Newman's general rule. He first gives, as a strict rendering of the Greek, 'The Trojans knocked forward (or, thumped, butted forward), in close pack.' I need not say that, as a 'strict rendering of the Greek,' this is good,—all Mr. Newman's 'strict renderings of the Greek' are sure to be, as such, good; but 'in close pack,' for ἀολλέες, seems to me to be what Mr.

Newman's renderings are not always,—an excellent *poetical rendering* of the Greek; a thousand times better, certainly, than Cowper's 'embattled close.' Well, but Mr. Newman goes on: 'I believe, that "forward in pack the Trojans pitched," would not be really unfaithful to the Homeric colour.' Here, I say, the Homeric colour is half washed out of Mr. Newman's happy rendering of ἀολλέες; while in 'pitched' for προὔτυψαν, the literal fidelity of the first rendering is gone, while certainly no Homeric colour has come in its place. Finally, Mr. Newman concludes: 'I maintain that "forward in mass the Trojans pitched," would be an irreprovable rendering.' Here, in what Mr. Newman fancies his final moment of triumph, Homeric colour and literal fidelity have alike abandoned him altogether; the last stage of his translation is much worse than the second, and immeasurably worse than the first.

All this to show that a looser, easier method than Mr. Newman's must be taken, if we are to arrive at any good result in these questions. I now go on to follow Mr. Newman a little further, not at all as wishing to dispute with him, but as seeking (and this is the true fruit we may gather from criticisms upon us) to gain hints from him for the establishment of some useful truth about our subject, even when I think him wrong. I still retain, I confess, my conviction that Homer's characteristic qualities are rapidity of movement, plainness of words and style, simplicity and directness of ideas, and, above all, nobleness, the grand manner. Whenever Mr. Newman drops a word, awakens a train of thought, which leads me to see any of these characteristics more clearly, I am grateful to him; and one or two suggestions of this kind which he affords, are all that now,—having expressed my sorrow that he should have misconceived my feelings towards him, and pointed out what I think the vice of his method of criticism,—I have to notice in his Reply.

Such a suggestion I find in Mr. Newman's remarks on my assertion that the translator of Homer must not adopt a quaint and antiquated style in rendering him, because the impression which Homer makes upon the living scholar is not that of a poet quaint and antiquated, but that of a poet perfectly simple, perfectly intelligible. I added that we cannot, I confess, really know how Homer seemed to Sophocles, but that it is impossible to me to believe that he seemed to him quaint and antiquated. Mr. Newman asserts, on the other hand, that I am absurdly wrong here; that Homer seemed 'out and out' quaint and antiquated to the Athenians; that 'every sentence of him was more or less antiquated to Sophocles, who could no more help feeling at every instant the foreign and antiquated character of the poetry than an Englishman can help feeling the same in reading Burns's poems.' And not only does Mr. Newman say this, but he has managed thoroughly to convince some of his readers of it. 'Homer's Greek,' says one of them, 'certainly seemed antiquated to the historical times of Greece. Mr. Newman, taking a far broader historical and philological view than Mr. Arnold, stoutly maintains that it did seem so.' And another says: 'Doubtless Homer's dialect and diction were as hard and obscure to a later Attic Greek as Chaucer to an Englishman of our day.'

Mr. Newman goes on to say, that not only was Homer antiquated relatively to Pericles, but he is antiquated to the living scholar; and, indeed, is in himself 'absolutely antique, being the poet of a barbarian age.' He tells us of his 'inexhaustible quaintnesses,' of his 'very eccentric diction;' and he infers, of course, that he is perfectly right in rendering him in a quaint and antiquated style.

Now this question,—whether or no Homer seemed quaint and antiquated to Sophocles,—I call a delightful question to raise. It is not a barren verbal dispute; it is a question 'drenched in matter,' to use an expression of Bacon; a question full of flesh and blood, and of which the scrutiny, though I still think we cannot settle it absolutely, may yet give us a directly useful result. To scrutinise it may lead us to see more clearly what sort of a style a modern translator of Homer ought to adopt.

Homer's verses were some of the first words which a young Athenian heard. He heard them from his mother or his nurse before he went to school; and at school, when he went there, he was constantly occupied with them. So much did he hear of them that Socrates proposes, in the interests of morality, to have selections from Homer made, and placed in the hands of mothers and nurses, in his model republic; in order that, of an author with whom they were sure to be so perpetually conversant, the young might learn only those parts which might do them good. His language was as familiar to Sophocles, we may be quite sure, as the language of the Bible is to us.

Nay, more. Homer's language was not, of course, in the time of Sophocles, the spoken or written language of ordinary life, any more than the language of the Bible, any more than the language of poetry, is with us; but for one great species of composition—epic poetry—it was still the current language; it was the language in which every one who made that sort of poetry composed. Every one at Athens who dabbled in epic poetry, not only understood Homer's language,—he possessed it. He possessed it as every one who dabbles in poetry with us, possesses what may be called the poetical vocabulary, as distinguished from the vocabulary of common speech and of modern prose: I mean, such expressions as *perchance* for *perhaps*, *spake* for *spoke*, *aye* for *ever*, *don* for *put on*, *charméd* for *charm'd*, and thousands of others.

I might go to Burns and Chaucer, and, taking words and passages from them, ask if they afforded any parallel to a language so familiar and so possessed. But this I will not do, for Mr. Newman himself supplies me with what he thinks a fair parallel, in its effect upon us, to the language of Homer in its effect upon Sophocles. He says that such words as *mon*, *londis*, *libbard*, *withouten*, *muchel*, give us a tolerable but incomplete notion of this parallel; and he finally exhibits the parallel in all its clearness, by this poetical specimen:—

> Dat mon, quhich hauldeth Kyngis-af
> Londis yn féo, niver
> (I tell 'e) feereth aught; sith hee
> Doth hauld hys londis yver.

Now, does Mr. Newman really think that Sophocles could, as he says, 'no more help feeling at every instant the foreign and antiquated character of Homer, than an Englishman can help feeling the same in hearing' these lines? Is he quite sure of it? He says he is; he will not allow of any doubt or hesitation in the matter. I had confessed we could not really know how Homer seemed to Sophocles;—'Let Mr. Arnold confess for himself,' cries Mr. Newman, 'and not for me, who know perfectly well.' And this is what he knows! 5

Mr. Newman says, however, that I 'play fallaciously on the words familiar and unfamiliar;' that 'Homer's words may have been familiar to the Athenians (*i.e.* often heard) even when they were either not understood by them or else, being understood, were yet felt and known to be utterly foreign. Let my renderings,' he continues, 'be heard, as Pope or even Cowper has been heard, and no one will be "surprised."' 10

But the whole question is here. The translator must not assume that to have taken place which has not taken place, although, perhaps, he may wish it to have taken place,—namely, that his diction is become an established possession of the minds of men, and therefore is, in its proper place, familiar to them, will not 'surprise' them. If Homer's language was familiar,—that is, often heard,—then to this language words like *londis* and *libbard*, which are not familiar, offer, for the translator's purpose, no parallel. For some purpose of the philologer they may offer a parallel to it; for the translator's purpose they offer none. The question is not, whether a diction is antiquated for current speech, but whether it is antiquated for that particular purpose for which it is employed. A diction that is antiquated for common speech and common prose, may very well not be antiquated for poetry or certain special kinds of prose. 'Peradventure there shall be ten found there,' is not antiquated for Biblical prose, though for conversation or for a newspaper it is antiquated. 'The trumpet spake not to the armèd throng,' is not antiquated for poetry, although we should not write in a letter, 'he *spake* to me,' or say, 'the British soldier is *armèd* with the Enfield rifle.' But when language is antiquated for that particular purpose for which it is employed,—as numbers of Chaucer's words, for instance, are antiquated for poetry,—such language is a bad representative of language which, like Homer's, was never antiquated for 15 20 25 30 35 that particular purpose for which it was employed. I imagine that Πηληϊάδεω for Πηλείδου, in Homer, no more sounded antiquated to Sophocles, than *armèd* for *arm'd*, in Milton, sounds antiquated to us; but Mr. Newman's *withouten* and *muchel* do sound to us antiquated, even for poetry, and therefore they do not correspond in their effect upon us with Homer's words in their effect upon Sophocles. When Chaucer, who uses such words, is to pass current amongst us, to be familiar to us, as Homer was familiar to the Athenians, he has to be modernised, as Wordsworth and others set to work to modernise him; but an Athenian no more needed to have Homer modernised, than we need to have the Bible modernised, or Wordsworth himself.

Therefore, when Mr. Newman's words *bragly, bulkin,* and the rest, are an established possession of our minds, as Homer's words were an established possession of an Athenian's mind, he may use them; but not till then. Chaucer's words, the words of Burns, great poets as these were, are yet not thus an established possession of an Englishman's mind, and therefore they must not be used in rendering Homer into English.

Mr. Newman has been misled just by doing that which his admirer praises him for doing, by taking a 'far broader historical and philological view than' mine. Precisely because he has done this, and has applied the 'philological view' where it was not applicable, but where the 'poetical view' alone was rightly applicable, he has fallen into error.

It is the same with him in his remarks on the difficulty and obscurity of Homer. Homer, I say, is perfectly plain in speech, simple, and intelligible. And I infer from this that his translator, too, ought to be perfectly plain in speech, simple, and intelligible; ought not to say, for instance, in rendering

Οὔτε κε σὲ στέλλοιμι μάχην ἐς κυδιάνειραν . . .

'Nor liefly thee would I advance to man-ennobling battle,' —and things of that kind. Mr. Newman hands me a list of some twenty hard words, invokes Buttmann, Mr. Malden, and M. Benfey, and asks me if I think myself wiser than all the world of Greek scholars, and if I am ready to supply the deficiencies of Liddell and Scott's *Lexicon!* But here, again, Mr. Newman errs by not perceiving that the question is one not of scholarship, but of a poetical translation of Homer. This, I say, should be perfectly simple and intelligible. He replies by telling me that ἀδινὸς, εἰλίποδες, and σιγαλόεις are hard words. Well, but what does he infer from that? That the poetical translator, in his rendering of them, is to give us a sense of the difficulties of the scholar, and so is to make his translation obscure? If he does not mean that, how, by bringing forward these hard words, does he touch the question whether an English version of Homer should be plain or not plain? If Homer's poetry, as poetry, is in its general effect on the poetical reader perfectly simple and intelligible, the uncertainty of the scholar about the true meaning of certain words can never change this general effect. Rather will the poetry of Homer make us forget his philology, than his philology make us forget his poetry. It may even be affirmed that every one who reads Homer perpetually for the sake of enjoying his poetry (and no one who does not so read him will ever translate him well), comes at last to form a perfectly clear sense in his own mind for every important word in Homer, such as ἀδινὸς, or ἠλίβατος, whatever the scholar's doubts about the word may be. And this sense is present to his mind with perfect clearness and fulness, whenever the word recurs, although as a scholar he may know that he cannot be sure whether this sense is the right one or not. But poetically he feels clearly about the word, although philologically he may not. The scholar in him may hesitate, like the father in Sheridan's play; but the reader of poetry in him is, like the governor, fixed. The same thing happens to us with our own language. How many words occur in the Bible, for instance, to which thousands of hearers do not feel sure they attach the precise real meaning; but they make out *a* meaning for them out of what materials they have at hand; and the words, heard over and over again, come to convey this meaning with a certainty which poetically is adequate, though not philologically. How many have attached a clear and poetically adequate sense to 'the *beam*' and 'the *mote*,' though not precisely the right one!

How clearly, again, have readers got a sense from Milton's words, 'grate on their *scrannel* pipes,' who yet might have been puzzled to write a commentary on the word *scrannel* for the dictionary! So we get a clear sense from ἀδινὸς as an epithet for grief, after often meeting with it and finding out all we can about it, even though that all be philologically insufficient; so we get a clear sense from εἰλίποδες as an epithet for cows. And this his clear poetical sense about the words, not his philological uncertainties about them, is what the translator has to convey. Words like *bragly* and *bulkin* offer no parallel to these words; because the reader, from his entire want of familiarity with the words *bragly* and *bulkin*, has no clear sense of them poetically.

Perplexed by his knowledge of the philological aspect of Homer's language, encumbered by his own learning, Mr. Newman, I say, misses the poetical aspect, misses that with which alone we are here concerned. 'Homer *is* odd,' he persists, fixing his eyes on his own philological analysis of μῶνυξ, and μέροψ, and Κυλλοποδίων, and not on these words in their synthetic character;—just as Professor Max Müller, going a little farther back, and fixing his attention on the elementary value of the word θυγάτηρ, might say Homer was 'odd' for using *that* word;—'if the whole Greek nation, by long familiarity, had become inobservant of Homer's oddities,'—of the oddities of this 'noble barbarian,' as Mr. Newman elsewhere calls him, this 'noble barbarian' with the 'lively eye of the savage,'—'that would be no fault of mine. That would not justify Mr. Arnold's blame of me for rendering the words correctly.' *Correctly*,—ah, but what *is* correctness in this case? This correctness of his is the very rock on which Mr. Newman has split. He is so correct that at last he finds peculiarity everywhere. The true knowledge of Homer becomes at last, in his eyes, a knowledge of Homer's 'peculiarities, pleasant and unpleasant.' Learned men know these 'peculiarities,' and Homer is to be translated because the unlearned are impatient to know them too. 'That,' he exclaims, 'is just why people want to read an English Homer,—*to know all his oddities, just as learned men do*.' Here I am obliged to shake my head, and to declare that, in spite of all my respect for Mr. Newman, I cannot go these lengths with him. He talks of my 'monomaniac fancy that there is nothing quaint or antique in Homer.' Terrible learning,—I cannot help in my turn exclaiming,—terrible learning, which discovers so much! 5

Here, then, I take my leave of Mr. Newman, retaining my opinion that his version of Homer is spoiled by his making Homer odd and ignoble; but having, I hope, sufficient love for literature to be able to canvass works without thinking of persons, and to hold this or that production cheap, while re- 10 taining a sincere respect, on other grounds, for its author.

In fulfilment of my promise to take this opportunity for giving the translator of Homer a little further advice, I proceed to notice one or two other criticisms which I find, in like manner, *suggestive;* which give us an opportunity, that is, of 15 seeing more clearly, as we look into them, the true principles on which translation of Homer should rest. This is all I seek in criticisms; and, perhaps (as I have already said) it is only as one seeks a positive result of this kind, that one can get any fruit from them. Seeking a negative result from them,— 20 personal altercation and wrangling,—one gets no fruit; seeking a positive result,—the elucidation and establishment of one's ideas,—one may get much. Even bad criticisms may thus be made suggestive and fruitful. I declared, in a former lecture on this subject, my conviction that criticism is not the strong 25 point of our national literature. Well, even the bad criticisms on our present topic which I meet with, serve to illustrate this conviction for me. And thus one is enabled, even in reading remarks which for Homeric criticism, for their immediate subject, have no value,—which are far too personal in spirit, 30 far too immoderate in temper, and far too heavy-handed in style, for the delicate matter they have to treat,—still to gain light and confirmation for a serious idea, and to follow the Baconian injunction, *semper aliquid addiscere,* always to be adding to one's stock of observation and knowledge. Yes, even 35 when we have to do with writers who,—to quote the words of an exquisite critic, the master of us all in criticism, M. Sainte-Beuve,—remind us, when they handle such subjects as our present, of 'Romans of the fourth or fifth century, coming to hold forth, all at random, in African style, on papers found in the desk of Augustus, Mæcenas, or Pollio,'—even then we may instruct ourselves if we regard ideas and not persons; even then we may enable ourselves to say, with the same critic describing the effect made upon him by D'Argenson's *Memoirs:* 'My taste is revolted, but I learn something;—*Je suis choqué mais je suis instruit.*'

But let us pass to criticisms which are suggestive directly and not thus indirectly only,—criticisms by examining which we may be brought nearer to what immediately interests us,—the right way of translating Homer.

I said that Homer did not rise and sink with his subject, was never to be called prosaic and low. This gives surprise to many persons, who object that parts of the *Iliad* are certainly pitched lower than others, and who remind me of a number of absolutely level passages in Homer. But I never denied that a *subject* must rise and sink, that it must have its elevated and its level regions; all I deny is, that a poet can be said to rise and sink when all that he, as a poet, can do, is perfectly well done; when he is perfectly sound and good, that is, perfect as a poet, in the level regions of his subject as well as in its elevated regions. Indeed, what distinguishes the greatest masters of poetry from all others is, that they are perfectly sound and poetical in these level regions of their subject,—in these regions which are the great difficulty of all poets but the very greatest, which they never quite know what to do with. A poet may sink in these regions by being falsely grand as well as by being low; he sinks, in short, whenever he does not treat his matter, whatever it is, in a perfectly good and poetic way. But, so long as he treats it in this way, he cannot be said to *sink*, whatever his matter may do. A passage of the simplest narrative is quoted to me from Homer:—

> ὤτρυνεν δὲ ἕκαστον ἐποιχόμενος ἐπέεσσιν,
> Μέσθλην τε, Γλαῦκόν τε, Μέδοντά τε, Θερσίλοχόν τε . . .[1]

---

[1] *Iliad*, xvii. 216.

and I am asked, whether Homer does not sink *there;* whether he '*can* have intended such lines as those for poetry?' My answer is: Those lines are very good poetry indeed, poetry of the best class, *in that place*. But when Wordsworth, having to narrate a very plain matter, tries *not* to sink in narrating it, 5
tries, in short, to be what is falsely called poetical, he does sink, although he sinks by being pompous, not by being low.

> Onward we drove beneath the Castle; caught,
> While crossing Magdalene Bridge, a glimpse of Cam,
> And at the Hoop alighted, famous inn. 10

That last line shows excellently how a poet may sink with his subject by resolving not to sink with it. A page or two farther on, the subject rises to grandeur, and then Wordsworth is nobly worthy of it:—

> The antechapel, where the statue stood 15
> Of Newton with his prism and silent face,
> The marble index of a mind for ever
> Voyaging through strange seas of thought, alone.

But the supreme poet is he who is thoroughly sound and poetical, alike when his subject is grand, and when it is plain: 20
with him the subject may sink, but never the poet. But a Dutch painter does not rise and sink with his subject,—Defoe, in *Moll Flanders*, does not rise and sink with his subject,—in so far as an artist cannot be said to sink who is sound in his treatment of his subject, however plain it is: yet Defoe, yet a 25
Dutch painter, may in one sense be said to sink with their subject, because though sound in their treatment of it, they are not *poetical*,—poetical in the true, not the false sense of the word; because, in fact, they are not in the grand style. Homer can in no sense be said to sink with his subject, because 30
his soundness has something more than literal naturalness about it; because his soundness is the soundness of Homer, of a great epic poet; because, in fact, he is in the grand style. So he sheds over the simplest matter he touches the charm of his grand manner; he makes everything noble. Nothing has raised more 35

questioning among my critics than these words,—*noble, the grand style*. People complain that I do not define these words sufficiently, that I do not tell them enough about them. 'The grand style,—but what *is* the grand style?'—they cry; some with an inclination to believe in it, but puzzled; others mockingly and with incredulity. Alas! the grand style is the last matter in the world for verbal definition to deal with adequately. One may say of it as is said of faith: 'One must feel it in order to know what it is.' But, as of faith, so too one may say of nobleness, of the grand style: 'Woe to those who know it not!' Yet this expression, though indefinable, has a charm; one is the better for considering it; *bonum est, nos hic esse;* nay, one loves to try to explain it, though one knows that one must speak imperfectly. For those, then, who ask the question,—What is the grand style?—with sincerity, I will try to make some answer, inadequate as it must be. For those who ask it mockingly I have no answer, except to repeat to them, with compassionate sorrow, the Gospel words: *Moriemini in peccatis vestris,*—Ye shall die in your sins.

But let me, at any rate, have the pleasure of again giving, before I begin to try and define the grand style, a specimen of what it *is*.

> Standing on earth, not rapt above the pole,
> More safe I sing with mortal voice, unchanged
> To hoarse or mute, though fall'n on evil days,
> On evil days though fall'n, and evil tongues. . . .

There is the grand style in perfection; and any one who has a sense for it, will feel it a thousand times better from repeating those lines than from hearing anything I can say about it.

Let us try, however, what *can* be said, controlling what we say by examples. I think it will be found that the grand style arises in poetry, *when a noble nature, poetically gifted, treats with simplicity or with severity a serious subject*. I think this definition will be found to cover all instances of the grand style in poetry which present themselves. I think it will be found to exclude all poetry which is not in the grand style.

And I think it contains no terms which are obscure, which themselves need defining. Even those who do not understand what is meant by calling poetry noble, will understand, I imagine, what is meant by speaking of a noble nature in a man. But the noble or powerful nature—the *bedeutendes Individuum* of Goethe—is not enough. For instance, Mr. Newman has zeal for learning, zeal for thinking, zeal for liberty, and all these things are noble, they ennoble a man; but he has not the poetical gift: there must be the poetical gift, the 'divine faculty,' also. And, besides all this, the subject must be a serious one (for it is only by a kind of license that we can speak of the grand style in comedy); and it must be treated *with simplicity or severity*. Here is the great difficulty: the poets of the world have been many; there has been wanting neither abundance of poetical gift nor abundance of noble natures; but a poetical gift so happy, in a noble nature so circumstanced and trained, that the result is a continuous style, perfect in simplicity or perfect in severity, has been extremely rare. One poet has had the gifts of nature and faculty in unequalled fulness, without the circumstances and training which make this sustained perfection of style possible. Of other poets, some have caught this perfect strain now and then, in short pieces or single lines, but have not been able to maintain it through considerable works; others have composed all their productions in a style which, by comparison with the best, one must call secondary.

The best model of the grand style simple is Homer; perhaps the best model of the grand style severe is Milton. But Dante is remarkable for affording admirable examples of both styles; he has the grand style which arises from simplicity, and he has the grand style which arises from severity; and from him I will illustrate them both. In a former lecture I pointed out what that severity of poetical style is, which comes from saying a thing with a kind of intense compression, or in an allusive, brief, almost haughty way, as if the poet's mind were charged with so many and such grave matters, that he would not deign to treat any one of them explicitly. Of this severity the last line of the following stanza of the *Purgatory* is a good example. Dante has been telling Forese that Virgil had guided him through Hell, and he goes on:—

> Indi m' han tratto su gli suoi conforti,
> Salendo e rigirando la Montagna
> *Che drizza voi che il mondo fece torti.*[1]

'Thence hath his comforting aid led me up, climbing and circling the Mountain, *which straightens you whom the world made crooked.*' These last words, 'la Montagna *che drizza voi che il mondo fece torti,*'—'the Mountain *which straightens you whom the world made crooked,*'—for the Mountain of Purgatory, I call an excellent specimen of the grand style in severity, where the poet's mind is too full charged to suffer him to speak more explicitly. But the very next stanza is a beautiful specimen of the grand style in simplicity, where a noble nature and a poetical gift unite to utter a thing with the most limpid plainness and clearness:—

> Tanto dice di farmi sua compagna
> Ch' io sarò là dove fia Beatrice;
> Quivi convien che senza lui rimagna.[2]

'So long,' Dante continues, 'so long he (Virgil) saith he will bear me company, until I shall be there where Beatrice is; there it behoves that without him I remain.' But the noble simplicity of that in the Italian no words of mine can render.

Both these styles, the simple and the severe, are truly grand; the severe seems, perhaps, the grandest, so long as we attend most to the great personality, to the noble nature, in the poet its author; the simple seems the grandest when we attend most to the exquisite faculty, to the poetical gift. But the simple is no doubt to be preferred. It is the more *magical:* in the other there is something intellectual, something which gives scope for a play of thought which may exist where the poetical gift is either wanting or present in only inferior degree: the severe is much more imitable, and this a little spoils its charm. A kind

[1] *Purgatory*, xxiii. 124.

[2] *Purgatory*, xxiii. 127.

You may say, if you like, when you find Homer's verse, even in describing the plainest matter, neither humdrum nor jaunty, that this is because he is so incomparably better a poet than other balladists, because he is Homer. But take the whole range 5 of Greek epic poetry,—take the later poets, the poets of the last ages of this poetry, many of them most indifferent,—Coluthus, Tryphiodorus, Quintus of Smyrna, Nonnus. Never will you find in this instrument of the hexameter, even in their hands, the vices of the ballad-style in the weak moments of this last: 10 everywhere the hexameter—a noble, a truly epical instrument —rather resists the weakness of its employer than lends itself to it. Quintus of Smyrna is a poet of merit, but certainly not a poet of a high order; with him, too, epic poetry, whether in the character of its prosody or in that of its diction, is no 15 longer the epic poetry of earlier and better times, nor epic poetry as again restored by Nonnus: but even in Quintus of Smyrna, I say, the hexameter is still the hexameter; it is a style which the ballad-style, even in the hands of better poets, cannot rival. And in the hands of inferior poets, the ballad-style sinks 20 to vices of which the hexameter, even in the hands of a Tryphiodorus, never can become guilty.

But a critic, whom it is impossible to read without pleasure, and the disguise of whose initials I am sure I may be allowed to penetrate,—Mr. Spedding,—says that he 'denies altogether 25 that the metrical movement of the English hexameter has any resemblance to that of the Greek.' Of course, in that case, if the two metres in no respect correspond, praise accorded to the Greek hexameter as an epical instrument will not extend to the English. Mr. Spedding seeks to establish his proposition by 30 pointing out that the system of accentuation differs in the English and in the Virgilian hexameter; that in the first, the accent and the long syllable (or what has to do duty as such) coincide, in the second they do not. He says that we cannot be so sure of the accent with which Greek verse should be 35 read as of that with which Latin should; but that the lines of Homer in which the accent and the long syllable coincide, as in the English hexameter, are certainly very rare. He suggests a type of English hexameter in agreement with the Virgilian model, and formed on the supposition that 'quantity is as distinguishable in English as in Latin or Greek by any ear that will attend to it.' Of the truth of this supposition he entertains no doubt. The new hexameter will, Mr. Spedding thinks, at least have the merit of resembling, in its metrical movement, the classical hexameter, which merit the ordinary English hexameter has not. But even with this improved hexameter he is not satisfied; and he goes on, first to suggest other metres for rendering Homer, and finally to suggest that rendering Homer is impossible.

A scholar to whom all who admire Lucretius owe a large debt of gratitude,—Mr. Munro,—has replied to Mr. Spedding. Mr. Munro declares that 'the accent of the old Greeks and Romans resembled our accent only in name, in reality was essentially different;' that 'our English reading of Homer and Virgil has in itself no meaning;' and that 'accent has nothing to do with the Virgilian hexameter.' If this be so, of course the merit which Mr. Spedding attributes to his own hexameter, of really corresponding with the Virgilian hexameter, has no existence. Again; in contradiction to Mr. Spedding's assertion that lines in which (in our reading of them) the accent and the long syllable coincide,[1] as in the ordinary English hexameter, are 'rare even in Homer,' Mr. Munro declares that such lines, 'instead of being rare, are among the very commonest types of Homeric rhythm.' Mr. Spedding asserts that 'quantity is as distinguishable in English as in Latin or Greek by any ear that will attend to it;' but Mr. Munro replies, that in English 'neither his ear nor his reason recognises any real distinction of quantity except that which is produced by accentuated and unaccentuated syllables.' He therefore arrives at the conclusion that in constructing English hexameters, 'quantity must be utterly discarded; and longer or shorter unaccentuated syllables can have no meaning, except so far as they may be made to produce sweeter or harsher sounds in the hands of a master.'

[1] Lines such as the first of the *Odyssey:*

Ἄνδρα μοι ἔννεπε, Μοῦσα, πολύτροπον, ὃς μάλα πολλὰ . . .

It is not for me to interpose between two such combatants; and indeed my way lies, not up the highroad where they are contending, but along a bypath. With the absolute truth of their general propositions respecting accent and quantity, I have nothing to do; it is most interesting and instructive to me to hear such propositions discussed, when it is Mr. Munro or Mr. Spedding who discusses them; but I have strictly limited myself in these Lectures to the humble function of giving practical advice to the translator of Homer. He, I still think, must not follow so confidently, as makers of English hexameters have hitherto followed, Mr. Munro's maxim,—*quantity may be utterly discarded*. He must not, like Mr. Longfellow, make *seventeen* a dactyl in spite of all the length of its last syllable, even though he can plead that in counting we lay the accent on the first syllable of this word. He may be far from attaining Mr. Spedding's nicety of ear;—may be unable to feel that 'while *quantity* is a dactyl, *quiddity* is a tribrach,' and that '*rapidly* is a word to which we find no parallel in Latin;'—but I think he must bring himself to distinguish, with Mr. Spedding, between '*th' o'er*-wearied eyelid,' and '*the* wearied eyelid,' as being, the one a correct ending for a hexameter, the other an ending with a false quantity in it; instead of finding, with Mr. Munro, that this distinction 'conveys to his mind no intelligible idea.' He must temper his belief in Mr. Munro's dictum,—*quantity must be utterly discarded*,—by mixing with it a belief in this other dictum of the same author,—*two or more consonants take longer time in enunciating than one*.[1]

[1] Substantially, however, in the question at issue between Mr. Munro and Mr. Spedding, I agree with Mr. Munro. By the italicised words in the following sentence, 'The rhythm of the Virgilian hexameter depends entirely on *cæsura, pause,* and a due arrangement of words,' he has touched, it seems to me, in the constitution of this hexameter, the central point, which Mr. Spedding misses. The accent, or *heightened tone*, of Virgil in reading his own hexameters, was probably far from being the same thing as the accent or *stress* with which we read them. The general effect of each line, in Virgil's mouth, was probably therefore something widely different from what Mr. Spedding assumes it to have been: an ancient's accentual reading was something which allowed the metrical

Criticism is so apt in general to be vague and impalpable, that when it gives us a solid and definite possession, such as is Mr. Spedding's parallel of the Virgilian and the English hexameter with their difference of accentuation distinctly marked, we cannot be too grateful to it. It is in the way in which Mr. Spedding proceeds to press his conclusions from the parallel which he has drawn out, that his criticism seems to me to come a little short. Here even he, I think, shows (if he will allow me to say so) a little of that want of pliancy and suppleness so common among critics, but so dangerous to their criticism; he is a little too absolute in imposing his metrical laws; he too much forgets the excellent maxim of Menander, so applicable to literary criticism:—

> Καλὸν οἱ νόμοι σφόδρ' εἰσίν · ὁ δ' ὁρῶν τοὺς νόμους
> λίαν ἀκριβῶς, συκοφάντης φαίνεται ·

'Laws are admirable things; but he who keeps his eye too closely fixed upon them, runs the risk of becoming'—let us say, a purist. Mr. Spedding is probably mistaken in supposing that Virgil pronounced his hexameters as Mr. Spedding pronounces them. He is almost certainly mistaken in supposing that Homer pronounced his hexameters as Mr. Spedding pronounces Virgil's. But this, as I have said, is not a question for us to treat; all we are here concerned with is the imitation, by the English hexameter, of the ancient hexameter *in its effect upon us moderns.* Suppose we concede to Mr. Spedding that his parallel proves our accentuation of the English and of the Virgilian hexameter to be different: what are we to conclude from that; how will a criticism—not a formal, but a substantial

---

beat of the Latin line to be far more perceptible than our accentual reading allows it to be.

On the question as to the *real* rhythm of the ancient hexameter, Mr. Newman has in his *Reply* a page quite admirable for force and precision. Here he is in his element, and his ability and acuteness have their proper scope. But it is true that the *modern* reading of the ancient hexameter is what the modern hexameter has to imitate, and that the English reading of the Virgilian hexameter is as Mr. Spedding describes it. Why this reading has not been imitated by the English hexameter, I have tried to point out in the text.

criticism—deal with such a fact as that? Will it infer, as Mr. Spedding infers, that the English hexameter, therefore, must not pretend to reproduce better than other rhythms the movement of Homer's hexameter for us,—that there can be no correspondence at all between the movement of these two hexameters,—that if we want to have such a correspondence, we must abandon the current English hexameter altogether, and adopt in its place a new hexameter of Mr. Spedding's Anglo-Latin type,—substitute for lines like the

> Clearly the rest I behold of the dark-eyed sons of Achaia . . .

of Dr. Hawtrey, lines like the

> Procession, complex melodies, pause, quantity, accent,
> After Virgilian precedent and practice, in order . . .

of Mr. Spedding? To infer this, is to go, as I have complained of Mr. Newman for sometimes going, a great deal too fast. I think prudent criticism must certainly recognise, in the current English hexameter, a fact which cannot so lightly be set aside; it must acknowledge that by this hexameter the English ear, the genius of the English language, have, in their own way, adopted, have *translated* for themselves the Homeric hexameter; and that a rhythm which has thus grown up, which is thus, in a manner, the production of nature, has in its general type something necessary and inevitable, something which admits change only within narrow limits, which precludes change that is sweeping and essential. I think, therefore, the prudent critic will regard Mr. Spedding's proposed revolution as simply impracticable. He will feel that in English poetry the hexameter, if used at all, must be, in the main, the English hexameter now current. He will perceive that its having come into existence as the representative of the Homeric hexameter, proves it to have, for the English ear, a certain correspondence with the Homeric hexameter, although this correspondence may be, from the difference of the Greek and English languages, necessarily incomplete. This incompleteness he will endeavour,[1] as he may find or fancy himself able, gradually somewhat to lessen through minor changes, suggested by the ancient hexameter, but respecting the general constitution of the modern: the notion of making it disappear altogether by the critic's inventing in his closet a new constitution of his 5 own for the English hexameter, he will judge to be a chimerical dream.

When, therefore, Mr. Spedding objects to the English hexameter, that it imperfectly represents the movement of the ancient hexameters, I answer: We must work with the tools 10 we have. The received English type, in its general outlines, is,

[1] Such a minor change I have attempted by occasionally shifting, in the first foot of the hexameter, the accent from the first syllable to the second. In the current English hexameter, it is on the first. Mr. Spedding, who proposes radically to subvert the constitution of this hexameter, 15 seems not to understand that any one can propose to modify it partially; he can comprehend revolution in this metre, but not reform. Accordingly he asks me how I can bring myself to say, '*Bétween* that and the ships,' or '*Thére* sat fifty men;' or how I can reconcile such forcing of the accent with my own rule, that 'hexameters must *read themselves*.' Presently 20 he says that he cannot believe I do pronounce these words so, but that he thinks I leave out the accent in the first foot altogether, and thus get a hexameter with only five accents. He will pardon me: I pronounce, as I suppose he himself does, if he reads the words naturally, 'Be*twéen* that and the ships,' and 'There *sát* fifty men.' Mr. Spedding is familiar enough 25 with this accent on the second syllable in Virgil's hexameters; in 'et *té* montosæ,' or 'Ve*ló*ces jaculo.' Such a change is an attempt to relieve the monotony of the current English hexameter by occasionally altering the position of one of its accents; it is not an attempt to make a wholly new English hexameter by habitually altering the position of four of them. 30 Very likely it is an unsuccessful attempt; but at any rate it does not violate what I think is the fundamental rule for English hexameters,—that they be such as to *read themselves* without necessitating, on the reader's part, any non-natural putting-on or taking-off of accent. Hexameters like these of Mr. Longfellow, 35

> 'In that delightful land which is washed by the Delaware's waters,'

and,

> 'As if they fain would appease the Dryads, whose haunts they molested,'

violate this rule; and they are very common. I think the blemish of Mr. Dart's recent meritorious version of the *Iliad* is that it contains too 40 many of them.

for England, the necessary given type of this metre; it is by rendering the metrical beat of its pattern, not by rendering the accentual beat of it, that the English language has adapted the Greek hexameter. To render the metrical beat of its
5 pattern is something; by effecting so much as this the English hexameter puts itself in closer relations with its original, it comes nearer to its movement than any other metre which does not even effect so much as this; but Mr. Spedding is dissatisfied with it for not effecting more still, for not rendering
10 the accentual beat too. If he asks me *why* the English hexameter has not tried to render this too, *why* it has confined itself to rendering the metrical beat, *why*, in short, it is itself, and not Mr. Spedding's new hexameter,—that is a question which I, whose only business is to give practical advice to a trans-
15 lator, am not bound to answer; but I will not decline to answer it nevertheless. I will suggest to Mr. Spedding that, as I have already said, the modern hexameter is merely an attempt to imitate the effect of the ancient hexameter, as read by us moderns; that the great object of its imitation has been the
20 hexameter of Homer; that of this hexameter such lines as those which Mr. Spedding declares to be so rare, even in Homer, but which are in truth so common,—lines in which the quantity and the reader's accent coincide,—are, for the English reader, just from that simplicity (for him) of rhythm which they owe to
25 this very coincidence, the master-type; that so much is this the case, that one may again and again notice an English reader of Homer, in reading lines where his Virgilian accent would not coincide with the quantity, abandoning this accent, and reading the lines (as we say) *by quantity*, reading them as if
30 he were scanning them; while foreigners neglect our Virgilian accent even in reading Virgil, read even Virgil by quantity, making the accents coincide with the long syllables. And no doubt the hexameter of a kindred language, the German, based on this mode of reading the ancient hexameter, has had a
35 powerful influence upon the type of its English fellow. But all this shows how extremely powerful accent is for us moderns, since we find not even Greek and Latin quantity perceptible enough without it. Yet in these languages, where we have

been accustomed always to look for it, it is far more perceptible to us Englishmen than in our own language, where we have not been accustomed to look for it. And here is the true reason why Mr. Spedding's hexameter is not and cannot be the current English hexameter, even though it is based on the accentuation which Englishmen give to all Virgil's lines, and to many of Homer's,—that the quantity which in Greek or Latin words we feel, or imagine we feel, even though it be unsupported by accent, we do not feel or imagine we feel in English words when it is thus unsupported. For example, in repeating the Latin line,

> Ipsa tibi blandos *fundent* cunabula flores,

an Englishman feels the length of the second syllable of *fundent*, although he lays the accent on the first; but in repeating Mr. Spedding's line,

> Softly cometh slumber *closing* th' o'erwearied eyelid,

the English ear, full of the accent on the first syllable of *closing*, has really no sense at all of any length in its second. The metrical beat of the line is thus quite destroyed.

So when Mr. Spedding proposes a new Anglo-Virgilian hexameter he proposes an impossibility; when he 'denies altogether that the metrical movement of the English hexameter has *any* resemblance to that of the Greek,' he denies too much; when he declares that, 'were every other metre impossible, an attempt to translate Homer into English hexameters might be permitted, *but that such an attempt he himself would never read*,' he exhibits, it seems to me, a little of that obduracy and over-vehemence in liking and disliking,—a remnant, I suppose, of our insular ferocity,—to which English criticism is so prone. He ought to be enchanted to meet with a good attempt in any metre, even though he would never have advised it, even though its success be contrary to all his expectations; for it is the critic's first duty—prior even to his duty of stigmatising what is bad—*to welcome everything that is good*. In welcoming this, he must at all times be ready, like the Christian convert, even to burn what he used to worship, and to worship what he used to burn. Nay, but he need not be thus inconsistent in welcoming it; he may retain all his principles: principles endure, circumstances change; absolute success is one thing, relative success another. Relative success may take place under the most diverse conditions; and it is in appreciating the good in even relative success, it is in taking into account the change of circumstances, that the critic's judgment is tested, that his versatility must display itself. He is to keep his idea of the best, of perfection, and at the same time to be willingly accessible to every second best which offers itself. So I enjoy the ease and beauty of Mr. Spedding's stanza,

Therewith to all the gods in order due . . .

I welcome it, in the absence of equally good poetry in another metre,[1] although I still think the stanza unfit to render Homer

[1] As I welcome another more recent attempt in stanza,—Mr. Worsley's version of the *Odyssey* in Spenser's measure. Mr. Worsley does me the honour to notice some remarks of mine on this measure: I had said that its greater intricacy made it a worse measure than even the ten-syllable couplet to employ for rendering Homer. He points out, in answer, that 'the more complicated the correspondences in a poetical measure, the less obtrusive and absolute are the rhymes.' This is true, and subtly remarked; but I never denied that the single shocks of rhyme in the couplet were more *strongly felt* than those in the stanza; I said that the more frequent recurrence of the same rhyme, in the stanza, necessarily made this measure more *intricate*. The stanza repacks Homer's matter yet more arbitrarily, and therefore changes his movement yet more radically, than the couplet. Accordingly, I imagine a nearer approach to a perfect translation of Homer is possible in the couplet, well managed, than in the stanza, however well managed. But meanwhile Mr. Worsley,—applying the Spenserian stanza, that beautiful romantic measure, to the most romantic poem of the ancient world; making this stanza yield him, too (what it never yielded to Byron), its treasures of fluidity and sweet ease; above all, bringing to his task a truly poetical sense and skill,—has produced a version of the *Odyssey* much the most pleasing of those hitherto produced, and which is delightful to read.

For the public this may well be enough, nay, more than enough; but for the critic even this is not yet quite enough.

thoroughly well,—although I still think other metres fit to render him better. So I concede to Mr. Spedding that every form of translation, prose or verse, must more or less break up Homer in order to reproduce him; but then I urge that that form which needs to break him up least is to be preferred. So I concede to him that the test proposed by me for the translator —a competent scholar's judgment whether the translation more or less reproduces for him the effect of the original—is not perfectly satisfactory; but I adopt it as the best we can get, as the only test capable of being really applied; for Mr. Spedding's proposed substitute—the translation's making the same effect, more or less, upon the unlearned which the original makes upon the scholar—is a test which can never really be applied at all. These two impressions—that of the scholar, and that of the unlearned reader—can, practically, never be accurately compared; they are, and must remain, like those lines we read of in Euclid, which, though produced ever so far, can never meet. So, again, I concede that a good verse-translation of Homer, or, indeed, of any poet, is very difficult, and that a good prose-translation is much easier; but then I urge that a verse-translation, while giving the pleasure which Pope's has given, might at the same time render Homer more faithfully than Pope's; and that this being possible, we ought not to cease wishing for a source of pleasure which no prose-translation can ever hope to rival.

Wishing for such a verse-translation of Homer, believing that rhythms have natural tendencies which, within certain limits, inevitably govern them; having little faith, therefore, that rhythms which have manifested tendencies utterly un-Homeric can so change themselves as to become well adapted for rendering Homer,—I have looked about for the rhythm which seems to depart least from the tendencies of Homer's rhythm. Such a rhythm I think may be found in the English hexameter, somewhat modified. I look with hope towards continued attempts at perfecting and employing this rhythm; but my belief in the immediate success of such attempts is far less confident than has been supposed. Between the recognition of this rhythm as ideally the best, and the recommenda-

tion of it to the translator for instant practical use, there must come all that consideration of circumstances, all that pliancy in foregoing, under the pressure of certain difficulties, the absolute best, which I have said is so indispensable to the critic.
5 The hexameter is, comparatively, still unfamiliar in England; many people have a great dislike to it. A certain degree of unfamiliarity, a certain degree of dislike, are obstacles with which it is not wise to contend. It is difficult to say at present whether the dislike to this rhythm is so strong and so wide-
10 spread that it will prevent its ever becoming thoroughly familiar. I think not, but it is too soon to decide. I am inclined to think that the dislike of it is rather among the professional critics than among the general public; I think the reception which Mr. Longfellow's *Evangeline* has met with indicates
15 this. I think that even now, if a version of the *Iliad* in English hexameters were made by a poet who, like Mr. Longfellow, has that indefinable quality which renders him popular,—something *attractive* in his talent, which communicates itself to his verses,—it would have a great success among the general pub-
20 lic. Yet a version of Homer in hexameters of the *Evangeline* type would not satisfy the judicious, nor is the definite establishment of this type to be desired; and one would regret that Mr. Longfellow should, even to popularise the hexameter, give the immense labour required for a translation of Homer, when
25 one could not wish his work to stand. Rather it is to be wished that by the efforts of poets like Mr. Longfellow in original poetry, and the efforts of less distinguished poets in the task of translation, the hexameter may gradually be made familiar to the ear of the English public; at the same time that there
30 gradually arises, out of all these efforts, an improved type of this rhythm; a type which some man of genius may sign with the final stamp, and employ in rendering Homer; a hexameter which may be as superior to Voss's as Shakspeare's blank verse is superior to Schiller's. I am inclined to believe
35 that all this travail will actually take place, because I believe that modern poetry is actually in want of such an instrument as the hexameter.

In the meantime, whether this rhythm be destined to success

or not, let us steadily keep in mind what originally made us turn to it. We turned to it because we required certain Homeric characteristics in a translation of Homer, and because all other rhythms seemed to find, from different causes, great difficulties in satisfying this our requirement. If the hexameter is impossible, if one of these other rhythms must be used, let us keep this rhythm always in mind of our requirements and of its own faults, let us compel it to get rid of these latter as much as possible. It may be necessary to have recourse to blank verse; but then blank verse must *de-Cowperise* itself, must get rid of the habits of stiff self-retardation which make it say '*Not fewer* shone,' for '*So many* shone.' Homer moves swiftly: blank verse *can* move swiftly if it likes, but it must remember that the movement of such lines as

> A thousand fires were burning, and by each . . .

is just the slow movement which makes us despair of it. Homer moves with noble ease: blank verse must not be suffered to forget that the movement of

> Came they not over from sweet Lacedæmon . . .

is ungainly. Homer's expression of his thought is simple as light: we know how blank verse affects such locutions as

> While the steeds *mouthed their corn aloof* . . .

and such modes of expressing one's thought are sophisticated and artificial.

One sees how needful it is to direct incessantly the English translator's attention to the essential characteristics of Homer's poetry, when so accomplished a person as Mr. Spedding, recognising these characteristics as indeed Homer's, admitting them to be essential, is led by the ingrained habits and tendencies of English blank verse thus repeatedly to lose sight of them in translating even a few lines. One sees this yet more clearly, when Mr. Spedding, taking me to task for saying that the blank verse used for rendering Homer 'must not be Mr. Tennyson's blank verse,' declares that in most of Mr. Tennyson's blank verse all Homer's essential characteristics—'rapidity of movement, *plainness of words and style, simplicity and directness of ideas*, and, above all, nobleness of manner—are as conspicuous as in Homer himself.' This shows, it seems to me, how hard it is for English readers of poetry, even the most accomplished, to feel deeply and permanently what Greek plainness of thought and Greek simplicity of expression really are: they admit the importance of these qualities in a general way, but they have no ever-present sense of them; and they easily attribute them to any poetry which has other excellent qualities, and which they very much admire. No doubt there are plainer things in Mr. Tennyson's poetry than the three lines I quoted; in choosing them, as in choosing a specimen of ballad-poetry, I wished to bring out clearly, by a strong instance, the qualities of thought and style to which I was calling attention; but when Mr. Spedding talks of a plainness of thought *like Homer's*, of a plainness of speech *like Homer's*, and says that he finds these constantly in Mr. Tennyson's poetry, I answer that these I do not find there at all. Mr. Tennyson is a most distinguished and charming poet; but the very essential characteristic of his poetry is, it seems to me, an extreme subtlety and curious elaborateness of thought, an extreme subtlety and curious elaborateness of expression. In the best and most characteristic productions of his genius, these characteristics are most prominent. They are marked characteristics, as we have seen, of the Elizabethan poets; they are marked, though not the essential, characteristics of Shakspeare himself. Under the influences of the nineteenth century, under wholly new conditions of thought and culture, they manifest themselves in Mr. Tennyson's poetry in a wholly new way. But they are still there. The essential bent of his poetry is towards such expressions as—

> Now lies the Earth all Danaë to the stars;
>
> O'er the sun's bright eye
> Drew the vast eyelid of an inky cloud;

> When the cairned mountain was a shadow, sunned
> The world to peace again;
>
> The fresh young captains flashed their glittering teeth,
> The huge bush-bearded barons heaved and blew;
>
> He bared the knotted column of his throat, 5
> The massive square of his heroic breast,
> And arms on which the standing muscle sloped
> As slopes a wild brook o'er a little stone,
> Running too vehemently to break upon it.

And this way of speaking is the least *plain*, the most *un-Homeric*, which can possibly be conceived. Homer presents his thought to you just as it wells from the source of his mind: Mr. Tennyson carefully distils his thought before he will part with it. Hence comes, in the expression of the thought, a heightened and elaborate air. In Homer's poetry it is all natural thoughts in natural words; in Mr. Tennyson's poetry it is all distilled thoughts in distilled words. Exactly this heightening and elaboration may be observed in Mr. Spedding's

> While the steeds *mouthed their corn aloof*,

(an expression which might have been Mr. Tennyson's) on which I have already commented; and to one who is penetrated with a sense of the real simplicity of Homer, this subtle sophistication of the thought is, I think, very perceptible even in such lines as these,—

> And drunk delight of battle with my peers, 25
> Far on the ringing plains of windy Troy,—

which I have seen quoted as perfectly Homeric. Perfect simplicity can be obtained only by a genius of which perfect simplicity is an essential characteristic.

So true is this, that when a genius essentially subtle, or a genius which, from whatever cause, is in its essence not truly and broadly simple, determines to be perfectly plain, determines not to admit a shade of subtlety or curiosity into its expression, it cannot even then attain real simplicity; it can only attain a semblance of simplicity.[1] French criticism, richer in its vocabulary than ours, has invented a useful word to distinguish this semblance (often very beautiful and valuable) 5 from the real quality. The real quality it calls *simplicité*, the semblance *simplesse*. The one is natural simplicity, the other is artificial simplicity. What is called simplicity in the productions of a genius essentially not simple, is, in truth, *simplesse*. The two are distinguishable from one another the moment 10 they appear in company. For instance, let us take the opening of the narrative in Wordsworth's *Michael*:—

> Upon the forest-side in Grasmere Vale
> There dwelt a shepherd, Michael was his name;
> An old man, stout of heart, and strong of limb.
> 15 His bodily frame had been from youth to age
> Of an unusual strength; his mind was keen,
> Intense, and frugal, apt for all affairs;
> And in his shepherd's calling he was prompt
> And watchful more than ordinary men.

20 Now let us take the opening of the narrative in Mr. Tennyson's *Dora*:—

> With Farmer Allan at the farm abode
> William and Dora. William was his son,
> And she his niece. He often looked at them,
> 25 And often thought, 'I'll make them man and wife.'

The simplicity of the first of these passages is *simplicité;* that of the second, *simplesse*. Let us take the end of the same two poems; first, of *Michael*:—

[1] I speak of poetic genius as employing itself upon narrative or dramatic 30 poetry,—poetry in which the poet has to go out of himself and to create. In lyrical poetry, in the direct expression of personal feeling, the most subtle genius may, under the momentary pressure of passion, express itself simply. Even here, however, the native tendency will generally be discernible.

The cottage which was named the Evening Star
Is gone,—the ploughshare has been through the ground
On which it stood; great changes have been wrought
In all the neighbourhood: yet the oak is left
That grew beside their door: and the remains 5
Of the unfinished sheepfold may be seen
Beside the boisterous brook of Green-head Ghyll.

And now, of *Dora:*—

So those four abode
Within one house together; and as years
Went forward, Mary took another mate: 10
But Dora lived unmarried till her death.

A heedless critic may call both of these passages simple if he will. Simple, in a certain sense, they both are; but between the simplicity of the two there is all the difference that there is between the simplicity of Homer and the simplicity of 15 Moschus.

But—whether the hexameter establish itself or not, whether a truly simple and rapid blank verse be obtained or not, as the vehicle for a standard English translation of Homer—I feel sure that this vehicle will not be furnished by the ballad-form. 20 On this question about the ballad-character of Homer's poetry, I see that Professor Blackie proposes a compromise: he suggests that those who say Homer's poetry is pure ballad-poetry, and those who deny that it is ballad-poetry at all, should split the difference between them; that it should be agreed that Homer's 25 poems are ballads *a little*, but not so much as some have said. I am very sensible to the courtesy of the terms in which Mr. Blackie invites me to this compromise; but I cannot, I am sorry to say, accept it; I cannot allow that Homer's poetry is ballad-poetry at all. A want of capacity for sustained noble- 30 ness seems to me inherent in the ballad-form when employed for epic poetry. The more we examine this proposition, the more certain, I think, will it become to us. Let us but observe how a great poet, having to deliver a narrative very weighty and serious, instinctively shrinks from the ballad-form as from 35 a form not commensurate with his subject-matter, a form too narrow and shallow for it, and seeks for a form which has more amplitude and impressiveness. Every one knows the *Lucy Gray* and the *Ruth* of Wordsworth. Both poems are excellent; but the subject-matter of the narrative of *Ruth* is much more weighty and impressive to the poet's own feeling than that of the narrative of *Lucy Gray*, for which latter, in its unpretending simplicity, the ballad-form is quite adequate. Wordsworth, at the time he composed *Ruth*,—his great time, his *annus mirabilis*, about 1800,—strove to be simple; it was his mission to be simple; he loved the ballad-form, he clung to it, because it was simple. Even in *Ruth* he tried, one may say, to use it; he would have used it if he could: but the gravity of his matter is too much for this somewhat slight form; he is obliged to give to his form more amplitude, more augustness, to shake out its folds.

> The wretched parents all that night
> Went shouting far and wide;
> But there was neither sound nor sight
> To serve them for a guide.

That is beautiful, no doubt, and the form is adequate to the subject-matter. But take this, on the other hand:—

> I, too, have passed her on the hills,
> Setting her little water-mills
> By spouts and fountains wild;
> Such small machinery as she turned,
> Ere she had wept, ere she had mourned,
> A young and happy child.

Who does not perceive how the greater fulness and weight of his matter has here compelled the true and feeling poet to adopt a form of more *volume* than the simple ballad-form?

It is of narrative poetry that I am speaking; the question is about the use of the ballad-form for *this*. I say that for this poetry (when in the grand style, as Homer's is) the ballad-form is entirely inadequate; and that Homer's translator must not adopt it, because it even leads him, by its own weakness, away from the grand style rather than towards it. We must remember that the matter of narrative poetry stands in a different relation to the vehicle which conveys it,—is not so independent of this vehicle, so absorbing and powerful in itself,—as the matter of purely emotional poetry. When there comes in poetry what I may call the *lyrical cry*, this transfigures everything, makes everything grand; the simplest form may be here even an advantage, because the flame of the emotion glows through and through it more easily. To go again for an illustration to Wordsworth;—our great poet, since Milton, by his performance, as Keats, I think, is our great poet by his gift and promise;—in one of his stanzas to the Cuckoo, we have:—

> And I can listen to thee yet;
> Can lie upon the plain
> And listen, till I do beget
> That golden time again.

Here the lyrical cry, though taking the simple ballad-form, is as grand as the lyrical cry coming in poetry of an ampler form, as grand as the

> An innocent life, yet far astray!

of *Ruth;* as the

> There is a comfort in the strength of love

of *Michael.* In this way, by the occurrence of this lyrical cry, the ballad-poets themselves rise sometimes, though not so often as one might perhaps have hoped, to the grand style.

> O lang, lang may their ladies sit,
> Wi' their fans into their hand,
> Or ere they see Sir Patrick Spence
> Come sailing to the land.
>
> O lang, lang may the ladies stand,
> Wi' their gold combs in their hair,

Waiting for their ain dear lords,
For they'll see them nae mair.

But from this impressiveness of the ballad-form, when its subject-matter fills it over and over again,—is, indeed, in itself, 5 all in all,—one must not infer its effectiveness when its subject-matter is not thus overpowering, in the great body of a narrative.

But, after all, Homer is not a better poet than the balladists, because he has taken in the hexameter a better instrument; he 10 took this instrument because he was a *different* poet from them; so different,—not only so much better, but so essentially different,—that he is not to be classed with them at all. Poets receive their distinctive character, not from their subject, but from their application to that subject of the ideas (to 15 quote the *Excursion*)

On God, on Nature, and on human life,

which they have acquired for themselves. In the ballad-poets in general, as in men of a rude and early stage of the world, in whom their humanity is not yet variously and fully de- 20 veloped, the stock of these ideas is scanty, and the ideas themselves not very effective or profound. [For] them the narrative itself is the great matter, not the spirit and significance which underlies the narrative. Even in later times of richly developed life and thought, poets appear who have what may be called 25 a *balladist's mind;* in whom a fresh and lively curiosity for the outward spectacle of the world is much more strong than their sense of the inward significance of that spectacle. When they apply ideas to their narrative of human events, you feel that they are, so to speak, travelling out of their own province: 30 in the best of them you feel this perceptibly, but in those of a lower order you feel it very strongly. Even Sir Walter Scott's efforts of this kind,—even, for instance, the

Breathes there the man with soul so dead,

or the

> O woman! in our hours of ease,—

even these leave, I think, as high poetry, much to be desired; far more than the same poet's descriptions of a hunt or a battle. But Lord Macaulay's 5

> Then out spake brave Horatius,
> The captain of the gate:
> 'To all the men upon this earth
> Death cometh soon or late,'

(and here, since I have been reproached with undervaluing 10 Lord Macaulay's *Lays of Ancient Rome*, let me frankly say that, to my mind, a man's power to detect the ring of false metal in those Lays is a good measure of his fitness to give an opinion about poetical matters at all),—I say, Lord Macaulay's 15

> To all the men upon this earth
> Death cometh soon or late,

it is hard to read without a cry of pain. But with Homer it is very different. This 'noble barbarian,' this 'savage with the lively eye,'—whose verse, Mr. Newman thinks, would affect 20 us, if we could hear the living Homer, 'like an elegant and simple melody from an African of the Gold Coast,'—is never more at home, never more nobly himself, than in applying profound ideas to his narrative. As a poet he belongs—narrative as is his poetry, and early as is his date—to an incomparably 25 more developed spiritual and intellectual order than the balladists, or than Scott and Macaulay; he is here as much to be distinguished from them, and in the same way, as Milton is to be distinguished from them. He is, indeed, rather to be classed with Milton than with the balladists and Scott; for 30 what he has in common with Milton—the noble and profound application of ideas to life—is the most essential part of poetic greatness. The most essentially grand and characteristic things of Homer are such things as—

> ἔτλην δ', οἷ' οὔ πώ τις ἐπιχθόνιος βροτὸς ἄλλος,
> ἀνδρὸς παιδοφόνοιο ποτὶ στόμα χεῖρ' ὀρέγεσθαι,[1]

5 or as—

> καὶ σὲ, γέρον, τὸ πρὶν μὲν ἀκούομεν ὄλβιον εἶναι,[2]

or as—

> ὧς γὰρ ἐπεκλώσαντο θεοὶ δειλοῖσι βροτοῖσιν,
> ζώειν ἀχνυμένους · αὐτοὶ δέ τ' ἀκηδέες εἰσίν,[3]

10 and of these the tone is given, far better than by anything of the balladists, by such things as the

> Io non piangeva: sì dentro impietrai:
> Piangevan elli . . .[4]

of Dante; or the

15 > Fall'n Cherub! to be weak is miserable

of Milton.

I suppose I must, before I conclude, say a word or two about my own hexameters; and yet really, on such a topic, I am almost ashamed to trouble you. From those perishable

20 [1] 'And I have endured—the like whereof no soul upon the earth hath yet endured—to carry to my lips the hand of him who slew my child.' —*Iliad*, xxiv. 505.

[2] 'Nay and thou too, old man, in times past wert, as we hear, happy.' —*Iliad*, xxiv. 543. In the original this line, for mingled pathos and dignity,
25 is perhaps without a rival even in Homer.

[3] 'For so have the gods spun our destiny to us wretched mortals,—that we should live in sorrow; but they themselves are without trouble.' —*Iliad*, xxiv. 525.

[4] '*I* wept not: so of stone grew I within:—*they* wept.'—*Hell*, xxxiii. 49
30 (Carlyle's Translation, slightly altered).

objects I feel, I can truly say, a most Oriental detachment. You yourselves are witnesses how little importance, when I offered them to you, I claimed for them,—how humble a function I designed them to fill. I offered them, not as specimens of a competing translation of Homer, but as illustrations of certain canons which I had been trying to establish for Homer's poetry. I said that these canons they might very well illustrate by failing as well as by succeeding: if they illustrate them in any manner, I am satisfied. I was thinking of the future translator of Homer, and trying to let him see as clearly as possible what I meant by the combination of characteristics which I assigned to Homer's poetry,—by saying that this poetry was at once rapid in movement, plain in words and style, simple and direct in its ideas, and noble in manner. I do not suppose that my own hexameters are rapid in movement, plain in words and style, simple and direct in their ideas, and noble in manner; but I am in hopes that a translator, reading them with a genuine interest in his subject, and without the slightest grain of personal feeling, may see more clearly, as he reads them, what I mean by saying that Homer's poetry is all these. I am in hopes that he may be able to seize more distinctly, when he has before him my

> So shone forth, in front of Troy, by the bed of the Xanthus,

or my

> Ah, unhappy pair, to Peleus why did we give you?

or my

> So he spake, and drove with a cry his steeds into battle,

the exact points which I wish him to avoid in Cowper's

> So numerous seemed those fires the banks between,

or in Pope's

Unhappy coursers of immortal strain,

or in Mr. Newman's

He spake, and, yelling, held a-front his single-hoofed horses.

At the same time there may be innumerable points in mine which he ought to avoid also. Of the merit of his own compositions no composer can be admitted the judge.

But thus humbly useful to the future translator I still hope my hexameters may prove; and he it is, above all, whom one has to regard. The general public carries away little from discussions of this kind, except some vague notion that one advocates English hexameters, or that one has attacked Mr. Newman. On the mind of an adversary one never makes the faintest impression. Mr. Newman reads all one can say about diction, and his last word on the subject is, that he 'regards it as a question about to open hereafter, whether a translator of Homer ought not to adopt the old dissyllabic *landis, houndis, hartis*' (for lands, hounds, harts), and also 'the final *en* of the plural of verbs (we *dancen*, they *singen*, etc.),' which 'still subsists in Lancashire.' A certain critic reads all one can say about style, and at the end of it arrives at the inference that, 'after all, there is some style grander than the grand style itself, since Shakspeare has not the grand manner, and yet has the supremacy over Milton;' another critic reads all one can say about rhythm, and the result is, that he thinks Scott's rhythm, in the description of the death of Marmion, all the better for being *saccadé*, because the dying ejaculations of Marmion were likely to be 'jerky.' How vain to rise up early, and to take rest late, from any zeal for proving to Mr. Newman that he must not, in translating Homer, say *houndis* and *dancen;* or to the first of the two critics above quoted, that one poet may be a greater poetical force than another, and yet have a more unequal style; or to the second, that the best art, having to represent the death of a hero, does not set about imitating his dying noises! Such critics, however, provide for an opponent's vivacity the charming excuse offered by Rivarol for his, when he was reproached with giving offence by it:—'Ah!' he exclaimed, 'no one considers how much pain every man of taste has had to *suffer*, before he ever inflicts any.'

It is for the future translator that one must work. The successful translator of Homer will have (or he cannot succeed) that true sense for his subject, and that disinterested love of it, which are, both of them, so rare in literature, and so precious; he will not be led off by any false scent; he will have an eye for the real matter, and, where he thinks he may find any indication of this, no hint will be too slight for him, no shade will be too fine, no imperfections will turn him aside,—he will go before his adviser's thought, and help it out with his own. This is the sort of student that a critic of Homer should always have in his thoughts; but students of this sort are indeed rare.

And how, then, can I help being reminded what a student of this sort we have just lost in Mr. Clough, whose name I have already mentioned in these lectures? He, too, was busy with Homer; but it is not on that account that I now speak of him. Nor do I speak of him in order to call attention to his qualities and powers in general, admirable as these were. I mention him because, in so eminent a degree, he possessed these two invaluable literary qualities,—a true sense for his object of study, and a single-hearted care for it. He had both; but he had the second even more eminently than the first. He greatly developed the first through means of the second. In the study of art, poetry, or philosophy, he had the most undivided and disinterested love for his object in itself, the greatest aversion to mixing up with it anything accidental or personal. His interest was in literature itself; and it was this which gave so rare a stamp to his character, which kept him so free from all taint of littleness. In the saturnalia of ignoble personal passions, of which the struggle for literary success, in old and crowded communities, offers so sad a spectacle, he never mingled. He had not yet traduced his friends, nor flattered his enemies, nor disparaged what he admired, nor praised what he despised. Those who knew him well had the conviction that, even with time, these literary arts would never be his. His poem, of which I before spoke, has some admirable Homeric qualities;—out-of-doors freshness, life, naturalness, buoyant rapidity. Some of the expressions in that poem,—'*Dangerous Corrievreckan . . . Where roads are unknown to* 5 *Loch Nevish*,'—come back now to my ear with the true Homeric ring. But that in him of which I think oftenest is the Homeric simplicity of his literary life.

Critical and Explanatory Notes

[PREFACE TO FIRST EDITION OF *Poems* (1853)]

Arnold brought out his first two volumes of poetry through his father's publisher, Fellowes, with only his initial, "A.," on the title page, on February 26, 1849, and October 27, 1852. In May, 1853, he wrote to his mother that he had just completed "Sohrab and Rustum" and had "settled with Fellowes to publish this, and one or two more new ones, with the most popular of the old ones, next winter or spring, with a preface, and my name." On August 25 he told Clough that J. A. Froude "rather discounsels from a preface, but I shall try my hand at it, at any rate," and by October 1 it was completed. "There is a certain *Geist* in it I think," he told Clough nine days later, "but it is far less *precise* than I had intended. How difficult it is to write prose: and why? because of the *articulations of the discourse:* one leaps these over in Poetry—places one thought cheek by jowl with another without introducing them and leaves them—but in prose this will not do." The volume of *Poems*, with its Preface, was published by Longman on November 18 at Arnold's risk, at the price of 5*s*. 6*d*.

Like almost all Arnold's prose writing, the Preface is essentially polemic—part of a running debate with the popular currents of opinion in his day as expressed in the literary journals—and the journals were not slow to accept the challenge: the Preface attracted their attention from the poems to an extent far out of proportion to the merit of the latter. Though the notes from which Arnold worked as he wrote it have not survived, there is evidence that he jotted down useful phrases from his reading as he encountered them (just as the *Note-Books* show that he did for the rest of his life): the statements of contemporary critics that he confutes are debated out of their context, and in their original surroundings are not always so opposed to Arnold's view as he here makes them appear. The two principal studies of the Preface as a debate with the journalists are H. W. Garrod, "Matthew Arnold's 1853 Preface," *Review of English Studies* XVII, 310–21 (July, 1941), and J. D. Jump, "Matthew Arnold and the *Spectator*," *ibid.* XXV, 61–64 (January, 1949).

Unlike much of his later writing, however, this Preface was not directed at a popular audience; it was the work of a poet and critic addressed to other poets and critics, and has therefore a seriousness and even solemnity that Arnold later dropped when he addressed a wider audience. It depends heavily upon Aristotle's *Poetics,* but the central point it makes is one that Arnold had turned over in his mind for several years and had often discussed (with developments and modifications that amounted to a reversal of his initial position) in his letters to Clough (ed. H. F. Lowry; London, 1932). One of the principal causes of misunderstanding was his failure to announce that by "poetry" he meant (as Aristotle did) epic and dramatic poetry; that he did mean this, however, is clear not only from his discussion but also from the first paragraph of his Preface to the edition of 1854. The first long poem in the volume the 1853 Preface introduced was the epic "episode" of "Sohrab and Rustum" and the one that had been withdrawn was the "dramatic poem" "Empedocles on Etna." A splendid study of the significance of the Preface, its origins in the Clough correspondence, and its dependence upon Aristotle is the ninth chapter of A. H. Warren's *English Poetic Theory, 1825–1865* (Princeton, 1950).

The Second Edition of the *Poems,* which reprinted the first Preface with the addition of the brief new one, appeared about June 17, 1854 (5*s.* 6*d.*), and the Third Edition, which reprinted both, on June 6, 1857 (also 5*s.* 6*d.*). Thereafter, both were dropped from the succeeding editions of Arnold's poetry, but they were printed again in *Irish Essays and Others* (1882), where Arnold introduced them with the remark: "Some of the readers of my poetry have expressed a wish for their reappearance, and with that wish I here comply. Exactly as they stand, I should not have written them now; but perhaps they are none the worse on that account."

1:5. "Empedocles on Etna," not reprinted by Arnold until 1867.

1:29–2:4. *Poetics* 4. 1–5.

2:17–18. *Theogony* 55; cf. also 102–3.

2:19–20. Cf. Horace *Ars Poetica* 333–34:

Aut prodesse volunt aut delectare poetae,
Aut simul et jucunda et idonea dicere vitae.

To teach—to please—comprise the poet's views,
Or else at once to profit and amuse.
—tr. Francis Howes

2:21–24. Preface to *Die Braut von Messina*, in *Sämmtliche Werke* (Stuttgart, 1862), V, 344.

3:2–6. Arnold seems to have in mind Aristotle's *Poetics* 4. 3 (though he draws a different conclusion), and 11. 6: "No less universal is the pleasure felt in things imitated. . . . Objects which in themselves we view with pain, we delight to contemplate when reproduced with minute fidelity: such as the forms of the most ignoble animals and of dead bodies." "A third part [of Plot] is the Scene of Suffering. The Scene of Suffering is a destructive or painful action, such as death on the stage, bodily agony, wounds and the like."—tr. S. H. Butcher.

3:20–23. The sentence appears in a review of Edwin Arnold's *Poems Narrative and Lyrical* (*Spectator*, April 2, 1853, p. 325); the word "therefore" is italicized by Arnold. When Arnold later attributed the review to R. S. Rintoul, editor of the *Spectator*, he omitted the modifying adverb from his original phrase, "an apparently intelligent critic."—*Unpublished Letters of Matthew Arnold*, ed. Arnold Whitridge (New Haven, 1923), p. 22.

3:31–34. Cf. Aristotle *Poetics* 6. 9–10: "Most important of all is the structure of the incidents. For Tragedy is an imitation, not of men, but of an action and of life, and life consists in action, and its end is a mode of action, not a quality. Now character determines men's qualities, but it is by their actions that they are happy or the reverse. Dramatic action, therefore, is not with a view to the representation of character: character comes in as subsidiary to the actions. Hence the incidents and the plot are the end of a tragedy; and the end is the chief thing of all." —tr. S. H. Butcher.

4:4–26. Cf. *ibid.* 13. 1–2, 5; 9. 2–4, 9: "We must proceed to consider what the poet should aim at, and what he should avoid, in constructing his plots; and by what means the specific effect of Tragedy will be produced. A perfect tragedy should . . . imitate actions which excite pity and fear, this being the distinctive mark of tragic imitation. . . . The practice of the stage bears out our view. At first the poets recounted any legend that came in their way. Now, the best tragedies are founded on the story of a few houses,—on the fortunes of Alcmaeon, Oedipus, Orestes, Meleager, Thyestes, Telephus, and those others who have done or suffered something terrible." "The true difference [between the poet and the historian] is that one relates what has happened, the other what may happen. Poetry, therefore, is a more philosophical and a higher thing than history: for poetry tends to express the universal, history the particular. By the universal I mean how a person of a certain type will on occasion speak or act, according to the law of probability or necessity; and it is this universality at which poetry aims in the names she attaches to the personages. . . . The poet or 'maker' should be the maker of plots rather than of verses; since he is a poet because he imitates, and what he imitates are actions. And even if he chances to take an historical subject, he is none the less a poet; for there is no reason why some events that have actually happened should not conform to the law of the probable and possible, and in virtue of that quality in them he is their poet or maker."—tr. S. H. Butcher.

4:27. A hero from epic and tragedy (the *Iliad* and Aeschylus' *Prometheus Bound*) and a heroine from tragedy and epic (Aeschylus' *Agamemnon* and Vergil's *Aeneid* iv).

4:35–36. A domestic epic by Goethe (1797), Byron's "pageant of his bleeding heart" (1812–18), a narrative poem by Alphonse de Lamartine (1836), and Wordsworth's long philosophical poem (1814).

6:13. All three of these are mentioned by Aristotle as subjects of Greek tragedy, but Orestes alone is the subject of tragedies now extant.

6:18–28. Aristotle also speaks of the advantage of the dramatist's using a story already known to the audience, though not in Arnold's terms (*Poetics* 9. 6–8).

7:7. Polybius commonly uses πραγματεία for historical writing, but not for epic or dramatic poetry. Can Arnold be punning on πραγματικὸν ποιῆσαι (iii. 116, 7)? Polybius' use of "pragmatic" is discussed in K. O. Mueller, *History of the Literature of Ancient Greece*, tr. and continued by J. W. Donaldson (London, 1858), III, 77.

7:12–14. Cf. Aristotle *Poetics* 17. 1–2: "In constructing the plot and working it out with the proper diction, the poet should place the scene, as far as possible, before his eyes. . . . Again, the poet should work out his play, to the best of his power, with appropriate gestures; for those who feel emotion are most convincing through natural sympathy with the characters they represent."—tr. S. H. Butcher. And see also Arnold's citation, in *Note-Books* (ed. Lowry), p. 533, of a passage from Voltaire's letter to Cideville, November 6, 1733: "Le succès est dans le sujet même. Si le sujet n'est pas intéressant, les vers de Virgile et de Racine, les éclairs et les raisonnements de Corneille, ne feraient pas réussir l'ouvrage."

7:20–24. Plutarch tells this story (*Moralia* 347 E-F) to make precisely the same point Arnold is making.

8:12–15. See [David Masson], "Theories of Poetry and a New Poet," *North British Review*, American edition, XIX, 180 (August 1853): "There is, indeed, [in Alexander Smith's 'A Life Drama'] an attempt, as in the *Faust* of Goethe and other poems, to make the poem a kind of sublimated biography. . . . Now, as we have already said, a true allegory of the state of one's own mind in a representative history, whether narrative or dramatic in form, is perhaps the highest thing that one can attempt in the way of fictitious art." Masson has already alluded (p. 170) to "Goethe's theory of poetical or creative literature, [which] was, that it is nothing else than the moods of its practitioners objectivized as they rise. . . . Scheming out some plan or story, which is in itself a sort of allegory of his mood as a whole, he fills up the sketch with minor incidents, scenes, and characters."

8:25–26. "Der Faust ist doch ganz etwas Inkommensurabeles, und alle Versuche, ihn dem Verstand näher zu bringen, sind vergeblich. Auch muss man bedenken, dass der erste Teil aus einem etwas dunkelen Zustand des Individuums hervorgegangen. Aber eben dieses Dunkel reizt die Menschen, und sie mühen sich daran ab, wie an allen unauflösbaren Problemen."—Eckermann, *Gespräche mit Goethe*, Jan. 3, 1830.

9:25–29. Goethe, "Über den sogennanten Dilettantismus" (1799), *Werke* (Stuttgart, 1833), XLIV, 262–63: "Was dem Dilettanten eigentlich fehlt, ist Architektonik im höchsten Sinne, diejenige ausübende Kraft, welche erschafft, bildet, constituirt. Er hat davon nur eine Art von Ahnung, giebt sich aber durchaus dem Stoff dahin, anstatt ihn zu beherrschen." The Weimar ed. (XLVII, 326) gives a slightly different version.

10:5–6. Arnold's remark may fairly summarize a review of Gautier's *Emaux et Camées* and other books, Alfred Crampon's "Les Fantaisistes," *Revue des deux mondes*, n.s., XVI, 582–97 (November 1, 1852), but I do not find these words.

10:7–32. The notions here expressed may be traced in Arnold's correspondence with Clough and in Clough's review of *Empedocles on Etna, and Other Poems.* See especially Arnold to Clough, October 28, 1852: "More and more I feel that the difference between a mature and a youthful age of the world compels the poetry of the former to use great plainness of speech as compared with that of the latter: and that Keats and Shelley were on a false track when they set themselves to reproduce the exuberance of expression, the charm, the richness of images, and the felicity, of the Elizabethan poets. Yet critics cannot get to learn this, because the Elizabethan poets are our greatest, and our canons of poetry are founded on their works. They still think that the object of poetry is to produce exquisite bits and images—such as Shelley's *clouds shepherded by the slow unwilling wind*, and Keats passim: whereas modern poetry can only subsist by its *contents:* by becoming a complete magister vitae as the poetry of the ancients did: by including, as theirs did, religion with poetry, instead of existing as poetry only, and leaving religious wants to be supplied by the Christian religion, as a power existing independent of the poetical power. But the language, style and general proceedings of a poetry which has such an immense task to perform, must be very plain direct and severe: and it must not lose itself in parts and episodes and ornamental work, but must press forwards to the whole." Clough's article in the *North American Review* LXXVII, 1–30 (July, 1853) discusses Alexander Smith's "A Life Drama" along with Arnold's volume; of the former he remarks that its antecedents "are to be found in the 'Princess,' in parts of Mrs. Browning, in the love of Keats, and the *habit* of Shakespeare. . . . We have before us, we may say, the latest disciple of the school of Keats, who was indeed no well of English undefiled, though doubtless the fountain-head of a true poetic stream. Alexander Smith . . . has given us, so to say, his Endymion." "He writes, it would almost seem, under the impression that the one business of the poet is to coin metaphors and similes. . . . The attention, which the reader desires to devote to the pursuit of the main drift of what calls itself a single poem, *simplex et unum,* is so incessantly called off to look at this and look at that; . . . that on the whole, though there *is* a real continuity of purpose, we cannot be surprised that the critic of the 'London Examiner' failed to detect it. Keats and Shelley, and Coleridge, perhaps, before them, with their extravagant love for

Elizabethan phraseology, have led to this mischief. Has not Tennyson followed a little too much in their train?"—A. H. Clough, *Prose Remains* (London, 1888), pp. 355–56, 374–76. See also Arnold's letters to Clough, c. 1848–49 (ed. H. F. Lowry, pp. 96–101).

10:13–14. See [David Masson], "Theories of Poetry and a New Poet," *North British Review*, American edition, XIX, 172 (August, 1853): "Leisurely compositions of the sweet sensuous order such as Keats' *Endymion* and Spenser's *Faery Queene*."

10:29. Boccaccio, *Decameron*, IV, 5.

11:12–16. Henry Hallam, *Introduction to the Literature of Europe in the Fifteenth, Sixteenth, and Seventeenth Centuries* (2d edition; London, 1843), III, 91–92.

11:24–26. Guizot conceives that Shakespeare wrote his Sonnets "dans un temps où l'esprit, comme tourmenté de son inexpérience et de sa jeunesse, essayait de toutes les formes, excepté de la simplicité."—*Shakspeare et son temps* (Paris, 1852), p. 114.

13:19. "It's hard to be good." Recorded by Diogenes Laertius i. 76, and by Plato *Protagoras* 343 C.

13:27–28. Alexander Smith, "A Life Drama," sc. II, *Poems* (Boston, 1853), p. 24:

> "My Friend! a Poet must ere long arise
> And with a regal song sun-crown this age, . . .
> A mighty Poet whom this age shall choose
> To be its spokesman to all coming times."

The passage is quoted by the reviewer in *North British Review*, American edition, XIX, 177–78 (August, 1853), as "a crudity, a piece of immature thought, and that too of a rather inferior quality."

14:11–12. See, for example, Niebuhr's letter to Savigny, February 19, 1830, in which after high praise of Goethe, he remarks, "How barren and dumb is our literature now! How apathetic are all hearts!"—*Life and Letters of Barthold George Niebuhr* (New York, 1852), p. 519. See also Goethe's remark to Eckermann, January 29, 1826: "Alle im Rückschreiten und in der Auflösung begriffenen Epochen sind subjektiv, dagegen aber haben alle vorschreitenden Epochen eine objektive Richtung. Unsere ganze jetzige Zeit ist eine rückschreitende, denn sie ist eine subjektive. Dieses sehen Sie nicht bloss an der Poesie, sondern auch an der Malerei und vielem anderen."

15:1–2. Vergil *Aeneid* xii. 894–95.

15:3–9. Goethe, "Über den sogenannten Dilettantismus," *Werke* (Stuttgart, 1833), XLIV, 281: "Der poetische Dilettantismus kann doppelter Art sein. Entweder vernachlässigt er das (unerlässliche) Mechanische, und glaubt genug gethan zu haben, wenn er Geist und Gefühl zeigt, oder er sucht die Poesie bloss im Mechanischen, worin er sich eine handwerksmässige Fertigkeit erwerben kann, und ist ohne Geist und Gehalt. Beide sind schädlich, doch schadet jener mehr der Kunst, dieser mehr dem Subjekt selbst."

[PREFACE TO SECOND EDITION OF *Poems* (1854)]

16:15–17:5. See *Spectator*, no. 1327 (December 3, 1853), Supplement, p. 5, in the review of Arnold's *Poems* (1853): "Because the historical Macbeth lived a thousand years ago, Mr. Arnold classes the Macbeth of our great dramatist as a subject of the past, in the same sense as the mythic legend of Oedipus, which belongs to an epoch of religion, social relations, and philosophy, difficult to apprehend even by close study of its fragments, quite impossible to present to oneself as a concrete and living whole. With the exception of the objective form given to the temptings of Macbeth's ambition, nothing in the thought or passion of the play is alien from the spirit of modern life. . . . *Macbeth* . . . is raised upon a moral and intellectual groundwork of feelings and ideas, the same as that on which the life of the audience to which it addresses itself is based, [and] appeal[s] to conceptions and sympathies already in existence and in daily exercise."

17:6–19. See J. A. Froude, review of Arnold's *Poems*, *Westminster Review*, American edition, LXI, 84 (January, 1854): "Why dwell with such apparent exclusiveness on classic antiquity, as if there was no antiquity except the classic, and as if time were divided into the eras of Greece and Rome and the nineteenth century? The Hellenic poet sang of the Hellenes, why should not the Teutonic poet sing of the Teutons? . . . the German epic Criemhilda and Von Tronjè Hagen. . . . It seems as if Teutonic tradition, Teutonic feeling, and Teutonic thought had the first claim on English and German poets." Also J. D. Coleridge, review of Arnold's *Poems*, *Christian Remembrancer* XXVII, 318–20 (April, 1854): "Ancient subjects . . . whatever those may be, are to be preferred, and, as we gather, almost exclusively preferred, to those of modern times. . . . It is, in reality, a low and narrow view of poetic art that . . . proposes to a poet as his best subject a story of classical times, to be treated in a classical style, and adorned with classical illustrations."

[ON THE MODERN ELEMENT IN LITERATURE]

Arnold was elected Professor of Poetry at Oxford on May 5, 1857, and delivered his inaugural lecture on November 14 following in the Sheldonian Theatre.[1] Wordsworth's grandson William reported the occasion to Crabb Robinson a few weeks later: "As a composition it was pointed & telling: tho' the matter was little to my taste: he seems to lust after a system of his own: and systems are not made in a day: or if they are—like a hastily-built fort, the stronger they are at one point, so much the weaker are they at another." Arnold conceived of this as the first lecture in a course on "The Modern Element in Literature," the whole of which he proposed to collect and publish as a book. None of the titles of the individual lectures in this first series has survived, but his letters to his mother give a notion of the content of some of them. Of that delivered on May 8, 1858, we know nothing except that his wife was not pleased with it; the third, on May 29, she liked better. The fourth, on December 4, was mainly on the feudal state of society and the scholastic philosophy, and at that time at least he intended to devote the fifth, on March 12, 1859, to "Dante, the troubadours, and the early Drama," and to "examine the origin of what is called the 'romantic' sentiment about women, which the Germans quite falsely are fond of giving themselves the credit of originating"; as the date grew closer he referred to it (February 16) only as a lecture "on the Troubadours." (Not until June 8, 1861, did he lecture on "The Claim of the Celtic Race, and the Claim of the Christian Religion, to Have Originated Chivalrous Sentiment," not until March 29, 1862, on "The Modern Element in Dante.") It was put together in some haste on the eve of his journey to the Continent to study elementary education there. Of the sixth lecture, on May 19, 1860, we know nothing.

[1] The newspaper announcements of the first three lectures stated that they would be delivered in the Clarendon Building, but both young Wordsworth and Arnold himself indicate the Sheldonian.

From the first Arnold was somewhat uncertain about the reception of his lectures. The audience for the second was not so large as for the first, and contained hardly any undergraduates; the theatre was "depressingly too big for us." Furthermore, his attempt to form general ideas was, he conceived, one which the Englishman naturally sets himself against. He had no doubt that his second lecture would be more satisfactory in print than it had seemed when he delivered it. Of the fourth (delivered, like all the later ones, in the smaller quarters of the Taylor Institution) he remarked that though he was not badly satisfied with it and it was necessary to the development of his course it would probably not be found interesting. In the end only the inaugural lecture was published, and that more than eleven years after it was delivered; he received £20 from *Macmillan's Magazine* for it.

Arnold's apology for its tone owes something to the fact that both the public press and (more significantly to him) his sister Jane Forster had found the published lectures *On Translating Homer* too dogmatic in their manner.

A brief and interesting restatement of the ideas in the inaugural lecture will be found in Arnold's letter to his brother Thomas on December 28, 1857, published by R. L. Lowe, *Modern Philology* LII, 262–64 (May, 1955).

18:2–4. The lecture had been summarized briefly in the review of *Merope* in *Saturday Review* (London) V, 19 (January 2, 1858).

18:25–19:10. Mr. Kenneth Allott points out that this story is taken from Eugène Burnouf, *Introduction à l'histoire du Buddhisme indien* (Paris, 1844), I, 253–54: "Va, Pûrṇá; délivré, délivre; arrivé à l'autre rive, fais-y arriver les autres; consolé, console; parvenu au Nirvâṇa complet, fais-y arriver les autres."

20:13–15. Some eight years earlier, Arnold wrote to Clough that the fault of modern English poets like Browning and Keats was that "they will not be patient neither understand that they must begin with an Idea of the world in order not to be prevailed over by the world's multitudinousness: or if they cannot get that, at least with isolated ideas: and all other things shall (perhaps) be added unto them."—*Letters of Arnold to Clough*, ed. H. F. Lowry (London, 1932), p. 97.

21:6–14. Prince Albert's address at the opening of the exhibition of art treasures at Manchester, May 5, 1857; see *The Times*, May 6, p. 9, and Arnold, *Note-Books*, ed. Lowry *et al* (London, 1952), p. 4.

23:1–3. "Life of Pope," *Six Chief Lives of the Poets*, ed. Matthew Arnold (London, 1881), p. 417.

24:10–29. Thucydides I. vi.

24:30–33. See the review of Casaubon's Diary (*Ephemerides*), *Quarterly Review*, American edition, XCIII, 264 (October, 1853).

24:37–25:3. *Kenilworth*, Chaps. 30–31. The expression "fierce vanities" appears early in the former chapter, just before the queen's arrival.

25:4–6. Reported in Thucydides II. xxxviii.

25:9–12. *Ibid.* II. xxxvii.

25:25–27. *Ibid.* I. i.

25:33–26:2. *Ibid.* I. ix–xi.

26:6–9. *Ibid.* I. xx.

26:9–17. *Ibid.* I. xxii.

26:35–38. Raleigh, *History of the World* (11th ed.; London, 1736), "Preface," p. xxx. Arnold's other references to this book are specific enough.

28:29–30. In the sonnet "To a Friend," line 12.

28:33–35. According to Plutarch, *Life of Pericles*, Sophocles and Pericles were generals together.

29:19–30. Plutarch *Moralia* 853–54. Arnold paraphrases in particular 854 B-C. Aristophanes wrote in the late fifth century, B.C., Menander in the late fourth and early third centuries.

29:32–33. Aristophanes of Byzantium (a grammarian, not the dramatist); ed. A. Nauck (1848), p. 249 (Chap. VI, fragment V).

31:8–10. W. E. Gladstone, *Homer and the Homeric Age* (Oxford, 1858), I, 10, 15 (reprinted from *Oxford Essays*, 1857).

32:24. For a comparable use of *ennui*, see Sainte-Beuve, *Chateaubriand et son groupe littéraire* (new ed.; Paris, 1889), I, 101.

32:36–33:6. A close paraphrase of *De rerum natura* iii. 1060–68.

33:8–17. A summary of *ibid.* iii. 1034–52.

33:17–20. *Ibid.* iii. 944–45.

33:28. *Ibid.* iii. 1072.

34:1–3. Almost the only biographical record of Lucretius is the statement in Jerome's addition to the Eusebian chronicle, under the year 94 B.C., "Titus Lucretius poeta nascitur. Postea amatorio poculo in furorem versus cum aliquot libros per intervalla insaniae conscribsisset quos postea Cicero emendavit, propria se manu interfecit anno aetatis XLIIII."—Lucretius *De rerum natura*, ed. H. A. J. Munro (4th edition; London, 1905), ii. 1. There is a kinship between Lucretius and the subject of Arnold's early drama,

Empedocles; furthermore, Arnold long clung to the notion of writing a tragedy about Lucretius and his age, an account of which is given in C. B. Tinker and H. F. Lowry, *The Poetry of Matthew Arnold. A Commentary* (London, 1940), pp. 340–47.

34:35–36. See Arnold, "Preface" (1853), p. 3:31–34 and note.

35:31–34. Niebuhr, like Arnold, was convinced that it was impossible for Vergil to give vitality in his epic to matter "der nicht seit Jahrhunderten als nationales Gemeingut in Volksliedern und Erzählungen lebt, so dass die cyklische Geschichte die ihn begreift, und alle die darin handeln, jedermann bekannt sind. . . . Sicher ahndete auch Virgil dass aller fremde Schmuck mit dem er sein Werk zierte wohl Reichtum des Gedichts aber nicht der seinige ward, und dass die Nachwelt dies einst erkennen werde. Dass er ungeachtet dieses quälenden Bewusstseins auf dem ihm offenen Wege dahin strebte einem Gedicht, welches er nicht aus freier Wahl schrieb, die grösste Schönheit zu geben die es aus seinen Händen empfangen konnte; . . . dass er, als der nahende Tod ihn von den Fesseln bürgerlicher Rücksichten lösste, vernichten wollte was er in diesen ernsten Stunden eben als den Stoff falsches Ruhms wehmütig betrachten musste, das macht ihn achtungswürdig, und soll uns für alle Schwächen seines Gedichts nachsichtig machen."—B. G. Niebuhr, *Römische Geschichte.* Neue Ausgabe von M. Isler (Berlin, 1873), I, 161–62 (3d ed., 1829, I, 218–19).

36:30–31. Horace *Odes* IV. vii. 13–14; Horace concludes his sentence, "pulvis et umbra sumus." Do Arnold's own words echo Landor's "I warmed both hands before the fire of life"?

[PREFACE TO *Merope*]

Merope, Arnold explained to his friend Fanny Blackett du Quaire, was "calculated rather to inaugurate my Professorship with dignity than to move deeply the present race of *humans*." He was well in the middle of it when he wrote to his sister Jane Forster on July 25, 1857, that he pleased himself pretty well with it, "though between indolence and nervousness I am a bad worker. What I learn in studying Sophocles for my present purpose is, or seems to me, wonderful; so far exceeding all that one would learn in years' reading of him without such a purpose. And what a man! What works!" Its publication was calculated to follow hard upon his inaugural lecture: Longmans (publishing as usual at Arnold's risk) announced it prematurely on December 5 as "just ready," then a fortnight later promised it for the twenty-third and advertised it as "now ready" on the day after Christmas. But again they were premature; binding had been delayed by the holidays and the book appeared on the twenty-ninth, with title page dated 1858, at a price of 5*s*. The *Saturday Review* immediately linked the work with Arnold's inaugural lecture and supported Arnold's campaign for simplicity and objectivity in poetry: "We think Mr. Arnold has rendered a real service to contemporary English literature by insisting on this; nor could he have effected his object in a better way than that he has adopted" (January 2, 1858).

The drama was not reprinted until it was incorporated in the three-volume "Library" edition of Arnold's poems in 1885; Arnold never reprinted the Preface. A "Historical Introduction" that followed the Preface in 1858 now regularly accompanies the drama in Arnold's collected poetical works and is not here reprinted.

The separate edition of *Merope* by John Churton Collins (Oxford, 1906) ignores the greater part of Arnold's Preface. An edition of Voltaire's *Mérope* by T. E. Oliver (New York, 1925) gives a scholarly survey of the history of the story in modern drama that supplements Arnold's account.

38:5–7. Mr. Kenneth Allott tells me he has always taken the critic of "fine intelligence" to be John Wilson, "Christopher North" (1785–1854). When the biography of Wilson by his daughter Mary Gordon appeared, Arnold wrote to his mother on December 3, 1862, that he planned to review it for *Fraser's*. But this is not one of the articles his *Note-Books* show him to have been working on, and apparently he never wrote it.

38:9–10. "When Phrynicus brought out upon the stage his drama of the Capture of Miletus, the whole theatre burst into tears, and the people sentenced him to pay a fine of a thousand drachmas, for recalling to them their own misfortunes. They likewise made a law that no one should ever again exhibit that piece."—Herodotus vi. 21, tr. G. Rawlinson. The story is repeated in K. O. Mueller, *History of the Literature of Ancient Greece*, tr. and continued by J. W. Donaldson (London, 1858), I, 389.

39:15–18. "I cannot in language less than hyperbolical express my admiration for this work considered in itself; but as a drama, I think an instructive parallel might be drawn between it and the *Iphigeneia* of Euripides. The enormous superiority of Goethe in intellectual stature, even aided by the immeasurable advantage he has to us of writing in a language which is in some sort our own, would not cover his inferiority as a *dramatist.*"—G. H. Lewes, *Life and Works of Goethe* (London, 1855), II, 13–14.

40:7–8. In the Epistle Dedicatory of his *Mérope* to Maffei, Voltaire remarks: "Enfin, j'ai hasardé ma tragédie, et notre nation a fait connaître qu'elle ne dédaignait pas de voir la même matière différemment traitée."—*Oeuvres complètes* (Paris, 1877–83), IV, 189.

40:26–33. Maffei in the Dedicatory Epistle of his *Merope* to Duke Rinaldo I of Modena.

40:34–37. Lessing devotes fifteen papers (nos. 36–50) of his *Hamburgische Dramaturgie* to Voltaire's *Mérope* and its antecedents. The sentence here quoted appears in no. 39, last paragraph.

41:7–11. See "Lettre du P. [René Joseph] de Tournemine, Jésuite . . . sur la tragédie de Mérope," December 23, 1738, printed by Voltaire with his play.—Voltaire, *Oeuvres complètes,* IV, 177.

41:11–14. Dedicatory Epistle of Voltaire's *Mérope* to Maffei, *ibid.*, IV, 180.

41:15–17. Aristotle *Poetics* 14. 9.

41:18–27. Plutarch *Moralia* 998 E.

41:29–31. Cicero *Tusculan Disputations* I. xlviii. 115; for scholiasts, see *Tragicorum Graecorum Fragmenta*, ed. A. Nauck, *s. v.* Euripides, *Kresphontes.* The fragments Arnold incorporated in his play are nos. 457 and 462 in Nauck's first edition (Leipzig, 1856).

42:14–34. Hyginus *Fabulae*, ed. M. Schmidt (Jena, 1872), no. 137.

42:36–43:6. Apollodorus *Library* II. viii. 5.

43:7–10. Pausanias IV. iii. 3–8. Arnold's "Historical Introduction" is printed in the Tinker and Lowry edition of his *Poetical Works* (London, 1950), pp. 325–29.

43:12–32. Arnold draws heavily on Voltaire's Epistle Dedicatory of *Mérope* to Maffei.—*Oeuvres complètes*, IV, 181–82, 184.

44:12–28. Arnold depends on Voltaire's account of the English play in the Epistle Dedicatory of *Mérope* to Maffei (*Oeuvres complètes*, IV, 184), but he adds the name of its author and the fact that it was "professedly taken from . . . Maffei." Condorcet, in his *Life of Voltaire*, tells the story of Voltaire's being forced to add a love-intrigue to his *Oedipe* (*ibid.*, I, 196). Jeffreys, whose tragedy was published in 1731, referred to "the Spirit of the Original" and "the native Beauties of my Author," and spoke of his play's being "accommodated" to the English stage. Aaron Hill supplied a Prologue for him that alluded to Merope's history on the Tuscan and the Roman stage and pointed out Jeffreys' addition of a love intrigue. Neither Jeffreys nor Hill mentioned Maffei by name.

44:31–34. Arnold, *Merope*, 349; Maffei, *La Merope*, I, i, 108–9.

45:34–47:25. Voltaire, *Oeuvres complètes*, IV, 185–89, 195. The story of the audience's "calling for" the author is told by Condorcet, *ibid.*, I, 221. The Latin line is Martial I. iii. 6.

47:36–48:7. *Hamburgische Dramaturgie*, no. 41, third paragraph: "Der Stil dieses de la Lindelle ist ziemlich der Voltairische Stil; es ist Schade, dass eine so gute Feder nicht mehr geschrieben hat und übrigens so unbekannt geblieben ist." Lessing's papers first appeared in September and October, 1767.

48:9–14. "La lettre que vous m'avez fait l'honneur de m'écrire, monsieur, doit vous valoir le nom d'hypercritique, qu'on donnait à Scaliger. Vous me paraissez bien redoutable; et si vous traitez ainsi M. Maffei, que n'ai-je point à craindre de vous! J'avoue que vous avez trop raison sur bien des points. Vous vous êtes donné la peine de ramasser beaucoup de ronces et d'épines: mais pourquoi ne vous êtes-vous pas donné le plaisir de cueillir les fleurs? . . . Je ne vous le dissimulerai pas: je trouve que M. Maffei a mis plus d'art que moi dans le manière dont il s'y prend pour faire penser à Mérope que son fils est l'assassin de son fils même."—Voltaire, *Oeuvres complètes*, IV, 196–97.

48:20–21. Not very severely in J. F. La Harpe, *Lycée, ou cours de littérature ancienne et moderne* (Paris, 1799), X, 3: "L'amertume de la censure formait comme une espèce d'antidote contre les louanges prodiguées à la *Mérope* italienne dans la dédicace de Voltaire. Le procédé n'était pas très-loyal, mais les critiques étaient justes, et l'on doit convenir que s'il a dû beaucoup à Maffei, il doit encore plus à son génie."

48:23–24. *Hamburgische Dramaturgie*, no. 37, beginning.

51:18–21. *Hamburgische Dramaturgie*, no. 50, conclusion, citing Voltaire's Dedicatory Epistle of *Mérope* to Maffei, third paragraph.

51:26–52:10. Arnold's sketch of Hill is probably drawn from *Biographia Britannica* (1766), Supplement, pp. 95–96, and from

Theophilus Cibber's *Lives of the Poets* (1753), V, 252–76. No account I have seen makes Hill a soldier, and the land he planned to settle, described in these sources as "in the South of Carolina," was in fact Georgia, not Florida. Neither source mentions the anonymous *Four Essays* (of which Arnold cites three): he may have seen them in the British Museum, where a manuscript note on the title page attributes them to Hill. Hill's *Zara* is in Mrs. Inchbald's *British Theatre*, vol. VII.

52:5–6. *The British Theatre; or, a Collection of Plays, Which Are Acted at the Theatres Royal.* With biographical and critical remarks by Mrs. [Elizabeth] Inchbald (London, 1808), 25 vols.

52:20–21. Alfieri, *Merope*, I, ii, 117–18.

53:8–9. Aristotle did not say this explicitly; his remarks on the use of "received stories" are made in *Poetics* 9. 6–9 and 13. 5.

53:9–11. Perhaps the second part of "Del romanzo storico."

53:15–19. Pausanias VIII. xxii. 9. "Katabothra" is a modern Greek word; Pausanias used "barathron."

53:36–54:3. *Hamburgische Dramaturgie*, no. 40, middle.

54:28–55:2. Aristotle *Poetics* 13. 1–3.

56:5–7. Voltaire, *Oeuvres complètes*, IV, 197.

56:15–58:5. Arnold's account of the Greek drama is drawn from K. O. Mueller, *Literature of Ancient Greece* (London, 1858), I, 383–86, 391, 402–3, 396–98, 413–14, 394, 418. He used the edition of 1840, presumably, and these chapters were translated by George Cornewall Lewis.

56:32–34. Sophocles' *Oedipus at Colonus;* see Mueller, *op. cit.*, I, 403.

58:17–22. Aristotle *Poetics* 4. 11–12 (but Arnold quotes Aristotle's sentences in inverse order).

59:16–19. "The currents of these passions are forever kept in agitation, and the alternations of pity and terror close only with the closing of the scene. In other words, in spite of the slowness of its *evolution*, the [Greek] drama is distinguished by the very absence of the *repose* which is pronounced its characteristic." —G. H. Lewes, *Goethe*, II, 11.

59:21–25. "It is evident that the tragic situation in this story is the slaughter of a brother by a sister ignorant of a relationship perfectly known to the audience. So far from having developed the tragedy of such a situation, Goethe has scarcely touched upon it, and never once awakened our fears. . . . The tragedy evolved addresses the conscience rather than the emotions, being less the conflict of passions than the high conflict with Duty."—*Ibid.*, II, 20–22. Schiller's remark is quoted on II, 13.

60:4–8. "Life of Milton," *Six Chief Lives of the Poets*, ed. Matthew Arnold (London, 1881), p. 116.

60:11–12. The first two lines of Voltaire's Prologue to his *Ériphyle* (*Oeuvres complètes*, II, 457).

60:18–24. From the sixth of the prose letters that Voltaire prefixed to the first edition of his *Oedipe* in 1719, the year after the play was produced and about six years after it was written. The first sentence Arnold quotes from Voltaire's fourth paragraph, the second sentence from his third paragraph (*Oeuvres complètes*, II, 42).

60:29–30. K. O. Mueller, *op. cit.*, I, 411; A. W. Schlegel, *A Course of Lectures on Dramatic Art and Literature*, tr. John Black (2d edition; London, 1840), I, 80.

61:8–10. Professor Thomas M. Raysor suggests that Arnold may be thinking of Coleridge's explanation of Hamlet's levity after the appearance of the ghost (I, v), but that if so, Arnold has distorted Coleridge, who speaks of the character's relieving his own psychological tension. See Coleridge, *Complete Works*, ed. Shedd (New York, 1854), IV, 155–56, and *Shakespearean Criticism*, ed. T. M. Raysor (London: Constable, 1930), I, 39–40; II, 274. Or perhaps Arnold had some recollection of the following: "Shakespeare found the infant stage demanding an intermixture of ludicrous character as imperiously as that of Greece did the chorus, and high language accordant. And there are many advantages in this;—a greater assimilation to nature, a greater scope of power, more truths, and more feelings;—the effects of contrast, as in Lear and the Fool; and especially this, that the true language of passion becomes sufficiently elevated by your having previously heard, in the same piece, the lighter conversation of men under no strong emotion" (ed. Shedd, IV, 38; in a somewhat different version, ed. Raysor, II, 73–74).

61:20–22. Voltaire's "Réponse à M. de la Lindelle," *Oeuvres complètes*, IV, 197.

61:30–34. See Milton's note "Of that sort of Dramatic Poem which is call'd Tragedy," prefixed to his *Samson Agonistes*.

62:16–18. Goethe was even more emphatic than Arnold makes him: "[*Samson*] so im Sinne der Alten ist wie kein anderes Stück irgendeines neueren Dichters."—Eckermann, *Gespräche mit Goethe*, January 31, 1830.

63:24–25. "Life of Pope," *Six Chief Lives of the Poets*, ed. Matthew Arnold, p. 421, but reading "elegance of diction, or sweetness of versification." Johnson's sentence continues, "but what can form avail without better matter?"

[ENGLAND AND THE ITALIAN QUESTION]

On March 15, 1859, three days after delivering his fifth lecture from the chair of Poetry at Oxford, Arnold crossed to the Continent on the errand which led to the publication of his first two books on European education. Trouble was then brewing between Austria on the one hand and Sardinia and her ally Napoleon III of France on the other; when Austrian troops entered Sardinian territory on April 29 there was war. Five successive battles were won by the French and Sardinians, the last on the bloody field of Solferino on June 24 in the presence of both emperors. Ten days later Napoleon set in motion negotiations for an armistice which was signed at Villafranca on July 8 and then immediately invited Franz Joseph to meet with him; on the eleventh the two emperors at Villafranca agreed on preliminary terms for a peace which involved (1) the formation of an Italian Confederation under the honorary presidency of the Pope (who was to be urged to reform the administration of his own territories), (2) the cession of Lombardy from Austria to France and then from France to Sardinia, (3) the restoration (if it could be accomplished without arms) of the overthrown Grand Dukes of Modena and Tuscany (who would grant constitutions and general amnesties), and (4) the retention of Venetia by the Austrian crown, though as a member of the Italian Confederation. A European congress was to be called to discuss the modification of the treaties of 1815 insofar as they concerned Italy.

That the terms were not all carried out does not concern us; these were the events that occurred while Arnold was on the Continent and this was the state of matters when Arnold composed his pamphlet *England and the Italian Question*. On June 25 he wrote to his sister Frances after a forty-five minute discussion of events with the British ambassador in Paris that he would "put together for a pamphlet, or for *Fraser*, a sort of *résumé* of the present question as the result of what I have thought, read, and observed here about it." On July 9 he wrote to his sister Jane from Geneva, "I really think I shall finish and bring out my pamphlet." On the seventeenth he wrote from Lausanne, "I am getting on, and think I shall make an interesting pamphlet; but Heaven knows how the thing will look when all together. If it looks not as I mean it, I shall not publish it." Negotiations for publication must have proceeded rapidly: on July 30 Longmans advertised that it would be ready in two days. It sold for a shilling. Meanwhile, a conversation in Paris with Jane's husband, William Forster, led Arnold in the proofs to soften a passage about the prospective Italian Confederation.

Arnold was back in England from about July 30 to August 14 and so could watch the reception of his work by the English press and read the acknowledgments of at least some of the friends and political leaders to whom he had ordered copies sent. His remark in a letter of August 11 that on Clough's authority he would alter an expression in the pamphlet suggests that he had thoughts of reprinting it; when the supply was exhausted about November 21 he was still uncertain whether he should do so or not. As late as 1870, when Napoleon was defeated and overthrown by the Prussians in a war that would seem to have upset some of Arnold's firmest notions about European affairs, he still sent to the publisher of the *Pall Mall Gazette* (September 13) a passage from his pamphlet as perhaps worth quoting in that paper.

The best commentary on the framing of the pamphlet is to be found in Arnold's correspondence, which has been published with considerable fulness for this period by G. W. E. Russell (1895) and by Arnold Whitridge (1923). One of the replies to it, that by Fitzjames Stephen in the *Saturday Review* of August 13, has been published with Arnold's pamphlet by Merle M. Bevington (Durham, N.C., 1953). The reader will find many of Arnold's favorite convictions expressed here—the tremendous consequence of the ideas of 1789, for example; the conviction that "the *intelligence* of [the French] *idea-moved masses* . . . makes them, politically, as far superior to the *insensible masses* of England as to the Russian serfs," and the belief that the English aristocracy, strong and stubborn in action but altogether without sympathy for ideas, had reached its greatest triumph at Waterloo and then proved helpless in meeting the problems that Napoleon's defeat brought on. The failure of Arnold's pamphlet is the failure of all amateur diplomacy which has the notion that an intelligent man can learn the truth simply by reading the newspapers and talking at large to the man on the street and in the salons. There is no awareness in this pamphlet that "the war of 1859 was plotted with greater deliberation than any major conflict in modern history," as one of its most recent historians has observed.—Charles W. Hallberg, *Franz Joseph and Napoleon III* (New York, 1955), p. 154.

66:7–11. Charlemagne died in 814. Arnold's account of the history of Italy in the Middle Ages depends heavily, though not entirely, upon J. C. L. de Sismondi, *History of the Italian Republics, Being a View of the Origin, Progress, and Fall of Italian Freedom* (London, 1832).

68:13–14. Manfred was killed at the battle of Benevento in 1266 (not 1267). After honorable burial on the battlefield he was exhumed and reburied obscurely at Ceprano. Arnold appears to have read his history somewhat hastily.

71:19–20. Lombardy (which included Milan) and Venetia were ruled directly by the Austrian crown after the treaties of 1815 that ended the Napoleonic wars.

73:17–18. Most of Poland was ruled by Russia; Hungary was under the Austrian crown, and Ireland was united with England.

74:21–22. Nevertheless, in 1860 Napoleon III did annex Savoy to France.

74:38. The Legitimate branch of the Bourbons, restored to the throne after the Napoleonic wars, ceased to rule with the abdication of Charles X in 1830; in 1859 it was represented by Charles's grandson the Count de Chambord. The Orleans branch ceased to rule with the abdication of Louis Philippe in 1848 and was represented in 1859 by his grandson the Count of Paris.

78:3. Napoleon's famous manifesto, issued on the day of Austria's invasion of Piedmont (April 29, 1859), said in part, "Austria has brought things to this extremity, that either she must rule up to the Alps, or Italy be free to the Adriatic. . . . I wish for no conquest. . . . The object of this war is to restore Italy to herself, not to change her master."—R. H. Edleston, *Napoleon III and Italy* (Darlington, 1908), I, 51.

80:9–11. Montalembert was prosecuted for libel against the state and the Emperor in consequence of his article in the *Correspondant* of October 25, 1858. He was convicted a month later, but his sentence was remitted by Napoleon.

80:30–31. Napoleon I had established a kingdom of Etruria in 1801, which he incorporated into the French Empire in 1808; he placed his brother Joseph on the throne of Naples in 1806, and his brother-in-law Murat on it in 1808.

82:30–32. Vergil *Aeneid* i. 283–85.

83:18–19. Charles James Fox, great leader of the Whigs in opposition to the war against revolutionary France, was the third son of Lord Holland.

84:9–10. The Venetian aristocracy fell when Napoleon overthrew the Republic in 1797, the French aristocracy, of course, in the revolution of 1789.

84:16–19. The stemming of the militant evangelism of the Mohammedans at Tours in 732, only a hundred years after the death of Mohammed, did not prove the plurality of gods, since though the vanquished forces were monotheistic, so were the Christian victors. Liberalism seemed to Arnold as certain of triumph in the nineteenth century as monotheism was after the Christianization of Rome.

84:20–21. Sir Archibald Alison, arch-conservative Scottish judge, published a ten-volume *History of Europe During the French Revolution* and an eight-volume *History of Europe from the Fall of Napoleon in 1815 to the Accession of Louis Napoleon in 1852*, intended "to show the corruption of human nature and the divine superintendence of human affairs; or, as Disraeli said, . . . to prove that Providence was on the side of the tories."—*D.N.B.*

85:22–23. See Vergil *Aeneid* viii. 485–88.

86:5. Ferney, only four or five miles from Geneva, remained part of France by the settlement of 1815 that returned the French cantons to Switzerland.

87:26–27. Corrected as to fact by Clough, Arnold wrote to him on August 11, 1859: "If you assure me that you *know* that the *officers* of the Prussian army serve for longer than 3 years, I will change *man* to *private*."

87:30. The St. Marylebone Vestry was the popularly elected governing body of the Parish (now Borough) of St. Marylebone, in Arnold's day decidedly bourgeois in composition and one of the most outspoken of the local governing bodies in London.

88:15–16. Gallicanism was the view that tended to restrain the Pope's authority in the French church in favor of that of the bishops and the temporal ruler; ultramontanism looked beyond the mountains to the papal authority.

88:26–28. The Concordat of 1855 between Franz Joseph and Pope Pius IX defined the relation of church and state with respect to education, appointment of clergy, canon and civil law, endowment of religious institutions, etc.

89:20. Louis Veuillot (1813–83) published the *Univers* as a

Catholic journal from 1843. It was suppressed by the government from 1860 to 1867, however, for its stand on the Italian question, upon which it naturally took the side of the Pope against unification under Victor Emmanuel.

89:29–30. A premature revolt at Perugia on June 14, 1859, was put down with great severity by the papal troops.

91:26–27. Cavour, bitterly disappointed at the terms of the peace, resigned the premiership of Sardinia on July 12. He resumed office on January 20, 1860.

92:25. "Non tali auxilio, nec defensoribus istis Tempus eget." —Vergil *Aeneid* ii. 521–22.

93:20–22. Palmerston became Prime Minister on June 30, 1859, as a result of the defeat of the Conservatives in a general election; they had been in power only since February, 1858.

93:30–34. In the settlement of 1815, Cracow had been declared a free city; in 1846 it was absorbed by Austria over strenuous protests by Palmerston, then Foreign Minister.

95:14–15. At Ligny the Prussians were repulsed on June 16, 1815, by the armies of Napoleon advancing into Belgium; the French were defeated at Waterloo two days later.

95:26. Guizot, the most powerful French statesman under Louis Philippe, spent a year in exile in England after the abdication of the king in 1848; though he then returned to France he never again took part in public affairs. Alexis de Tocqueville's *Democracy in America* was much admired among English Liberals, and De Tocqueville himself visited England and married an Englishwoman. He retired from public life because of his opposition to Napoleon III's *coup d'état* and died on April 16, 1859. It was from a conversation with Guizot that Arnold first learned the war was inevitable, a week before the outbreak of hostilities.

[ON TRANSLATING HOMER]

On October 29, 1860, Arnold wrote to his mother: "I am in full work at my lecture on Homer, which you have seen advertised in the *Times*. I give it next Saturday [November 3]. I shall try to lay down the true principles on which a translation of Homer should be founded, and I shall give a few passages translated by myself to add practice to theory. This is an off lecture, given partly because I have long had in my mind something to say about

Homer, partly because of the complaints that I did not enough lecture on poetry. I shall still give the lecture, continuing my proper course, towards the end of the term." But a single lecture did not provide enough scope, nor was he able to finish all he had to say in a second lecture on Homer, delivered December 8: a third was needed on January 26, 1861. For the first time he seems really to have succeeded with his audience: "I feel very sure of my ground in these lectures, and that makes me do them, no doubt, all the better. I hear from Oxford that people were greatly pleased and interested by the first of the set." The editor of *Fraser's*, Parker, gained a commitment from Arnold to let him publish the lectures in that journal; when Parker died and was succeeded shortly after the first lecture was delivered by Arnold's friend J. A. Froude, the claim of *Fraser's* was pressed even more vigorously. "I should get at least £30 so it is a temptation, but I think as they are my first published Oxford lectures it is more decorous to publish them as a book than as magazine articles." By December 18 the third lecture was composed and on January 16, 1861, ten days before it was delivered, Arnold was halfway through the proofs of the book. As he completed the delivery of that last lecture, "to a full audience," he told his sister Jane, "I was cheered, which is very uncommon at Oxford." The book was advertised by Longmans in the *Times* for January 29, at 3*s.* 6*d.*

The subject was, in fact, one of very lively current interest. Arnold's lectures, allusive as they are to contemporary discussions of the problem, hardly more than hint at the magnitude of the debate; within the twelve months after the publication of his lectures, four new translations of Homer were published in England (*Iliad* i–xii by J. H. Dart, *Iliad* i by J. T. B. Landon, *Odyssey* i–xii by P. S. Worsley, and *Odyssey* i–xii by Dean Henry Alford). At the heart of the question was the revolutionary *Prolegomena ad Homerum* (1795) of Friedrich Wolf, who advanced the theory that the Homeric poems as we know them were a rather late blending of unconnected ancient lays handed down by oral recitation: if this were true, Wolf's followers argued, modern translation should somehow reflect the fact. Other scholars (among them Arnold's friend Clough) puzzled themselves with the question of precisely how the ancients read their hexameters and how best English verse could make somewhat the same combination of stress and quantity the Greeks made. Arnold's great merit in these lectures was to remove the question altogether from the realm of pedantry and apply to it, as one reviewer remarked, "delicacy of taste, keenness of insight, and evidence of true poetic culture" (*Spectator*, February 16, 1861). He uses here most effectively the touchstone technique of evaluating poetry that he was to advocate many years later in "The Study of Poetry."

A modern edition of the lectures by W. H. D. Rouse, himself a distinguished scholar and translator of Homer, contains a valuable Introduction that points out the solid merits of Arnold's theories (despite some faults) and evaluates subsequent translations (London, 1905). T. S. Omond covers some of the same ground in "Arnold and Homer," *Essays and Studies by Members of the English Association*, III, 71–91 (1912); Noel Annan gives an entertaining sketch of Newman's career and the debate with Arnold in *New Statesman* XXVII, 191 (March 18, 1944), and the first chapter of Basil Willey's *More Nineteenth Century Studies* (London, 1956) is a more serious discussion of Newman's intellectual position.

Motto: Juvenal I. 1.

97:11–15. *The Iliad of Homer*, faithfully translated into unrhymed English metre by F. W. Newman (London: Walton and Maberly, 1856).

The Iliad of Homer, translated into blank verse by Ichabod Charles Wright. 2 vols. (Cambridge: Macmillan and Co., 1859–65).

Wright's verse translation of the *Divine Comedy* first appeared in three volumes, 1833–40, and was published in Bohn's Illustrated Library in 1854. On the eve of the publication of the second volume of his *Iliad*, Wright brought out *A Letter to the Dean of Canterbury on the Homeric Lectures of Matthew Arnold* (London, 1864) that Arnold dismissed as "of no consequence."

97:25–98:2. Newman's Preface, pp. xv–xvi.

98:2–5. *National Review* XI, 310 (see n. to p. 101:28, below).

98:7–12. Newman's Preface, p. xvi. Arnold is paraphrasing, not quoting.

98:35–37. *Ibid.*, p. iii.

99:18–19. Edward Craven Hawtrey (1789–1862) was Provost of Eton College, who in 1847 contributed translations from Homer to a volume called *English Hexameter Translations*.

In his *Letter to the Dean of Canterbury* (1864), Wright quoted a letter from Hawtrey to himself about Arnold's lecture: "I do not quarrel with his judgment as to its [my translation of 'Hector and Andromache'] having been not successful; for I do not think it was: but with regard to his own version as compared with mine, I think I should candidly say, that they were *much of a muchness*" (p. 12; letter dated February 28, 1861). Wright also quoted Hawtrey's mature conviction that English is not a language in which hexameters can succeed, and his endorsement of Wright's translation.

William Hepworth Thompson (1810–86) was Regius Professor of Greek in the University of Cambridge, 1853–66. On February 13, 1861, Arnold forwarded to his mother, with obvious pride, a letter to himself from Professor Thompson expressing his approval of the lectures.

Benjamin Jowett (1817–93) was a fellow of Balliol College, Oxford, when Arnold was an undergraduate there, and was Regius Professor of Greek at Oxford from 1855.

99:21–22. This frequently repeated remark was quoted in the *National Review* XI, 286.

99:24. Aristotle *Nicomachean Ethics* 1107a *et passim.*

100:2–3. George Grote held that the poem was originally an *Achillêis,* built upon a narrower plan, then enlarged into an *Iliad.* —*History of Greece* (3d edition; London, 1851), II, 236–37.

100:5–6. "If therefore it has been shown, that the mythological character of Apollo is clearly the vehicle of the ancient tradition, known to us in the Book of Genesis, respecting the Seed of the woman, it seems plain that in Latona is represented the woman from whom that Seed was to spring. I do not presume to enter into the question whether we ought to consider that the Latona of Homer represents the Blessed Virgin, who was divinely elected to be the actual mother of our Lord; or rather our ancient mother Eve, whose seed He was also in a peculiar sense to be."— W. E. Gladstone, *Studies on Homer and the Homeric Age* (Oxford, 1858), II, 153. Gladstone was member of Parliament for the University of Oxford.

100:18–22. Newman's Preface, p. vi; Newman has "translation" for "translator."

100:28. Newman's translation, vi. 359, 440; Newman has "then" for "thus."

100:29. *Ibid.*, iii. 58.

100:32. *Ibid.*, xvii. 444.

101:12. Johann Heinrich Voss's translations of the *Odyssey* (1781) and the *Iliad* (1793) into hexameters became the standard German version.

101:28–102:4. "The English Translators of Homer" [review of Newman's and Books I–VI of Wright's *Iliad*], *National Review* (London) XI, 283–314 (October, 1860). The quotation from Ruskin's *Modern Painters*, Part IV, Chapter XII ("Of the Pathetic Fallacy"), sec. 12 is on p. 302. Of this book when it first appeared Arnold commented to his sister Jane Forster (March 31, 1856), "Full of excellent *aperçus*, as usual, but the man and character too febrile, irritable, and weak to allow him to possess the *ordo concatenatioque veri.*" On December 17, 1860, he told his sister Frances, "Gradually I mean to say boldly the truth about a great many English celebrities, and begin with Ruskin in these lectures on Homer."

102:9. In a letter to his mother on March 20, 1861, Arnold speaks of the praise Sainte-Beuve has given him as especially gratifying because it "is administered by the first of living critics, and with a delicacy for which one would look in vain here." The very expression is Sainte-Beuve's: "M. Joubert, le plus délicat des amis et des juges."—*Chateaubriand et son groupe littéraire* (new ed.; Paris, 1889), I, 263.

102:20–22. "Ich rudre in fremdem Element herum, ja, ich möchte sagen dass ich nur drin patsche, mit Verlust nach aussen und ohne die mindeste Befriedigung von innen oder nach innen. Da wir denn aber, wie ich nun immer deutlicher von Polygnot und Homer lerne, die Hölle eigentlich hier oben vorzustellen haben, so mag denn das auch für ein Leben gelten."—*Briefwechsel zwischen Schiller und Goethe* (Stuttgart und Tübingen, 1829), VI, 230–31, letter dated "Jena am 13. December 1803." Polygnotus was a fifth-century (B.C.) Athenian painter whose murals at Delphi on the destruction of Troy and on Odysseus' visit to the underworld are described by Pausanias X. xxv–xxxi; Goethe was supervising the printing of his paper on Polygnotus for the *Jenaische Allgemeine Literaturzeitung*, and at least part of the hell on earth was caused by the arduous editorial duties for that journal. Arnold had quoted this passage in a letter to his sister Jane Forster on May 2, 1857.

103:5. *The Iliad of Homer*, translated by William Sotheby, 2 vols. (London: John Murray, 1831).

103:14–15. The first two lines of an epigram on "Reason" published in *On the Constitution of the Church and State* (1830), p. 227.

104:6–12. *The Iliad of Homer*, translated into English blank verse by the late William Cowper, Esq. (2d edition; London: J. Johnson, 1802), I, xlii–xliii. Arnold used the edition by Southey (London, 1837), which prints the text of Cowper's first edition but has both prefaces.

104:14–19. *Ibid.*, I, xxix (Preface to the first edition).

104:31–33. *Ibid.*, I, 259 (*Iliad* viii. 643–45). Cowper's second edition reads "those fires between the stream."

105:3–8. *Ibid.*, II, 271 (*Iliad* xix. 491–95). Cowper's version in the second edition is very much altered.

105:18–22. *Ibid.*, I, xxxii, xxiii (Preface to the first edition).

105:26–28. In Part IV of *Modern Painters*, which Arnold earlier singled out for reproof, Ruskin several times praised highly "the noble Pre-Raphaelite movement of our own days."—E.g., Chap. VI, sec. 8, and Chap. X, sec. 21.

106:10–11. Newman's Preface, p. vii.

106:11–12. Cowper, *op. cit.*, I, xxi (Preface to the first edition).

107:29–30. Goethe, *Aus Meinem Leben: Dichtung und Wahrheit* (Frankfurt a. M., 1922), III, 128–29 (middle of Book XII). Goethe insisted, however, that the Homeric poems were by no means the product of a primitive society.

107:32–108:2. Arnold supplies the historical and biographical data.

111:6–8. Wordsworth to Walter Scott, November 7, 1805: "In his translation from Virgil, whenever Virgil can be fairly said to have his *eye* upon his object, Dryden always spoils the passage." —*Early Letters*, ed. E. de Selincourt (Oxford, 1935), p. 541.

112:15–17. *Literary Remains*, ed. H. N. Coleridge (London, 1836), I, 259.

112:17–18. Henry Hallam, *Introduction to the Literature of Europe in the Fifteenth, Sixteenth, and Seventeenth Centuries* (2d edition; London, 1843), II, 131.

112:18–23. *The Iliads of Homer, Prince of Poets* . . . Done According to the Greek by George Chapman. With introduction and notes by the Rev. Richard Hooper, M.A. 2 vols. (2d edition; London: John Russell Smith, 1865), I, xx–xxi. Hooper wrote "perfectly identified himself." The passages from Coleridge and Hallam that Arnold cites are quoted by Hooper, I, xvi, xv.

113:29. The epithet "clearest-soul'd" is Arnold's own, from his early sonnet "To a Friend."

113:30–33. Pope, "Preface to the *Iliad*," in *The Iliad of Homer*, translated by Alexander Pope, with an introduction and notes by the Rev. Theodore Alois Buckley (London, 1853), I, 68 (quoted by Hooper, *op. cit.*, I, xv). Pope's words were "[Chapman's translation] is something like what one might imagine Homer himself would have writ before he arrived at years of discretion." The sneer was Hallam's, *op. cit.*, II, 131.

114:3–8. Chapman, *op. cit.*, I, 23 (Commentarius on Book I).

116:30–117:1. Cowper, *op. cit.*, I, xliii (Preface to the second edition).

117:28–118:2. *National Review* XI, 311. For "scholastic" read "scholarlike."

118:26–28. Newman's Preface, p. xvi.

118:31–34. *Ibid.*, pp. vii–viii, v.

119:15–19. *Ibid.*, p. iv.

119:27–33. *Ibid.*, pp. iv, x, ix.

120:7, 10–12. *Troilus and Cressida*, Prologue, lines 2, 17–19.

120:30–31. *Epistulae* II. iii. 359 ("De Arte Poetica").

121:12–17. *Specimens of Early English Metrical Romances*, ed. George Ellis, revised by J. O. Halliwell (London, 1848), p. 326 (lines 5099–5104 in the edition of the romance by Karl Brunner, Vienna, 1913).

122:11. *Iliad* ii. 211–77 and *Odyssey* xviii. 1–109; both Thersites and Irus were vulgar characters.

122:22–25, 29–30. Newman's Preface, p. x.

124:8–14. Newman's Glossary, pp. xxi–xxii.

125:15–22. Newman's Preface, pp. v, iv.

125:23–28. *National Review* XI, 311.

125:28–126:2. Chapman, *op. cit.*, p. xxi (editor's Introduction).

126:3–7. William Maginn, *Homeric Ballads and Comedies of Lucian*, annotated by Shelton Mackenzie (New York, 1856), p. 5 (quoting from the London edition of 1850 by "J. C.," John Churchill).

126:20. "The Loving Ballad of Lord Bateman" was printed with illustrations by George Cruikshank in 1839. See F. J. Child, ed., *The English and Scottish Popular Ballads* (Boston, 1898), I, 476–77.

126:28–29. *Paradise Lost*, III, 35–36.

126:31–32. "King Estmere," lines 175–76.

127:1. "The Frolicksome Duke, or the Tinker's Good Fortune," line 43.

127:18–19. The metrical version of the Psalms in English by Nicholas Brady and Nahum Tate was published in 1696.

129:3–4. R. B. Sheridan, "Clio's Protest":

"You write with *ease*, to show your breeding;
But *easy writing*'s vile *hard reading*."

131:4–11. The English editor of Maginn's *Homeric Ballads* (p. 5) praises Macaulay's *Lays of Ancient Rome* as a ground-breaking work which "aims at resolving into their constituent elements, whether primary or not, the records of a nation's antiquity." Arnold quotes below parts of stanzas 3–4 of Maginn's first ballad, "The Bath of Odysseus."

132:11–13. Newman's Preface, p. vii.

132:20–23. George P. Marsh, *Lectures on the English Language*, First Series (4th edition; New York, 1863), pp. 520–21 n: "I am not disposed to question the spirit or fidelity of [Mr. Newman's] translation, and upon European ears, which are, of course, less familiar than ours with our national serio-comic melody, the metre may not produce a ludicrous effect; but to an American it has altogether the air of an attempt to set the Iliad to the tune of Yankee Doodle."

134:34–135:2. Newman's Preface, pp. viii, v. The Coryphaeus was leader of the grotesquely costumed chorus of the Greek Old Comedy.

135:2–6. Maginn, *op. cit.*, pp. 67–68.

136:18–19. The catechism in *The Book of Common Prayer* defines *Sacrament* as "an outward and visible sign of an inward and spiritual grace."

138:15–21. *Iliad* xvi. 74–79.

138:34–36. "Certainly I must confesse mine owne barbarousnesse, I never heard the old Song of *Percy* and *Duglas*, that I founde not my heart mooved more then with a Trumpet."—*The Defence of Poesie*, ed. A. Feuillerat (Cambridge, 1923), p. 24.

139:31–33. Newman's Preface, p. x.

142:19–20. John 6:63.

142:33–35. Maginn, *op. cit.*, p. 22.

144:3–4. Johnson, *Vanity of Human Wishes*, lines 349–50.

144:6–7. *Paradise Lost*, II, 1–2.

144:22. H. F. Cary's blank-verse translation of Dante's *Vision* (*Commedia*) was published in 1814.

145:36. "The wrath sing, O Goddess," *Iliad* i. 1.

146:1–6. *Paradise Lost*, I, 1–6.

146:11–12. *Paradise Lost*, IV, 1–2.

147:22–23. *The Task,* I, 264–65.

147:24–26. "Ulysses," lines 19–21. Tennyson wrote "Yet all," "margin fades," "ever when I move."

148:18–19. Medea's magic spells rejuvenated Jason's aged father Aeson; the daughters of Jason's wicked uncle Pelias, beholding the miracle, were induced to stab their father in the hope of effecting similar rejuvenation, but the experiment proved fatal.—Ovid *Metamorphoses* vii. 159–349.

148:26. "The question is resolved by action" (rather than logic).

149 n. *Iliad* iii. 234–44. Arnold misrepresents the critic in the *National Review* (XI, 312), who advocates, not the transliteration of Greek names, but the consistent use of Greek names of deities instead of the substitution of Roman equivalents—precisely, in other words, what Arnold himself wishes.

150:39–40. George Grote clung to the spellings "Sokratês," "Alkibiadês," "Empedoklês," but not "Thoukydidês." He justified his use of the "k" as "reproducing the Greek name to the eye as well as to the ear," but made "exception for such names as the English reader has been so accustomed to hear with the C, that they may be considered as being almost Anglicized" (hence "Thucydides").—*History of Greece* (3d edition; London, 1851), I, xxiv.

151:26–33. J. T. Freeman Mitford, Lord Redesdale, *Thoughts on English Prosody and Translations from Horace* and *Further Thoughts on English Prosody* (both 1859).

152:13. *Paradise Lost,* III, 36.

152:16. Chapman, *Iliad* i. 590.

152:23. Newman, *Iliad* xiv. 84.

152:29. "Tetrasticon," in a letter to Harvey; cited by Marsh, *op. cit.*, p. 520 n.

154:5–7. *Macbeth,* I, vii, 12–14.

154:9. *As You Like It,* IV, i, 168.

154:19. Chapman, *Iliad* ix. 307.

154:28–30. Cowper, *Iliad* (1802), I, xxxi–xxxii (Preface to the first edition).

155:10–11, 38–39. *Hamlet,* III, i, 77 and 67. Shakespeare wrote "weary life."

155:24–26. *Macbeth,* II, i, 58; I, vii, 7 and 20; *Hamlet,* III, i, 75–76.

156:3–5. Pope, *Iliad* (1853), I, 64 (Preface).

156:8–12. The Butcher and Lang prose translation of the *Odyssey* (1879) and the Lang, Leaf, and Myers *Iliad* (1883) show the influence of this remark; the Preface to the former says (p. xi): "We do not know whether it is necessary to defend our choice of a somewhat antiquated prose. Homer has no ideas which cannot be expressed in words that are 'old and plain,' and to words that are old and plain, and, as a rule, to such terms as, being used by the Translators of the Bible, are still not unfamiliar, we have tried to restrict ourselves." Earlier in the Preface (p. ix) the translators appeal to the authority of Sainte-Beuve and Arnold: "[The prospective reader] must recognise, with Mr. Matthew Arnold, that what he now wants, namely, the simple truth about the matter of the poem, can only be given in prose, 'for in a verse translation no original work is any longer recognisable.'"

156:25. *Hamlet*, III, i, 59.

157:1–3, 8–10. *Macbeth*, I, vii, 65–67, 49–51.

157:5. In a note to this passage in his "pictorial edition" of Shakespeare (Tragedies, II, 17), Charles Knight remarked, "Shakspere understood the construction of a still, in this happy comparison of the brain to that part of a vessel through which a distilled liquor passes."

157:21–22. Chapman, *Iliad* xix. 406–7.

157:24. Psalms 12:7: "The words of the Lord are pure words: even as the silver, . . . purified seven times in the fire."—Prayer Book version.

157:25–26. Arnold humorously perverts the meaning of Horace's "naturam expelles furca" (*Epistles* I. x. 24).

158:19–20. "Il Penseroso," 97–98. Milton wrote "In Scepter'd."

158:24. *Romeo and Juliet*, III, ii, 1.

158:26–27. "Elegy Written in a Country Church-yard," 87.

158:28–29. Newman, *Iliad* xiv. 83.

158:30–31. Matthew 16:22.

158:32–33. John 16:18.

159:10–13. Cowper, *Iliad* (1802), I, xxxiv (Preface to the first edition).

160:16–21. *Iliad* viii. 560–65.

161:27–33. *Iliad* xvii. 441–47.

162:15. *Iliad* vi. 448. See end of Lecture I.

163:25. *Iliad* vi. 441.

165:22. Goliath's? who had "a coat of mail: and the weight

of the coat *was* five thousand shekels of brass."—I Samuel 17:5.

165:34–35. Psalms 118:16, in the Prayer Book version and hence not in Cruden.

166:2. Alexander Cruden's *Complete Concordance to the Holy Scriptures* has gone through many editions and revisions from its first publication in 1738 and is still current.

166:7–8. Matthew 5:22; Luke 12:20; I Corinthians 15:36.

166:11. *Antony and Cleopatra*, V, ii, 308–9.

167:27. The standard translation of Shakespeare into German verse by A. W. Schlegel, Ludwig Tieck, and their collaborators (1797–1833).

167:28. Either the translation by B. Laroche that was first published in 1843 or that by F. V. Hugo, son of the great novelist and poet, that began to appear in 1859.

167:33. Abraham Hayward's prose translation of *Faust*, Part I, was first published in 1833 and remained current for many years. By the time Arnold spoke, however, Hayward was perhaps best known for *The Art of Dining; or, Gastronomy and Gastronomers* (1852).

168:10. John Wilson, *Works*, ed. J. F. Ferrier (Edinburgh, 1857), VIII, 1–389: seven essays on "Homer and His Translators" from *Blackwood's*, April 1831 to February 1834.

[ON TRANSLATING HOMER. LAST WORDS]

Arnold had told his mother that, having finished with Homer, he intended to resume his former series and plunge once more into the Middle Age. "I have a strong sense of the irrationality of that period, and of the utter folly of those who take it seriously, and play at restoring it; still, it has poetically the greatest charm and refreshment possible for me." On the very day he delivered his lecture on "The Claim of the Celtic Race, and the Claim of the Christian Religion, To Have Originated Chivalrous Sentiment," June 8, 1861, there was advertised a three-shilling pamphlet of 104 pages called *Homeric Translation in Theory and Practice. A Reply to Matthew Arnold, Esq.*, by Francis W. Newman.

As the most recent advocate and practitioner of the ballad metre for Homeric translation, Newman, younger brother of the cardinal-to-be and professor of Latin in University College, London, found himself uncomfortably close to the heart of Arnold's attack in the three lectures on Homer. That he should have taken offense at some of Arnold's spirited remarks is hardly surprising, yet Arnold seems to have been surprised, and when the *Saturday Review* sharply rebuked him for abusing the privilege of the Oxford chair of poetry, he determined to give a fourth lecture on Homer, in which he would "try to set things straight, at the same time soothing Newman's feelings—which I am really sorry to have hurt—as much as I can without giving up any truth of criticism." "The one feeling this answer of Newman's gives me is sorrow that he should be so deeply annoyed by what I intended far more as an illustration of the want of *justesse d'esprit* to which the English are prone, than as an attack upon him." He delivered his lecture at Oxford on November 30, 1861. Again, he promised it to *Fraser's*, but when he prepared it for printing he found it much too long and so published it as a little book of sixty-nine pages; Longmans advertised it in the *Times* of March 21 at 3*s.* 6*d.*

Newman's reply is verbose, badly ordered, and without the slightest perception of the real point at issue; even where he is right he is irrelevant. His essay has achieved undeserved immortality only by being printed in several modern editions of Arnold's essays (e.g., Oxford Standard Authors and Everyman's Library); readers who wish to see what provoked the best of Arnold's Homeric lectures may find it in one of those volumes, though page references in these notes are to the first edition. A dozen years later Newman attempted to engage Arnold in another arena when he reviewed *Literature and Dogma* in *Fraser's Magazine*, n.s. VIII, 114–34 (July, 1873).

168:23–24. Motto: Psalm 119:157. "Perhaps there is some little doubt about the motto . . . , but I put it in the Vulgate Latin, as I always do when I am not earnestly serious."—Arnold to his mother, March 19, 1862.

168:25–169:13. The entire paragraph is drawn from Sainte-Beuve's article, "Correspondance de Buffon," *Causeries du lundi* (Paris, n.d.), XIV, 326 (Monday, March 26, 1860). From the context of Arnold's lecture one may sense in his language about the Jansenist Gazetteer an allusion to *The Saturday Review* (see his letters to his mother on July 30, 1861, a few days after he had read its critique of his lectures, to his sister Jane on July 31, and to his mother again on August 15).

169:29–31. Sainte-Beuve, *Causeries*, XIV, 327.

170:17–19. See *Iliad* xvii. 384–99 *et passim.*

170:23–32. Francis W. Newman, *Homeric Translation in Theory and Practice. A Reply to Matthew Arnold, Esq., Professor of Poetry, Oxford.* By . . . a translator of the *Iliad* (London: Williams and Norgate, 1861), pp. 1 & 34, 18, 47, 20, 91, 91, 74–75, 22.

171:10–12. *Ibid.*, p. 47.

171:13–14. "Homeric Translators and Critics," *Saturday Review* XII, 95 (July 27, 1861). This article is a lively rebuke to Arnold for misusing the Poetry chair "elaborately to ridicule, with every kind of contemptuous and insulting language, a living scholar [whose] academical honours [at Balliol] were considerably higher than those of the present Poetry Professor." The reviewer is also severe upon Arnold's "outrageous self-conceit. . . . *Das grosse ich* reigns from one end to the other. . . . But it is not the mere number of I's in Mr. Arnold's lectures, it is the way in which 'I' always comes in—an authoritative, oracular way, something akin, we venture to guess, to 'the grand style,' something reminding us of what, many years ago, was known in the Oxford Union as the white pocket-handkerchief style of oratory."

172:30–173:16. *Werke* (Weimar, 1892), XXXV, 8 ("Tag- und Jahreshefte," "Bis 1786").

173:34–35. Newman, *op. cit.*, pp. 39–44.

173:37. Newman's own studies of the language of the Berbers were to lead to his *Libyan Vocabulary* (1882).

174:1–14. Newman, *Homeric Translation*, pp. 33, 35, 77.

174:32–33. Montaigne, *Essais*, II, x ("Des livres"): "Plutarque est plus uniforme et constant; Seneque, plus ondoyant et divers."

175:21–23. Newman, *op. cit.*, pp. 49, 103.

175:31–34. *Ibid.*, p. 50.

176:17–19. *Ibid.*, p. 52.

176:26–31. *Ibid.*, p. 89.

177:1–3. *Measure for Measure*, III, i, 34–36.

177:10–23. Newman, *op. cit.*, p. 95; *Iliad* xiii. 136.

179:1–10, 19–25. Newman, *op. cit.*, pp. 35–36, 48, 54.

179:12–15. *Saturday Review* XII, 96.

179:37–180:5. Plato *Republic* ii, 377–iii, 391.

180:24–181:6. Newman, *op. cit.*, pp. 36, 68, 35–36.

181:7–13. *Ibid.*, pp. 46–47.

181:29–30. Genesis 18:31–32.

181:31–32. Milton, "On the Morning of Christ's Nativity," line 58.

182:10. *Poems of Chaucer Modernized*, ed. R. H. Horne (London, 1841). Wordsworth did "The Cuckoo and the Nightingale" and 168 lines of "Troilus and Cresida"; earlier he had published a version of "The Prioress' Tale."

182:32. Newman's *Iliad* xii. 325.

182:33–183:1. Newman, *Homeric Translation*, pp. 36–37, 43.

183:28–30. *The Critic*, II, ii, 380–81: "The *father* softens—but the *governor* Is fixed!"

183:38. Matthew 7:3–5.

184:2. "Lycidas," line 124.

184:17–185:3. Newman, *op. cit.*, pp. 51, 79, 50, 51, 56, 59, 89; F. Max Müller, as a philologist, traced the Greek word for "daughter" to the Sanskrit "duhitar," from the root DUH, to milk. —"Comparative Mythology," *Oxford Essays, 1856* (London), pp. 16–17.

185:24–26. At the end of Lecture II.

186:6–8. "Journal et mémoires de Marquis d'Argenson," *Causeries du lundi* (Paris, n.d.), XIV, 241 (Monday, June 20, 1859).

187:8–10, 15–18. *Prelude*, III, 15–17, 60–63.

188:3–6. *Saturday Review* XII, 96 ("mockingly and with incredulity"); *Westminster Review*, American ed., LXXVII, 87 ("with an inclination to believe in it, but puzzled"). Ruskin only recently had tried his hand at defining the "Grand Style" in the third volume of *Modern Painters*, Part IV, chap. I and III (1856).

188:12–13. Matthew 17:4. Mark 9:5.

188:18–19. John 8:24.

188:23–26. *Paradise Lost*, VII, 23–26.

189:32–37. Lecture III, pp. 145–47.

191:5–10. Pindar *Pythian Odes* iii. 86–91.

191:14–17. "On Translating Homer," *Times* (London), October 28, 1861, p. 8, col. 5 (by E. S. Dallas).

192:5–7. There was a very late flowering of the Greek epic tradition in Quintus Smyrnaeus' *Posthomerica* (4th century A.D.) and in Nonnus of Panoplis' *Dionysiaca*, Tryphiodorus' *Iliu Halosis*, and Colluthus' *Rape of Helen* (5th century). These works, three of which treat of the Trojan War and related events, are all extant.

192:22–193:10. "Arnold on Translating Homer," by J. S., *Fraser's Magazine* LXIII, 703–14 (June, 1861). The passages Arnold quotes directly are on pp. 713 and 705.

193:12. H. A. J. Munro's reply to Spedding is appended to his paper on a metrical inscription at Cirta, *Cambridge Philosophical Society Transactions* X, 374–408 (1861).

194:12–13. *Evangeline*, I, i, 46.

195:31–34. Newman, *Homeric Translation,* pp. 13–14.

195:14–15. Fragment 635 of Th. Kock, *Comicorum Atticorum Fragmenta* (Leipzig, 1888).

196:8–14. Spedding, *loc. cit.*, p. 709, and Hawtrey quoted by Arnold, Lecture III, p. 149 n.

197:36, 38, 40. *Evangeline,* II, v, 1 and 6. Twelve books of J. Henry Dart's *Iliad of Homer, in English Hexameter Verse* were published in the spring of 1862; the entire work in 1865.

199:12. Vergil *Eclogues* iv. 23.

200 n. P. S. Worsley, *The Odyssey of Homer* Translated into English Verse in the Spenserian Stanza (Edinburgh and London, 1861–62). Arnold's lectures are mentioned respectfully in the prefaces to both volumes; the sentence Arnold quotes is on I. xii. Worsley also cited (I. xiii) the conclusion of *Childe Harold* as evidence that the Spenserian stanza could reach the grand style. On January 1, 1862, Arnold told his mother that he had had a very nice note from Worsley and intended to mention his translation in a footnote to the published lecture, since it was by far the most pleasing version of the *Odyssey* he had seen.

203:15, 19, 22. Examples by Spedding, *loc. cit.*, pp. 712–13.

204:35–205:9. *Princess,* vii, 182; "Merlin and Vivien," lines 633–34 and 638–39; *Princess,* v, 20–21; "Marriage of Geraint," lines 74–78.

205:25–26. Tennyson, "Ulysses," lines 16–17.

207:16. Moschus was a successor to Theocritus in the highly sophisticated Alexandrian pastoral tradition; like Homer, he wrote in hexameters. "Tennyson's devoted adherents will be very angry with me, but their ridiculous elevation of him above Wordsworth was one of the things which determined me to say what I did." —Arnold to his mother, March 19, 1862.

207:22–26. J. S. Blackie, "Homer and His Translators," *Macmillan's Magazine* IV, 272 (August, 1861). Arnold described Blackie to his sister Frances on June 19, 1859, as "an animated, pleasant man, with a liking for all sorts of things that are excellent. *Au reste,* an *esprit* as confused and hoity toity as possible, and as capable of translating Homer as of making the Apollo Belvedere."

209:28–210:2. The Percy version of "Sir Patrick Spence," lines 33–40.

210:16. The first line of the fragment from "The Recluse" that Wordsworth prefixed to the 1814 edition of *The Excursion.* Wordsworth wrote "On Man, on Nature, . . ."

210:33. *Lay of the Last Minstrel,* VI, 1.

211:2. *Marmion,* VI, xxx, 1.

211:6–9. *Lays of Ancient Rome,* "Horatius," stanza 27.

211:21–22. Newman, *op. cit.,* p. 14.

214:14–19. *Ibid.,* p. 104.

214:19–23. *Saturday Review* XII, 96.

214:27. "It is vain for you to rise up early, to sit up late."—Psalms 127:2 (King James version). "It is but lost labour that ye haste to rise up early, and so late take rest."—Psalms 127:3 (Prayer Book version).

214:35–215:3. Antoine Rivarol, quoted by Sainte-Beuve, *Causeries,* V, 69 (Monday, October 27, 1851): "L'esprit de critique est un esprit d'ordre; il connaît des délits contre le goût et les porte au tribunal du ridicule; car le rire est souvent l'expression de sa colère, et ceux qui le blâment ne songent pas assez que l'homme de goût a reçu vingt blessures avant d'en faire une."

215:18–19. Clough turned to the translation of Homer into English hexameters at various times; during the last years of his life it was almost the only poetical work he was able to undertake. He submitted specimens of it to Arnold as early as 1849.—*Letters of Matthew Arnold to Arthur Hugh Clough,* ed. H. F. Lowry (London, 1932), *passim.*

216:4–5. From Clough's hexameter "vacation pastoral," *The Bothie of Tober-Na-Vuolich,* IX, 79, and IV, 12.

Textual Notes

[TEXTS]

53.* Poems. | By | Matthew Arnold. | *A New Edition.* | London: | Longman, Brown, Green, and Longmans. | M DCCC LIII.
Preface, pp. v–xxxi.

54. Poems. | By | Matthew Arnold. | *Second Edition.* | London: | Longman, Brown, Green, and Longmans. | M DCCC LIV.
Preface, pp. v–viii.
Preface to the First Edition [1853], pp. ix–xxxv.

56. Poems. | By | Matthew Arnold. | *A New and Complete Edition.* | Boston: | Ticknor and Fields. | M DCCC LVI.
The Preface [1853] in this volume (pp. 9–26) has no independent textual authority and has not been collated.

57. Poems. | By | Matthew Arnold. | *Third Edition.* | London: | Longman, Brown, Green, Longmans, & Roberts. | 1857.
Advertisement to the Second Edition [1854], pp. v–viii.
Preface [1853], pp. ix–xxxvi.

58. Merope. | A Tragedy. | By | Matthew Arnold. | London: | Longman, Brown, Green, Longmans, & Roberts. | MDCCCLVIII.
Preface, pp. vii–xlviii.

59. England and the Italian Question. | By | Matthew Arnold. | "Sed nondum est finis." | *S. Matt.* xxiv. 6. | London | Longman, Green, Longman, and Roberts. | 1859

61. On Translating Homer | Three Lectures | Given at Oxford | By | Matthew Arnold, M.A. | Professor of Poetry in the University of Oxford, and | Formerly Fellow of Oriel College | London | Longman, Green, Longman, and Roberts | 1861

62. On Translating Homer | Last Words | A Lecture Given at Oxford | By | Matthew Arnold, M.A. | Professor of Poetry in

* For 53 read 1853, etc.

the University of Oxford, and | Formerly Fellow of Oriel College | London | Longman, Green, Longman, and Roberts | 1862

65. Essays in Criticism. | By | Matthew Arnold, | Professor of Poetry in the University of Oxford. | Boston: | Ticknor and Fields. | 1865.

    This edition, which contains "On Translating Homer" (pp. 284–424), has no textual authority and is not collated.

80. Passages from | the Prose Writings | of | Matthew Arnold | London | Smith, Elder, & Co., 15 Waterloo Place | 1880 | [*All rights reserved*]

    Also issued with the imprint: New York | Macmillan and Co., | 1880

82. Irish Essays | and Others | By | Matthew Arnold | London | Smith, Elder, & Co., 15 Waterloo Place | 1882 | *All rights reserved*

    Preface to First Edition of Poems. (1853.), pp. 281–305.
    Preface to Second Edition of Poems. (1854.), pp. 306–8.

83*o*. On the Study | of | Celtic Literature | and on | Translating Homer | By | Matthew Arnold | New York | Macmillan and Co. | 1883

83m. Mixed Essays | Irish Essays | and Others | By | Matthew Arnold | New York | Macmillan and Co. | 1883

    Preface to First Edition of Poems. (1853.), pp. 486–504.
    Preface to Second Edition of Poems. (1854.), pp. 505–7.

91. Irish Essays | and Others | By | Matthew Arnold | Popular Edition | London | Smith, Elder, & Co., 15 Waterloo Place | 1891 | *All rights reserved*

    Preface to First Edition of Poems. (1853.), pp. 202–19.
    Preface to Second Edition of Poems. (1854.), pp. 220–22.
    There is no evidence that this edition has any independent textual authority.

96. On | Translating Homer | By | Matthew Arnold | Popular Edition | London | Smith, Elder, & Co., 15 Waterloo Place | 1896 | [*All rights reserved*]

    There is no evidence that this edition has any independent textual authority.

[PREFACE TO FIRST EDITION OF *Poems* (1853)]

Texts: 53, 54, 56, 57, 82, 83m, 91 (56 not collated)

3:20. *footnote added* 54, 57, 82, 83m, 91
3:20. an apparently intelligent 53
3:30. who write it. 53, 54, 57
4:2. of it: he 53, 54, 57
5:1. three latter cases 53, 54, 57
5:33. *style:* but 53, 54, 57
6:6. stage; their significance 53, 54, 57
6:31. belonged; we 53, 54, 57
6:34. required; he 53, 54, 57
7:5. poem: such 53, 54, 57
7:9–10. permitted. But for all kinds of poetry . . . poem. Their theory 53 (*which omits this sentence below*)
8:3. danger; he 53, 54, 57
8:30. immense: what 53, 54, 57
11:28. audience: he 53, 54, 57
11:30. them: in 53, 54, 57
11:32. moderns: but 53, 54, 57
12:5. art; he 53, 54, 57
13:33. them: they 53, 54, 57
14:10–11. by the two men, the one of strongest head, the other of widest culture, whom 57
15:1. *turbida terrent* 53
15:13. ourselves: let 53, 54, 57
Dated, at end: Fox How, Ambleside, October 1. 1853. 53, 54, 57

[PREFACE TO SECOND EDITION OF *Poems* (1854)]

Texts: 54, 57, 82, 83m, 91

16:10–12. But neither have I time now to supply these deficiencies, nor is this the proper place for attempting it: on one 54, 57
16:15. ably urged 54, 57
16:21. mind, since Voltaire, has 54, 57
16:25. either; as 54, 57

16:29. Alcestis or Joan [*for "Prometheus or Joan"*] 57
17:2. another; each 54, 57
17:6. wish 54, 57, 82; wished 83*m*
17:8. not so: I 54, 57
Dated, at end: London, June 1, 1854. 54, 57

[ON THE MODERN ELEMENT IN LITERATURE]

Published in *Macmillan's Magazine* XIX, 304–14 (February, 1869). Not reprinted by Arnold.

24:21. prescribes *Macm.*
27:23–24. from Beda and his master *Macm.* (*corrected from Raleigh*)
27:28. being so near *Macm.* (*corrected from Raleigh*)

[PREFACE TO *Merope*]

Text: 58. Not reprinted by Arnold.

[ENGLAND AND THE ITALIAN QUESTION]

Text: 59. Not reprinted by Arnold.

[ON TRANSLATING HOMER]

Texts: 61, 65, 80, 83o, 96 (65 not collated)

The following passages appear in 80: 102:20–24 (p. 26); 112:34–113:14 (pp. 21–22); 137:26–138:24 (pp. 22–23); 140:3–11, 13–33 (pp. 8–10); 143:19–29 (p. 22); 155:29–156:12 (pp. 20–21); 168:7–22 (p. 20). These have sometimes been modified slightly to make them independent of their context.

102:4. just a 61
110:16. fortunate 83*o*, 96
114:6. confirm that the date 61, 83*o*, 96 (*corrected from Chapman*)
117:1. unreasonably 61, 83*o*, 96 (*corrected from Cowper*)
117:2. it; Homer 61
118:1. bold 83*o*, 96
118:1. scholarlike *National Review*
121:35. its subject 61, 83*o*

135:3. and *truly* 96
135:9. all stages 96
138:1. standard 96
138:17–18. shouting from out his 80
140:3. eccentricity, the 80
140:3–4. which Professor Francis Newman's 80
146:15. *The deluxe ed. of 1903 emends* heard the warning
153:27. pronounce certainly what 61
154:28. further 83*o*, 96; farther 61, *Cowper*
155:29. We shall find 80
157:23. such conceit 83*o*, 96
165:17. "brazen-coated:" Mr. 61
165:24. farther 61
167:9. grammar; in 61
168:9. boistering 83*o*, 96
168:13. is all very 80

[LAST WORDS]

Texts: 62, 65, 80, 83o, 96 (65 not collated)

The following passages appear in 80: 171:37–172:16 (p. 8); 206:2–27 (pp. 47–48); 210:8–212:1 (pp. 23–26); 215:16–216:7 (pp. 77–78).

172:27. happiest manifestations 96
183:7. translation, in 83*o*, 96
186:4. we may regard 83*o*, 96
187:21. ¶But a Dutch 62
197:33. that may be 96
197:34. taking-off accent 83*o*, 96
204:35–205:9. or *after the first four passages* 62
206:1. ever 83*o*, 96
206:4–5. distinguish the semblance of simplicity from 80
210:15. the 'Recluse' 80
210:16. On man, on nature, 80 *and Wordsworth*
210:21. From them 62, 83*o*, 96; In them 80
215:16–17. How can I help remembering what a mind and character we have lost in losing Mr. Clough, whose name has more than once occurred in my lectures on Homer? 80
216:1. poem, 'The Bothie of Toper-na-Fuosich,' has 80

Index

A reference to a page of text should be taken to include the notes to that page.